Developing
Habits *of* Mind
in Secondary Schools

An ASCD Action Tool

Developing Habits *of* Mind

in Secondary Schools

Karen Boyes

Graham Watts

ASCD

Alexandria, Virginia USA

1703 North Beauregard St. • Alexandria, VA 22311-1714 USA • Phone: 1-800-933-2723 or
1-703-578-9600 • Fax: 1-703-575-5400 • Web site: www.ascd.org • E-mail: member@ascd.org

Author guidelines: www.ascd.org/write

Gene R. Carter, *Executive Director*; Nancy Modrak, *Publisher*; John L. Brown, *Content Development*;
Mary Beth Nielsen, *Director, Editorial Services*; Judy Ochse, *Project Manager*; Gary Bloom, *Director,
Design and Production Services*; Georgia Park, *Senior Graphic Designer*; Mike Kalyan, *Production
Manager*; Valerie Younkin, *Desktop Publishing Specialist*

All Web links in this book are correct as of the publication date below but may have become inac-
tive or otherwise modified since that time. If you notice a deactivated or changed link, please e-mail
books@ascd.org with the words "Link Update" in the subject line. In your message, please specify the
Web link, the book title, and the page number on which the link appears.

PAPERBACK ISBN: 978-1-4166-0888-2 ASCD Product #109108 n10/09

Quantity discounts for the paperback edition only: 10–49 copies, 10%; 50+ copies, 15%; for 1,000
or more copies, call 1-800-933-2723, ext. 5634, or 1-703-575-5634.

Library of Congress Cataloging-in-Publication Data
Boyes, Karen.
    Developing habits of mind in secondary schools : an ASCD action tool / Karen Boyes, Graham
Watts.
        p. cm.
    Includes bibliographical references.
    ISBN 978-1-4166-0888-2 (pbk. : alk. paper)   1. Thought and thinking—Study and teaching
(Secondary)   2. Cognition in children.   I. Watts, Graham (Graham C.)   II. Association for
Supervision and Curriculum Development.   III. Title.
    LB1590.3.B696 2009
    373.1102—dc22
                                                                                          2009026220

16 15 14 13 12 11 10 09   1 2 3 4 5 6 7 8 9 10

Developing
Habits *of* Mind
in Secondary Schools

An ASCD Action Tool

TOOLS FOR EXPANDING CAPACITIES

TOOLS FOR INCREASING ALERTNESS

TOOLS FOR EXTENDING VALUES

TOOLS FOR BUILDING COMMITMENT

RESOURCES AND REFERENCES

Downloads

Electronic versions of the tools are available for download at **www.ascd.org/downloads**.

Enter this unique key code
to unlock the files:

GD134-05016-62411

If you have difficulty accessing the files,
e-mail webhelp@ascd.org or call 1-800-933-ASCD for assistance.

Acknowledgments

We would like to thank Art Costa and Bena Kallick for giving us the opportunity to work together on this learning journey and for believing in us, even though we were almost strangers at the start. We are eternally grateful for your insight and endless encouragement and hope this work does justice to the legacy you have created.

We also thank the team from ASCD for getting all the details sorted out and making this project a reality.

From Karen Boyes
I'd like to pay tribute to my teachers and colleagues who have inspired me and taught me so much about the Habits of Mind, especially Art Costa, Bena Kallick, Georgette Jensen, Adrian Rennie, Ross Kennedy, and Trudy Francis. A huge thanks goes to the team at Spectrum Education, in particular Jess Woodmass and Jenny Porter, who kept everything running smoothly so I could complete this project. Finally, I wish to acknowledge my family—my parents, Tui and Trevor, for always being there for me; my two gorgeous children, Hamish and Sasha, who embrace the Habits of Mind and grow each day because of them; and my wonderful husband, Denny, who is my rock, my foundation, my love.

From Graham Watts

I want to thank all those who have taught me, worked with me, and helped this work come to fruition. I offer particular thanks to Gill Hubble, Nola Tuckey, and Niki Phillips for their ideas and intellect, and to my parents for their generous support and endless belief in me.

Rationale and Planning

WHAT ARE HABITS OF MIND?

Habits of Mind are thoughtful behaviors—what some have called "intellectual dispositions"—that allow us to cope with a complex and rapidly changing world. They are powerful tools we can use to intelligently navigate the moral, ethical, and spiritual challenges we encounter in our increasingly complex world. Habits of Mind also serve as guiding principles to promote successful lifelong learning both within the classroom and in the world beyond it. Habits of Mind can be used to

- Establish and maintain positive relationships, including appreciation of the unique perspectives and points of view evident in our culturally diverse world.
- Develop and use effective communication techniques and strategies, including active listening, consensus building, and interpersonal awareness.
- Apply flexible thinking strategies to complex situations requiring authentic problem solving and decision making.
- Demonstrate powerful character traits, such as self-reflection and resilience, that have been labeled 21st century skills for our global economy and increasingly interdependent world.

Habits of Mind are as useful for adults as they are for students. When educators internalize these intellectual dispositions, they can better model the behaviors they want to see in their students. In addition, Habits of Mind are relevant to students of all ages and in all subjects. In essence, they can become catalysts for creating and sustaining a whole-school learning culture and promoting true communities of learning.

WHY DEVELOP HABITS OF MIND?

Habits of Mind can help us answer a range of powerful and essential questions: Just what do human beings do when they behave intelligently? What behaviors do efficient, effective problem solvers and decision makers demonstrate? How can we help students become lifelong learners who are increasingly proficient at using intelligent intellectual dispositions to explore their world? Research in effective thinking and intelligent behavior indicates that there are some identifiable characteristics of effective thinkers—characteristics that have been identified in successful people in all walks of life.

The critical attribute of intelligent human beings is not only having information but also knowing how to act on it. Employing Habits of Mind means having a disposition toward behaving intelligently when confronted with problems that have no immediately known answers. It means using a composite of many skills, attitudes, cues, past experiences, and proclivities. It means that for different problems, decisions, or situations, we need to determine the value of one pattern of thinking over another, making choices about which is most appropriate for a specific context. Over time, we learn to reflect on, evaluate, and modify our use of Habits of Mind, and we carry their impact forward to future applications.

UNIVERSAL CHARACTERISTICS OF PRODUCTIVE HABITS OF MIND

This ASCD Action Tool will help you to explore 16 significant Habits of Mind. As you explore and apply each, consider how they share the following characteristics:

Value	Choosing to employ a particular pattern of intellectual behavior (Habit of Mind) rather than other, less productive patterns.
Inclination	Feeling the need to use a pattern of intellectual behavior (Habit of Mind).
Sensitivity	Perceiving opportunities for and appropriateness of using a particular Habit of Mind.
Capability	Having the skills to apply the behaviors associated with key Habits of Mind.
Commitment	Constantly striving to reflect on and improve performance while using a Habit of Mind.

FOCUSING ON 16 IMPORTANT HABITS OF MIND

This ASCD Action Tool looks at 16 significant Habits of Mind. The habits reflect what intelligent people tend to do when they are confronted with problems or decisions about which there may not be a clear answer or preferred pathway for resolution. The habits are not meant to be seen as discrete or mutually exclusive; instead, they should be viewed as "permeable membranes," interacting with one another and mutually supporting the capacity for intelligent behavior as expressed through critical, creative, and self-regulated thinking. The 16 Habits of Mind we investigate are the following:

1. Persisting. Intelligent people stick to a task until it is completed. They don't give up easily. They take a systematic approach to solving problems—knowing how to begin, what steps must be performed, and what data need to be generated or collected. Because they are able to sustain a problem-solving process over time, persistent people are also comfortable with ambiguous or open-ended situations and tasks.

2. Managing Impulsivity. Intelligent, reflective individuals self-regulate and self-monitor, considering alternatives and consequences related to several possible directions prior to taking action. They decrease their need for trial and error by gathering information, taking time to reflect on an answer before giving it, making sure they understand directions, and listening to alternative points of view.

3. Listening to Others with Understanding and Empathy. The ability to listen to another person— to understand and empathize with another point of view or perspective—is one of the highest forms of intelligent behavior. Being able to paraphrase others' ideas, detecting indicators (cues) of their feelings or emotional states in their oral and body language (empathy), and accurately expressing their concepts, emotions, and problems are indicators of active listening and open and accurate communication.

4. Thinking Flexibly. People who think flexibly have the ability to change their mind as they receive additional data or expand their experience base. They can hypothesize multiple and simultaneous outcomes and activities related to a situation, drawing upon a repertoire of problem-solving strategies and practicing style flexibility—for example, knowing when it is appropriate to be broad and global in their thinking and when a situation requires detailed precision. They seek novel approaches and usually have a well-developed sense of humor.

5. Thinking About Thinking (Metacognition). Metacognition is the ability to perceive and analyze both what we know and what we don't know. It is our capacity for planning

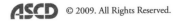

a strategy to produce the information needed to solve a problem, to be conscious of our own steps and strategies, and to reflect on and evaluate the productiveness of our thinking. The major components of metacognition involve developing a plan of action, keeping that plan in mind over a period of time, and reflecting on and evaluating the plan upon its completion.

6. Striving for Accuracy and Precision. People who value accuracy, precision, and craftsmanship take time to check over their products or performances. They review the rules by which they are to operate, the models and visions they are to follow, and the criteria they are to address. They also confirm that their finished product or performance matches the criteria exactly. Accurate and precise learners take pride in their work. They strive to attain the highest possible standards and pursue ongoing learning to focus their energies to accomplish tasks.

7. Questioning and Posing Problems. Effective problem solvers know how to ask questions to fill in the gaps between what they know and what they don't know. Effective questioners are inclined to ask a range of questions. They also recognize discrepancies and challenging phenomena in their environment, probing into causes and meanings. Successful questioners request data to support the conclusions and assumptions of others, pose questions about alternative points of view, pose questions to establish and confirm causal connections and relationships, and generate hypothetical problems and approaches to investigate them.

8. Applying Past Knowledge to New Situations. Intelligent human beings learn from experience. When confronted with a new and perplexing problem, they draw upon their store of knowledge and experience as sources of data to support ideas, theories to explain, analogies to compare, or processes to solve each new challenge. They are able to abstract meaning from one experience and carry it forth to another. Ultimately, they confirm their understanding of knowledge and skills by being able to apply them creatively and independently to novel, new, and unanticipated tasks, situations, and settings.

9. Thinking and Communicating with Clarity and Precision. Language and thinking are closely entwined. Intelligent people strive to communicate accurately in both written and oral forms. They take care to use precise language, define terms, and use correct names as well as universal labels and analogies. They strive to avoid overgeneralizations, deletions, and distortions. Instead, they support their statements with explanations, comparisons, quantification, and evidence. Clear and precise language plays a critical role in enhancing our cognitive maps and our ability to think critically. Enriching the complexity and specificity of language and how we use it produces more effective thinking.

10. Gathering Data Through All Senses. Intelligent people know that all information gets into the brain through the sensory pathways: gustatory, olfactory, tactile, kinesthetic, auditory, and visual. We derive most of our linguistic, cultural, and physical learning from the environment as we take it in through our senses and subsequently observe and analyze its patterns and processes. Those whose sensory pathways are open, alert, and acute absorb more information from the environment than those whose pathways are withered, immune, and oblivious to sensory stimuli.

11. Creating, Imagining, and Innovating. Creative human beings try to conceive solutions to problems differently from the norm, examining alternative possibilities from many angles. They tend to project themselves into different roles using analogies and visioning strategies. Creative people take risks, pushing the boundaries of perceived limits. They are intrinsically motivated, working on a task because of the aesthetic challenge rather than material rewards. Creative people are also positively responsive to criticism. They hold up their products for others to judge and seek feedback in an ongoing effort to refine their techniques and approaches.

12. Responding with Wonderment and Awe. We want our students to be curious, to commune with the world around them, to reflect on the changing formations of nature, and to experience awe in the face of creative expression. Ideally, they should feel engaged and passionate about learning. Students who respond with wonderment and awe can find beauty in a sunset, intrigue in the geometry of a spider web, and exhilaration at the iridescence of a hummingbird's wings. They continually think outside the boxes of tradition and norm-based perspectives, striving to see the unseen. They approach lifelong learning as a powerful and positive process that sustains and enriches them.

13. Taking Responsible Risks. Intelligent and creative people often seem to have a powerful urge to go beyond established limits, feeling compelled to place themselves in situations where they do not know what the outcome will be. They accept confusion, uncertainty, and higher risks of failure as part of the normal process of learning—and they tend to view setbacks as interesting, challenging, and growth producing. At the same time, they do not behave impulsively or recklessly. They take "educated" risks, drawing on their past knowledge about consequences with a well-trained sense of what is appropriate and inappropriate.

14. Finding Humor. People who engage in the mystery of humor have the ability to perceive situations from an original and often interesting vantage point. They tend to initiate humor more often, place greater value on having a sense of humor, and appreciate and understand others' humor, and they are often verbally playful when interacting with others. Those who have this Habit of Mind can distinguish between situations of human frailty and fallibility that are in need of compassion and those that are truly funny.

15. Thinking Interdependently. Working interdependently requires the ability to justify ideas and to test the feasibility of solution strategies on others. It also requires the development of a willingness and openness to accept feedback from a critical friend. Human beings who think interdependently typically express a range of observable and productive behaviors, including listening, consensus seeking, giving up an idea to work with someone else's, empathy, compassion, group leadership, knowing how to support group efforts, and altruism.

16. Learning Continuously. Intelligent people are in a continuous learning mode— striving for improvement, always growing, always learning, always modifying and improving themselves. They perceive and approach problems, situations, tensions, conflicts, and circumstances as valuable opportunities to learn. Our wish for our students should be that they become creative human beings who are eager to learn. That process includes the humility of knowing what we don't know, which—according to Kallick and Costa—is the highest form of thinking we will ever learn.

ORGANIZATION OF THIS ACTION TOOL

This ASCD Action Tool is arranged to follow five dimensions of growth that move from an initial exploration of each Habit of Mind through a comprehensive internalization of the habits in students and teachers. Designed to scaffold learning, each dimension represents a step students commonly take as they embrace intelligent behaviors during core learning experiences. This action tool guides students through the dimensions and helps both students and teachers create a deep understanding of each Habit of Mind. Students learn to recognize Habits of Mind and appreciate their usefulness in learning and in life. Each dimension is the focus of one section as follows:

- **Exploring Meanings.** This section contains a series of resources designed to help students understand the terminology, concepts, and definitions associated with the 16 Habits of Mind. The tools in this section can reinforce students' understanding of operational language. This language can serve as a cognitive anchor or trigger, allowing students to monitor and describe their own thinking as they acquire and apply each of the Habits of Mind. By using the resources included in this section, educators can help learners build a scaffold or platform from which they can extend and refine their use of the Habits of Mind that follow.

- **Expanding Capacities.** This section builds upon the foundations established in the Exploring Meanings section. As teachers and students become familiar with the 16 Habits of Mind, they can use them to become increasingly fluent in self-assessment and self-regulation. The tools and resources in this section will help educators extend and refine students' understanding and application of the Habits of Mind in their academic lives as well as beyond the classroom.

- **Increasing Alertness.** This section takes the previous two a step further by extending students' work with the habits to see their innate potential and applicability to academic and daily life. Thus, this section marks a shift from teacher-led growth toward student-led growth. It serves as a bridge between external understanding of the habits and true internal and personal understanding. The tools in this section lead educators and students to investigate people that matter to them—for example, famous people, world leaders, and local people they respect—and significant global and local issues. As they identify applications of the habits to the world around them via case studies, interviews, and research projects, they grow in their understanding of how the habits can be extremely beneficial in learning and in life.

- **Extending Values.** This section explores strategies that will help educators and students create a "school as a home for the mind," a theme that is central to Costa and Kallick's belief that the full potential of the 16 Habits of Mind cannot be realized unless this framework is applied schoolwide to all aspects of school culture. The activation model presented in this section is designed to integrate the Habits of Mind into all facets of school improvement planning and organization development. The tools and resources focus on leaders, teachers, students, parents, and the wider learning community.

- **Building Commitment.** The tools and materials presented in this final section are designed to take learners from thinking consciously about using the habits to internalizing them so that they become a regular part of how the learners think, behave, and live. In effect, the habits then become so much a part of the individual's mind, emotions, and consciousness that they unconsciously and automatically guide and inform the person's decision-making and problem-solving processes.

The Resources and References section contains two appendices:

- **Appendix A.** Appendix A offers greater depth and detail on each of the 16 Habits of Mind. It contains useful quotes, explanations, and icons to help broaden teachers' and students' understanding and application. An interesting activity to do with teachers and students is ask them to design an equivalent document with original icons, personal quotes, and new definitions.
- **Appendix B.** The planning, teaching, and assessing tools referred to throughout the action tool can be found in Appendix B. They are provided as black-line masters for easy use in classrooms, but their use is not limited to the form in which they appear. As you become more familiar with the Habits of Mind, you may want to adapt, combine, re-create, or improve these resources to meet your needs and the needs of your students.

STRUCTURE AND PLANNING

The first page of each section includes a summary and a list of contents. The individual tools (which can also be considered lessons) include step-by-step instructions, as well as worksheets, sample completed worksheets, and resource pages as appropriate. Teachers can pick and choose from the available tools. They may use each tool as a lesson plan as given; teachers who prefer to create their own lesson plan may want to use the lesson plan template available in Appendix B.

Teachers may adapt the tools and activities to meet specific age and curriculum goals. The idea is to set a solid foundation by first introducing the Habits of Mind to students and then developing students' understanding, appreciation, and commitment to the habits as they progress through the elementary and secondary grades. Thus, all of the worksheets and related resources in this action tool are intended to be starting points from which teachers can customize to suit the ability level and age range within different classroom environments.

ELECTRONIC TOOLS AND RESOURCES

The tools are available for download. To access these documents, visit www.ascd.org/downloads and enter the key code found on page viii. All files are saved in Adobe Portable Document Format (PDF). The PDF is compatible with both personal computers (PCs) and Macintosh computers. **Note: You must have the Adobe Acrobat Professional software on your machine to save your work.** The main menu will let you navigate through the various sections, and you can print individual tools or sections in their entirety. If you are having difficulties downloading or viewing the files, contact webhelp@ascd.org for assistance, or call 1-800-933-ASCD.

MINIMUM SYSTEM REQUIREMENTS

Program: The most current version of the Adobe Reader software is available for free download at www.adobe.com.

PC: Intel Pentium Processor; Microsoft Windows XP Professional or Home Edition (Service Pack 1 or 2), Windows 2000 (Service Pack 2), Windows XP Tablet PC Edition, Windows Server 2003, or Windows NT (Service Pack 6 or 6a); 128 MB of RAM (256 MB recommended); up to 90 MB of available hard-disk space; Internet Explorer 5.5 (or higher), Netscape 7.1 (or higher), Firefox 1.0, or Mozilla 1.7.

Macintosh: PowerPC G3, G4, or G5 processor, Mac OS X v.10.2.8–10.3; 128 MB of RAM (256 MB recommended); up to 110 MB of available hard-disk space; Safari 1.2.2 browser supported for MAC OS X 10.3 or higher.

GETTING STARTED

Select "Download files." Designate a location on your computer to save the zip file. Choose to open the PDF file with your existing version of Adobe Acrobat Reader, or install the newest version of Adobe Acrobat Reader from www.adobe.com. From the main menu, select a section by clicking on its title. To view a specific tool, open the Bookmarks tab in the left navigation pane and then click on the title of the tool.

PRINTING TOOLS

To print a single tool, select the tool by clicking on its title via the Bookmarks section and the printer icon, or select File then Print. In the Print Range section, select Current Page to print the page on the screen. To print several tools, enter the page range in the "Pages from" field. If you wish to print all of the tools in the section, select All in the Printer Range section and then click OK.

TOOLS FOR TEACHER TRAINING

Who dares to teach must never cease to learn.
—John Cotton Dana
Librarian and museum director

A teacher affects eternity; he can never tell where his influence stops.
—Henry Brooks Adams
Novelist, journalist, historian, and professor

Exposing the Habits of Mind to teachers can greatly enhance students' capacity to learn and apply the habits in multiple ways and can help to build a school culture infused with Habits of Mind. The following pages present lesson plans for two training sessions for colleagues, administrators, and other interested school staff. The materials put the bulk of learning and exploring onto the shoulders of the teachers, so it is not necessary to be an expert to facilitate these training sessions.

The first tool provides an introduction and launching pad for teachers to familiarize themselves with the habits and begin applying them. The second tool allows teachers to work together more extensively to share ideas and expand their capacity to teach these valuable lifelong skills. These tools, or lessons, may be presented at a staff meeting, in an after-school training session, or through work teams. Teachers generally respond well to the model as a viable way to develop intelligent behaviors within their students.

Action Tool 1: Exploring the Meaning of Habits of Mind with Teachers

PURPOSE OF THIS TOOL

A good starting point when introducing Habits of Mind into a school is to first introduce the habits to teachers and staff. The experience will be more powerful for students if teachers develop a deep understanding and appreciation of the habits themselves before they present them to students. They may have numerous initial questions: What do these habits mean? How will they work with my age group or in my subject? How can I put the model into practice? Rather than answering the questions, begin with the Y-Chart activity in this tool.

The resources in this action tool will enable participants to

- Identify the 16 Habits of Mind.
- Explore several Habits of Mind for personal meaning.
- Define each Habit of Mind and identify appropriate uses.
- Prepare to model the 16 Habits of Mind to students.
- Prepare to recognize the habits in students.t

HOW TO USE THIS TOOL

This tool presents a series of resources that can be used to introduce and reinforce for teachers the meaning of the 16 Habits of Mind. The following is the suggested sequence for exploring these habits, as well as a list of resources included to support this process:

- Summary of 16 Habits of Mind handout (Introductory Activity)
- Y-Chart worksheet (Introductory Activity)
- Defining Habits of Mind worksheet (Core Activity)
- Discussion (Reflection Activity)
- Describing16 Habits of Mind (Extension Activity)

The activities and tasks included in this tool should take about 60 minutes to complete. You will need the following materials:

- Summary of 16 Habits of Mind (Appendix B)
- Describing 16 Habits of Mind (Appendix A)

TIPS AND VARIATIONS

1. Introductory Activity

- Distribute the list of the 16 Habits of Mind. Read the names of the habits but do not discuss them yet.
- Have teachers form small groups. Assign the Habits of Mind to each group such that every group has at least one habit to consider, and all of the habits are covered. For instance, if you have four groups, each group will have four habits to consider.
- Give each group one copy of the Y-Chart worksheet (page XX) for each Habit of Mind they are considering; for example, if each group has four habits, they will need four copies of the worksheet. (Alternatively, teachers could write information for each of their Habits of Mind on one sheet.)
- Ask the groups to use the chart to unpack the meaning of their assigned Habits of Mind. For example, for the first habit, Persistence, they might ask themselves questions such as

    What does it look like when someone in class persists? What facial expressions might I see? What body language? What does persistence look like outside the classroom? On the baseball field? In a chess tournament? At the airport? At the beach?

    What does it feel like when I persist? Is there just one feeling or emotion, or several? Do my feelings change as I apply persistence? Does everyone experience the same feelings when they persist?

    What does it sound like when someone persists? What words might I hear? Other noises? How might I talk to myself? What advice might I offer a friend who needs to persist? How might the sounds change from the classroom to the football field?

- When teachers have finished, have each team discuss their Y-charts with the whole group. It can be very interesting to see the breadth of ideas teachers will produce.

2. Core Activity

- Give teachers a copy of the Defining Habits of Mind worksheet.
- Ask them to work individually to complete it, defining each habit in their own words (column 1) and listing two or three ideal times to use each (column 2) as well as two or three occasions when the habit would not be useful (column 3).

3. Reflection Activity

- Lead a group discussion about the value of Habits of Mind.
- Explain that teachers will really begin to see the benefits as they watch students apply the habits in learning situations.

4. Extension Activity

- Distribute the article "Describing 16 Habits of Mind," found in Appendix A.
- Encourage teachers to take the materials they have received with them to study as they prepare to introduce the Habits of Mind to their students.
- Suggest that teachers review Costa and Kallick's *Learning and Leading with Habits of Mind* (2008, ASCD), if they have not already done so.

ASCD ☐ 13

Name _____ Class _____ Date _____

Y-Chart

You can use this chart to explore your thoughts about the Habits of Mind.

Topic:

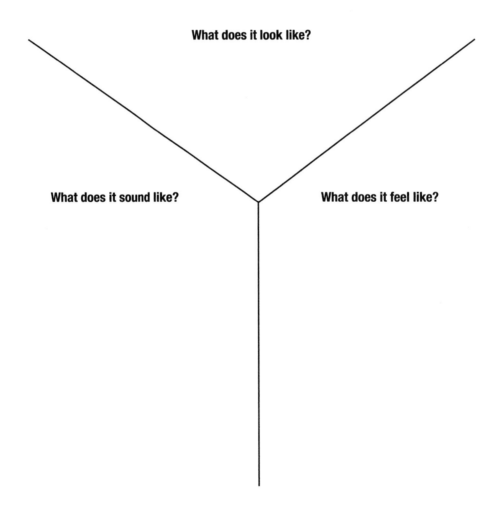

What does it look like?

What does it sound like?

What does it feel like?

Name _____ Class _____ Date _____

Defining Habits of Mind

Habit of Mind	My Definition	Good Times to Use	Bad Times to Use
Persisting			
Managing Impulsivity			
Listening with Understanding and Empathy			
Thinking Flexibly			
Thinking About Thinking (Metacognition)			
Striving for Accuracy and Precision			
Questioning and Posing Problems			
Applying Past Knowledge to New Situations			

Name _____ Class _____ Date _____

Defining Habits of Mind, *continued*

Habit of Mind	My Definition	Good Times to Use	Bad Times to Use
Thinking and Communicating with Clarity and Precision			
Gathering Data Through All Senses			
Creating, Imagining, and Innovating			
Responding with Wonderment and Awe			
Taking Responsible Risks			
Finding Humor			
Thinking Interdependently			
Learning Continuously			

Action Tool 2: Expanding Capacities with Teachers

PURPOSE OF THIS TOOL

This tool builds on the concepts developed in the previous tool. Teachers should now be familiar with all 16 Habits of Mind and have a working understanding of what they mean. This tool helps teachers gain more in-depth knowledge and understanding of the habits so that they will be better prepared to foster them among their students. The resources in this action tool will enable participants to

- Discuss with colleagues their experiences in applying the Habits of Mind so far.
- Define each Habit of Mind in as many ways as possible.
- Use analogies to gain perspective on each Habit of Mind.
- Describe how they can integrate each Habit of Mind into the classroom.
- Contribute to and build on the ideas of colleagues.

HOW TO USE THIS TOOL

This tool presents a series of resources that can be used to extend and refine teachers' understanding of the 16 Habits of Mind. The following is the suggested sequence for exploring these habits:

- How's It Going? (Introductory Discussion)
- Word Splash, Y-Chart, and Classroom Integration group activity (Core Activity)
- Final Review group activity and discussion (Synthesizing Activity)
- Results folders (Follow-Up)

The activities and tasks included in this tool should take two hours, best divided into two close-proximity days to complete. Note that you will need to complete some advance preparation as well as some follow-up action. You will need the following materials:

- Large roll of butcher paper or a couple of self-stick wall charts
- Package of markers
- A bell, whistle, or other noisemaker (optional)
- Folders (one per teacher)
- Clock or watch

TIPS AND VARIATIONS

1. Advance Preparation

• Set up stations around the room, one for each Habit of Mind. At each station, hang three poster-size pieces of butcher paper specific to one habit. (See the following pages as examples for the habit Persisting.) Have extra butcher paper on hand in case additional space is needed for recording ideas. Place a number of markers at each station.

• On the board, write three sample charts such as those shown on the following pages for the habit Persisting. These samples will serve as guides for the teachers.

2. Introductory Discussion

• Stimulate discussion about experiences teachers have had with the Habits of Mind so far by asking questions such as the following:

How have you used the Habits of Mind in the classroom?

What have you learned?

What problems have you encountered?

What questions do you have?

• Spend some time sharing your ideas and having other teachers do so as well.

3. Core Activity

• Tell teachers that to further help them think about and share ideas related to the Habits of Mind, you have created stations around the room, each with three charts: a Word Splash, a Y-Chart, and a chart titled Classroom Integration. Direct the teachers' attention to the examples on the board as you explain each type of chart.

• Explain that word splashes are brainstorming activities. Teachers should think of as many ways as they can to rephrase the name of the Habit of Mind. Tell them that by the time all ideas are recorded, everyone should have a thorough definition of the habit.

• Remind teachers of their previous experience with Y-charts. Say that this chart will allow them to draw analogies to express what they think, feel, and hear regarding each habit.

• Explain that the Classroom Integration chart serves as a tool for teachers to share their ideas about how they use or could use the Habits of Mind in the classroom, as well as times to avoid using the habits.

- Instruct teachers to get up and go to any station. Allow five minutes for teachers to add their ideas to each chart at that station, and then blow a whistle, ring a bell, or call "time" and instruct teachers to move to the next station.
- At about halfway through this activity, allow teachers to take a break. Ideally, they would return to the activity fresh the next day.

4. Synthesizing Activity

- When everyone has been through the 16 stations, allow them time to mingle around the room and look at everyone's comments.
- Lead a group discussion about the experience.

5. Follow-Up

- Tell teachers you will type up their collection of ideas. At a later time, give each teacher a folder with all the group's ideas and encourage them to apply the ideas in the days, weeks, and years to come.
- Have teachers add the handouts and materials they received in Action Tool 1 to the folders, so they will have a Habits of Mind resource available at all times.

Word Splash for Persisting

Persisting means ...

Y-Chart for Persisting

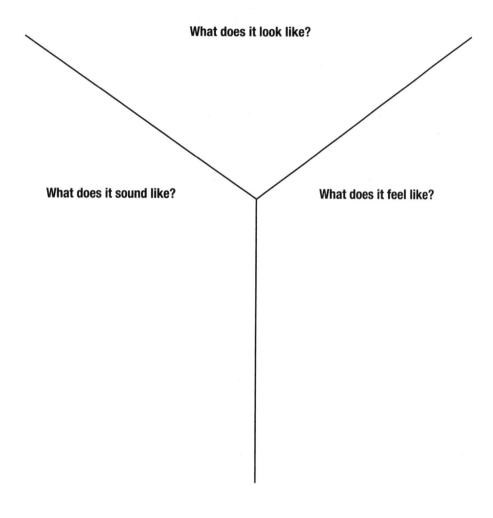

What does it look like?

What does it sound like?

What does it feel like?

Classroom Integration for Persisting

1. It is important to use this Habit of Mind when . . .

2. This Habit of Mind is not useful when . . .

3. I could introduce this Habit of Mind by . . .

Word Splash for Persisting

> The following is an example of what you are asking teachers to record on the appropriate posters at each station. These answers are simplified. Teachers should feel free to share any ideas they have.

Persisting means . . .

   . . . *to keep going.*

   . . . *not giving up.*

   . . . *sticking with it.*

   . . . *staying on task.*

   . . . *repeating.*

   . . . *practicing.*

   . . . *trying again.*

   . . . *trying a different way.*

Name _____ Class _____ Date _____

Y-Chart for Persisting

> The following is an example of what you are asking teachers to record on the appropriate posters at each station. These answers are simplified. Teachers should feel free to share any ideas they have.

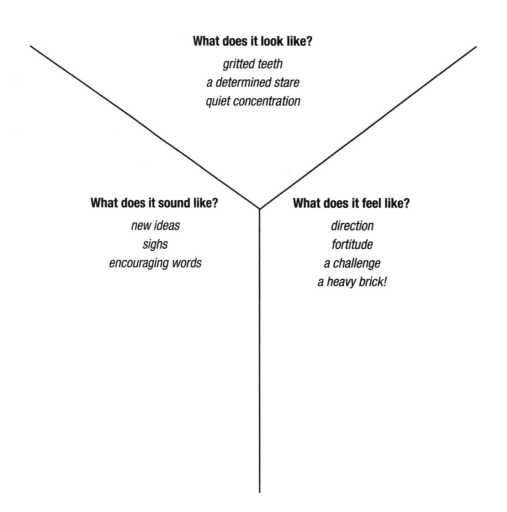

What does it look like?

gritted teeth
a determined stare
quiet concentration

What does it sound like?

new ideas
sighs
encouraging words

What does it feel like?

direction
fortitude
a challenge
a heavy brick!

Classroom Integration for Persisting

> The following is an example of what you are asking teachers to record on the appropriate posters at each station. These answers are simplified. Teachers should feel free to share any ideas they have.

1. It is important to use this Habit of Mind when ...

　　... students are struggling with new information.

　　... students are nervous about something.

　　... I'm pushing students to try something new.

2. This Habit of Mind is not useful when ...

　　... students need to brainstorm.

　　... I want students to relax and let things happen.

　　... persisting could cause mental, emotional, or physical harm.

3. I could introduce this Habit of Mind by ...

　　... giving students a task that takes several weeks to complete.

　　... giving students a tough group assignment they could figure out together.

　　... sharing a personal experience about persistence.

Exploring Meanings

We shall not cease from exploration, and the end of all our exploring will be to arrive where we started and know the place for the first time.

—T. S. Eliot, Author

Understanding the terminology, labels, and definitions of Habits of Mind is an important first step in exploring the habits and seeing the value they offer. Students report that simply being made aware of the Habits of Mind helps improve their thinking. The language alone seems to act as a cognitive anchor or trigger, allowing students to monitor and describe their own thinking. Once learners know the Habits of Mind they begin to connect them to their own experiences and recognize them in others. They become able to reflect on times when they have (or should have) used a particular habit.

The tools in this section build a solid foundation by helping students gather a range of examples and analogies that relate to the model. Soon students will be able to expand their simple definitions to more complex and complete ones.

CONTENTS

TITLE OF TOOL

Persisting

Exploring Meanings

PURPOSE OF THIS TOOL

Persisting is a Habit of Mind that relates to sticking to a task until it is completed. People who use this habit don't give up easily. They devise methods for analyzing the situation and create a plan for solving problems and accomplishing goals. With this tool, students become familiar with persisting as an important habit to develop.

The resources in this tool will enable students to

- Use persistence to solve several challenging puzzles.
- Examine how persistence helped a historical figure make a significant achievement.
- Identify and apply important steps in applying persistence.
- Examine how persistence has helped in their achievements.
- Self-evaluate their willingness to be persistent.
- Create an action plan for improving their ability to be persistent.

HOW TO USE THIS TOOL

The following list of resources includes the suggested sequence for using this tool:

- Waking Up the Brain worksheet (Motivating Activity)
- Inventing the Lightbulb worksheet (Core Activity 1)
- Persistence discussion (Class Discussion)
- How Well Do You Know Your ABCs? worksheet (Core Activity 2)
- Persistence Self-Evaluation worksheet (Reflection Activity)

The activities and tasks included in this tool should take 60–90 minutes to complete.

TIPS AND VARIATIONS

1. Motivating Activity

- Give students the Waking Up the Brain worksheet. Have them work independently to solve the problems. Check after a few minutes to see if students are struggling. If they are, you may wish to provide a few hints, such as the following:

  For teaser 1: Think outside the box, literally; that is, think past the lines.

  For teaser 2: Use a chart to organize what you know.

  For teaser 3: Think of common sayings that incorporate the given words in some way.

- If any students complete the teasers very quickly, suggest they create a few teasers of their own. Then put those teasers on the board for students to solve as they finish the worksheet.

2. Core Activity 1

- Tell students to find a partner. Distribute the Inventing the Lightbulb worksheet. Ask partners to read the quotation, then consider the process detailed in the chart. Ask them to pull examples from the quotation to show how Edison may have remained persistent as he attempted to invent the lightbulb.
- Next, have partners discuss two examples of their own persistence in accomplishing a goal. Suggest they consider one achievement at school and one extracurricular or other Habit of Mind achievement. After a few minutes of discussion, direct students to choose one of their examples and individually complete the "My Achievement" portion of the worksheet.

3. Class Discussion

- Tell students that Albert Einstein once defined insanity as doing the same thing over and over again but expecting a different outcome. Ask: What is the difference between the action Einstein describes and persistence? (Persistence requires applying a different approach if something isn't working. Instead of repeating the same thing exactly the same way, the person should review the situation, identify what can be done differently, and adjust as necessary to get different results. This is step 4 in the achievement chart: Know when to try another approach or strategy.)

4. Core Activity 2

- Give students the How Well Do You Know Your ABCs? worksheet. Encourage them to be methodical when solving the challenge.

5. Reflection Activity

- Have students complete the Persistence Self-Evaluation worksheet. Tell them that the point is not for them to judge themselves harshly but to reflect on their participation and performance so that they can learn and improve. You could have students find a partner to discuss their evaluations. Alternatively, you could meet with students one-on-one to discuss their evaluations or suggest that students come speak to you about their progress if they wish.

Name _____ Class _____ Date _____

Waking Up the Brain

Complete the following brain teasers. If you get stuck, don't give up. Persist by finding different approaches to solve the problems.

1. Without lifting your pen off the page, use only four straight lines to connect all of the dots below.

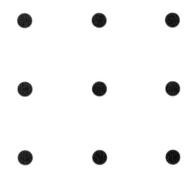

2. Aaron, Leo, and Jude work at the same cycle factory. One works on the assembly line, one in the paint shop, and the third in the packing department. The one in the packing department earns the most and has no brothers or sisters. Aaron, who is dating Leo's sister, earns less than the one in the paint shop. Who works in which department?

3. Unravel the hidden meaning in each of the squares below.

a.	b.	c.
JOB I'M JOB	house PRAIRIE	AGEBEAUTY
d. OFTEN NOT OFTEN NOT OFTEN	e. 	f. FIEPLAYLD
g. PETS A	h. UU IT'S	i. LOVE SIGHT SIGHT SIGHT

Name _____ Class _____ Date _____

Waking Up the Brain

Complete the following brain teasers. If you get stuck, don't give up. Persist by finding different approaches to solve the problems.

1. Without lifting your pen off the page, use only four straight lines to connect all of the dots below.

> Starting at the top left dot, draw down, then go up, past the middle dot, then come back around through the top dots and the middle dots as follows:

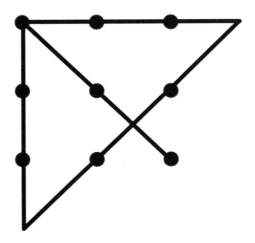

2. Aaron, Leo, and Jude work at the same cycle factory. One works on the assembly line, one in the paint shop, and the third in the packing department. The one in the packing department earns the most and has no brothers or sisters. Aaron, who is dating Leo's sister, earns less than the one in the paint shop. Who works in which department?

> Encourage students to organize the information they know in a chart. When the information is organized, the solution is fairly obvious.

Assembly Department	Paint Department	Packing Department
• Dates Leo's sister • Not Painting • Earns less than Painting	• Has sister • Not in Packing	• Earns the most • No brothers or sisters • Not Aaron • Not Leo
Aaron	Leo	Jude

3. Unravel the hidden meaning in each of the squares below.

> The answers are shown in each box below. If students have trouble getting started, give them one or two answers. If they have no trouble, suggest they create a few of their own.

a. JOB I'M JOB *I'm between jobs.*	b. house PRAIRIE *Little house on the prairie*	c. AGEBEAUTY *Age before beauty*
d. OFTEN NOT OFTEN NOT OFTEN *More often than not*	e. *Going round in circles*	f. FIEPLAYLD *PLAYIN' THE FIELD*
g. PETS A *A step backward*	h. UU IT'S *It's up to you. (It's up 2 u's.)*	i. LOVE SIGHT SIGHT SIGHT *Love at first sight*

Name _____ Class _____ Date _____

Inventing the Lightbulb

Read the quotation about Thomas Edison's experience in inventing the lightbulb. Then, for each step in the chart that follows, consider what Edison might have done to remain persistent while attempting to invent the lightbulb.

Inventing the Electric Lightbulb: A Story of Persistence

The invention of the electric lightbulb caused Thomas Edison a great amount of work, angst, and experimentation. He conducted hundreds of experiments in his attempt to find the perfect solution that would lead to creating the perfect lightbulb. Although he himself never lost faith in the value of his efforts, many of those around him did. As time passed, the nonbelievers became increasingly certain that he would not be successful.

Edison's method was to think of an idea or theory and then, through the process of trial and error, work through every possibility and variation until he exhausted all options. Then he would start from scratch again, with a different approach, and repeat the same deductive process, exploring all avenues. Edison believed that if he was thorough, learned from his mistakes, and held firm in his belief in himself, he would eventually succeed. And succeed he did!

Edison's Achievement

Steps to Persistence	Examples from Edison's Experience
1. Determine what needs to be solved, decided, or achieved.	
2. Know what range of approaches or strategies you can use.	
3. Find out who or what may be of assistance with this task.	
4. Know when to try another approach or strategy.	
5. Keep working toward solving the problem.	

Inventing the Light Bulb, *continued*

Now complete the chart using an example of your own personal persistence.

My Achievement

Steps to Persistence	Examples from My Experience
1. Determine what needs to be solved, decided, or achieved.	
2. Know what range of approaches or strategies you can use.	
3. Find out who or what may be of assistance with this task.	
4. Know when to try another approach or strategy.	
5. Keep working toward solving the problem.	

Would you add any extra steps to those shown above? If so, what and why?

Would you modify any of the steps? If so, explain how and why.

Name _____ Class _____ Date _____

How Well Do You Know Your ABCs?

Apply what you've learned about persistence so far to see this puzzle to the end.

Challenge

Write down the set of letters A, B, C in each of six possible orders so that when all 18 letters are written around a circle, adjacent letters are always different.

Possible combinations:

1.

2.

3.

4.

5.

6.

In a circle:

Exploring Meanings

Name _____ Class _____ Date _____

How Well Do You Know Your ABCs?

Apply what you've learned about persistence so far to see this puzzle to the end.

Challenge

Write down the set of letters A, B, C in each of six possible combinations so that when all 18 letters are written around a circle, adjacent letters are always different.

> Encourage students to be methodical when solving this challenge. Students can record the possible combinations in any order. The order of the letters in the circle can also vary—just be sure the same two letters do not appear side by side.

Possible combinations:

1. ABC

2. BCA

3. CAB

4. BAC

5. CBA

6. ACB

In a circle:

Name _____ Class _____ Date _____

Persistence Self-Evaluation

Review the activities, discussions, and challenges you've completed about persistence. Answer the following questions honestly to give yourself a sense of how you're doing so far.

1. What was I trying to learn?

2. Why is this topic important?

3. How have I succeeded in learning this topic?

4. Where did I fall short in learning this topic?

5. How can I persist better in the future?

Managing Impulsivity

PURPOSE OF THIS TOOL

This tool focuses on the Habit of Mind called Managing Impulsivity. When students learn to manage their desires instead of acting on them immediately, they are better able to prevent problems. They can cooperate with others to achieve goals and develop a vision to achieve personal progress. This Habit of Mind teaches students to clarify and understand directions, consider consequences of actions, and develop strategies for solving problems. Students are encouraged to make sure they understand a problem or situation before reacting to it and to withhold value judgments until they have a good understanding of the facts and consequences of the situation.

The resources in this tool will enable students to

- Define the term *impulsive*.
- Explore unseen consequences to following an impulse.
- Discuss positive situations for being impulsive.
- List several good and bad situations for being impulsive.

HOW TO USE THIS TOOL

The following list of resources includes the suggested sequence for using this tool:

- Impulse Buying (Introductory Discussion)
- Going to France Human Graph (Core Activity)
- Picasso's Impulsivity discussion (Core Activity)
- Good/Bad Impulsivity T-Chart worksheet (Synthesis Activity)

The activities and tasks included in this tool should take about 60 minutes to complete.

TIPS AND VARIATIONS

1. Introductory Discussion

- Ask students if anyone can define the term *impulse buying*. (Buying something because it seems right at the moment, without thinking in advance about the appropriateness, budget feasibility, or value for the money.) Ask students if they've ever picked up something while standing in the checkout line at a grocery store. Explain that supermarket managers place desirable items near the checkout stand to encourage impulse buying.

- Ask students if they've ever yelled out, jumped too soon, volunteered for the unknown, or said something they later regretted. These are often problematic impulses. On the other hand, explain that there are good times to let impulsivity take the lead. A key to developing the Habit of Mind of Managing Impulsivity is knowing when impulsivity will be constructive and when it may be detrimental.

2. Core Activity

- Ask the class to line up along the back wall of the classroom. Tell them they are going to become a human graph. Explain that you are going to tell them some things they can do. After each possibility, students who like the idea will move to one side of the room and students who really don't like the idea will move to the opposite wall. Students who don't have strong feelings about the idea can stand anywhere in between the two extremes. Tell students they can only listen to you—they can't ask questions or seek clarification. Then make statements such as the following:

    You won a free airline ticket to Paris.
    The ticket is for an economy seat.
    You will stay in an expensive hotel near the Eiffel Tower.
    You will have to go to the top of the Eiffel Tower.
    You will be required to bungee-jump from the top of the Eiffel Tower.
    You will have to write an essay describing your visit.
    You will be given spending money for the trip.
    The spending money is a loan; you will have to pay it back.
    You can take your best friend but no one else.
    You can stay for only two days.
    You can speak only French while you are there.

- As you make each statement, students will move from one side of the class to another or may stay somewhere in between. Most will probably like the idea of a free trip to Paris. Their response of crowding to one side of the room can be compared to an impulse decision. Many students wouldn't yet think about the possibility that there may be "strings attached." Some may have questions, but because they can't ask you about the conditions of the trip, they won't. As a result, when the conditions become clear, students will realize that there are drawbacks and the deal may not seem quite as great as it did originally. This lesson helps students see the need for asking a lot of questions and managing impulsive urges.

- Ask: When shouldn't we manage our impulsivity? One example relates to artistic urges. Tell students to consider the work of the famous Spanish artist Pablo Picasso. Picasso's artistic vision came from inspiration and an original view of the world. He embraced impulsivity. He allowed his mind to flow freely into his paintings without the filter of rational thinking. He might argue that if he had managed his impulsivity his painting would not have been so unusual or have spoken from his soul so deeply. So for Picasso, managing impulsivity was not a useful habit to have when he was beginning a new painting. Instead, he allowed thoughts and actions to flow without questions. Ask students if they can think of other examples or times when being impulsive is good. Ask if being impulsive might make those around them feel happy.

3. Synthesis Activity

Give students the Good/Bad Impulsivity T-Chart worksheet. Have them list examples of good and bad times to manage impulsivity.

Name _____ Class _____ Date _____

Good/Bad Impulsivity T-Chart

List at least two examples of good times to manage impulsivity and at least two examples of good times to be impulsive.

Good Times to Manage Impulsivity	Good Times to Be Impulsive

Name _____ Class _____ Date _____

Good/Bad Impulsivity T-Chart

List at least two examples of good times to manage impulsivity and at least two examples of good times to be impulsive.

> The following are sample answers. Encourage students to add more examples if time permits.

Good Times to Manage Impulsivity	Good Times to Be Impulsive
Accepting a gift from a stranger	*During an improvisational acting class*
Going shopping in preparation for a new job	*Jamming on the guitar with friends*
Hosting a party for a friend	*Going on an impromptu picnic with family*
Going on a long driving trip	*Following a spontaneous urge to write a poem*

> Good times to manage impulsivity include situations in which more information is needed or serious consequences could result from hasty action.

> Good times to be impulsive include experiences that benefit from quick reactions and experiences that may suffer from too much thought or planning.

Listening with Understanding and Empathy

Exploring Meanings

PURPOSE OF THIS TOOL

This action tool focuses on the Habit of Mind called Listening with Understanding and Empathy. Effective, intelligent people spend time listening to other people and can cue in to oral and body language to understand their feelings. Listening helps people understand diverse perspectives. Listening with understanding and empathy means paying close attention to words and the meaning and feelings beneath the words.

This tool focuses on teaching students how to paraphrase another person's ideas, detect cues of the person's feelings (empathy), and accurately express what the person is trying to say. Students need to practice withholding their own values and opinions in order to really hear and understand another person's thoughts. This complex skill is rarely taught in the classroom, yet it plays a vital role in a healthy life.

The resources in this tool will enable students to

- Discuss the value of listening.
- Define the terms *empathy* and *sympathy*.
- Identify words and actions that demonstrate effective listening and understanding.
- Demonstrate effective and ineffective listening skills.

HOW TO USE THIS TOOL

The following list of resources includes the suggested sequence for using this tool:

- Listening and Empathy (Introductory Discussion)
- Hear Me? worksheet (Core Activity)
- Listening role-play (Synthesis Activity)

The activities and tasks included in this tool should take about 45 minutes to complete.

TIPS AND VARIATIONS

1. Introductory Discussion

- Ask: How important is the ability to listen to other people? (It is an essential life skill.) Explain that listening to others may sound easy, but many people are not good listeners. In addition, listening is a skill that is rarely taught. Tell students that this Habit of Mind will help them learn how to become active listeners who not only really hear spoken words but also understand how the speaker is feeling. Effective listeners can share the feelings of the speaker.

• Ask: Can anyone define the term *empathy*? (Empathy is the ability to sense someone's feelings, attitudes, and motives and identify with them.) You may hear that empathy means feeling sorry for someone; feeling bad for someone is more like sympathy. Empathy means really feeling what someone else is saying. It means putting oneself in someone else's shoes and really knowing how that person feels.

2. Core Activity

• Explain that everyone likes to know that they are heard and that their words and feelings are understood. Give students the Hear Me? worksheet. The diagram lists statements a person might say to show understanding and empathy, as well as actions that display understanding and empathy. Ask students to read through the comments and then add three new examples of words they might say or actions they might take to show that they understand and empathize with someone.

3. Synthesis Activity

• Have students choose a partner. Explain that one person will be the listener and the other person will be the speaker, and that later they will swap roles.

• Ask the speaker to describe what he or she has done since leaving home this morning. Tell the listener to role-play a bad listener by acting in a way that shows little understanding of or empathy toward the speaker. For example, the listener may have his back turned to the speaker, interrupt the speaker, get distracted by classroom activities, or change the subject.

• After 2–3 minutes of "bad listening," tell the speakers to continue with the story, but this time the listeners will begin listening with understanding and empathy. Encourage the listeners to keep the Hear Me? worksheet handy to get some examples of statements and actions they can take to demonstrate effective listening.

• After 2–3 minutes of conversation, tell the partners to stop the role-play and discuss what happened. Encourage the speakers to explain how they felt as the listener changed behavior. Discuss how the speakers felt during the poor versus effective listening techniques.

• Have the partners change roles and repeat the activity.

Name _____ Class _____ Date _____

Hear Me?

At the top, the diagram lists statements a person might say to show understanding and empathy. At the bottom, it describes actions that display understanding and empathy. Read through both lists. Then fill in the empty speech bubbles and blank boxes with statements that demonstrate listening with compassion and empathy.

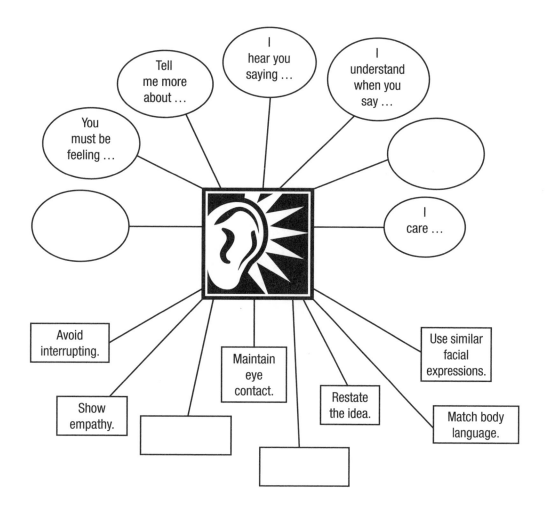

Thinking Flexibly

Exploring Meanings

PURPOSE OF THIS TOOL

Effective, intelligent people are able to change their mind as they receive additional data. They look for unique ways to solve problems, and they have a well-developed sense of humor. They are good at seeing consequences of different options. Thinking flexibly means approaching a problem from a new angle using a novel approach. Also called lateral thinking, this skill requires thinkers to have confidence in their intuition.

Students should be able to tolerate confusion and ambiguity to a point and let go of a problem, trusting that their subconscious can continue to apply creative strategies for solving the problem. As students explore this Habit of Mind, they learn to consider alternative points of view and different ways of solving problems. They learn that their initial ideas and strategies are not the only way, and that it is useful to be open-minded and creative.

The resources in this tool will enable students to

- Discuss the need for flexibility in planning and in daily life.
- Consider options for solving a dilemma.
- Use flexible thinking to analyze optical illusions.
- Explore an idea using the Thumbs Up, Thumbs Down, What If . . . model.
- Do research to understand how specific optical illusions are created.

HOW TO USE THIS TOOL

The following list of resources includes the suggested sequence for using this tool:

- An Ill Plan (Introductory Discussion)
- Bus Stop Dilemma worksheet (Motivating Activity)
- Thumbs Up, Thumbs Down, What If . . . worksheet (Reflection Activity)
- Understanding Optical Illusions research project (Extension Activity)

The activities and tasks included in this tool should take about 60 minutes to complete. You will need a clock or watch.

TIPS AND VARIATIONS

1. Introductory Discussion

- Write the following proverb on the board:

It's an ill plan that cannot be changed.

—Latin proverb

- Ask: What does this statement mean? (The best plans are plans that are open to being changed, molded, and reworked in the event of changing circumstances.) Then ask: To what extent do you agree?
- Tell students that in this lesson they will learn about the Habit of Mind called Thinking Flexibly. Alert them to get ready to change perspectives, generate alternatives, consider all options, and look at things in new and different ways. Explain that people who can think flexibly are those who can see when they need to change their mind and who can cope with confusion and contradiction. Being able to think flexibly allows us to be innovative, overcome obstacles, and reach reasoned and sound decisions.

2. Motivating Activity

- Give students the Bus Stop Dilemma worksheet. Have them find a partner, read the scenario, and decide what they would do in such a situation.
- After 3–5 minutes, have students join another pair of students to share answers and further discuss the scenario.
- Have groups share their ideas with the class.

3. Core Activity

- Select a suitable image of an optical illusion—for example, the Hermann Grid illusion, the Sander illusion, or the Triangle and Tuning Fork illusion. Many are available on the Internet. You may wish to provide a copy to each student, project it on a screen for all to see (if the technology is available at your school), or have students view it individually or in small groups on classroom computers (if your school has them). Ask students what they see. Have them continue to look at the image and ask again what they see.
- Show other optical illusions that you have selected. Have students spend some time carefully analyzing each image by looking at it from different angles, from near and from far, using a blank piece of paper to isolate parts of the image, and so on. Encourage them to persist and to interpret the lines and shapes they see in different ways. Suggest that they relax and open their minds to all the possibilities. If some students are having trouble "seeing" what each illusion is all about, let those who catch on early offer some advice to help their classmates.

• Point out that optical illusions force the mind to work a little harder—to think flexibly. Ask students if they know of or have seen other optical illusions and how they figured them out.

4. Reflection Activity

• Divide the class into small groups. Distribute the Thumbs Up, Thumbs Down, What If … worksheet. Each group should work for two minutes analyzing the given scenario from a thumbs-up perspective. Have them record notes asserting why the idea is a good one. Then give the groups two minutes to record thoughts from a thumbs-down perspective. Finally, give them two minutes to analyze the idea as if it were a very interesting formative idea. They should use it as a starting place to brainstorm new ideas.

• Discuss what students have learned. Ask: Did you like the Thumbs Up, Thumbs Down, What If … model? How is this model a good tool for lateral thinking? Can you think of occasions when it might be useful for you to use? Did you find the "What If" part of the model difficult? Explain.

5. Extension Activity

• Encourage interested students to do research to find out exactly how the optical illusions work and to report their findings with the class.

• To share students' findings even more, help students create a brochure titled "How to Design Optical Illusions" for teenage readers. The brochure could include instructions, examples, and tips for successful designs.

Name _____ Class _____ Date _____

Bus Stop Dilemma

Read through the scenario and determine what you would do in such a situation.

Imagine that you are driving down the road in your car on a wild, stormy night. You pass by a bus stop and see three people waiting for the bus. You just heard on the radio that all bus service has been canceled because of the storm.

The following people are at the bus stop:

1. An elderly lady who looks so ill she could possibly die.
2. An old friend who once saved your life.
3. The perfect partner you have been dreaming about.

You can transport only one person in your car. Which person would you choose? You could pick the elderly lady because she might die—you could save her life! But then again, you owe your old friend your life. This would be a perfect opportunity to pay your friend back. Then there is the perfect partner—you may never be able to find that person again! What would you do?

Your solution:

Exploring Meanings

Name _____ Class _____ Date _____

Bus Stop Dilemma

Read through the scenario and determine what you would do in such a situation.

Imagine that you are driving down the road in your car on a wild, stormy night. You pass by a bus stop and see three people waiting for the bus. You just heard on the radio that all bus service has been canceled because of the storm.

The following people are at the bus stop:

1. An elderly lady who looks so ill she could possibly die.
2. An old friend who once saved your life.
3. The perfect partner you have been dreaming about.

You can transport only one person in your car. Which person would you choose? You could pick the elderly lady because she might die—you could save her life! But then again, you owe your old friend your life. This would be a perfect opportunity to pay your friend back. Then there is the perfect partner—you may never be able to find that person again! What would you do?

Your solution:

Encourage students to be flexible thinkers and to "think outside of the box." The best answer suggested to date is this: Have your old friend drive the elderly lady to the hospital. In the meantime, you can keep your perfect partner company at the bus stop. When your friend returns, ask him or her to wait at the bus stop while you drive your perfect partner home. Then return to the bus stop, collect your old friend, and tell him or her all about your perfect new partner!

☐ 53

Exploring Meanings

Name _____ Class _____ Date _____

Thumbs Up, Thumbs Down, What If . . .

Consider the idea below. Record your thoughts from a thumbs-up, or positive, perspective on the issue. Then record your thoughts from a thumbs-down, or negative, perspective. Finally, consider the idea as a starting point in a brainstorming session. Come up with new ideas that stem from the original.

Idea:

Every city should install a vast network of bicycle lanes so people can easily and safely bike to school, work, and other places they want to go.

 Thumbs Up!

 Thumbs Down!

 What If . . .

Name _____ Class _____ Date _____

Thumbs Up, Thumbs Down, What If . . .

Consider the idea below. Record your thoughts from a thumbs-up, or positive, perspective on the issue. Then record your thoughts from a thumbs-down, or negative, perspective. Finally, consider the idea as a starting point in a brainstorming session. Come up with new ideas that stem from the original.

Idea:
Every city should install a vast network of bicycle lanes so people can easily and safely bike to school, work, and other places they want to go.

> Share the following sample answers with students to help them get started.

 Thumbs Up!

If more people rode bikes, pollution in cities would decrease.

We could reduce our dependence on fuel.

We could help improve global climate problems.

This is a way to encourage everyone to get more exercise.

This could help people lose weight and become healthier.

Exploring Meanings

Thumbs Up, Thumbs Down, What If . . .

Thumbs Down!

Building bike lanes is expensive.

Just building bike lanes would not guarantee that people would use them.

People can bike to school now if they want to, and most don't.

Many people are killed every year in bicycle accidents. As long as bikes and cars share any roads, there will be a public safety issue.

What If . . .

. . . cities created "bicycle transit stations" so that people could drive their cars to convenient locations and then bike, using car-free trails to high-use areas such as schools or downtown.

. . . cities mandated that everyone ride their bike one day per week, so, for example, on Mondays no one would be allowed to drive at all in certain areas.

. . . cities closed portions of downtown to cars, thereby enforcing pedestrian and cycling traffic only.

Exploring Meanings

Thinking About Thinking (Metacognition)

PURPOSE OF THIS TOOL

The Habit of Mind called Thinking About Thinking (Metacognition) focuses on our ability to know what we know and what we don't know. The major components of metacognition are developing a plan of action, maintaining that plan over a period of time, and then evaluating the plan upon its completion.

As students develop their metacognition, they become increasingly aware of their actions and the effects of those actions on others and the environment. They become better able to form internal questions as they search for meaning and information. They develop mental maps and plans for actions, mentally rehearse their plans, and reshape plans as needed during implementation. Finally, students become more skilled at self-evaluation and improving personal performance.

The resources in this tool will enable students to

- Observe how a person's opinion can change when other opinions and facts are introduced.
- Map their thinking process.
- Use a flowchart to organize their thoughts and solve a problem.
- Discuss different models for organizing their thoughts.

HOW TO USE THIS TOOL

The following list of resources includes the suggested sequence for using this tool:

- Changing Thinking discussion (Motivating Activity)
- Should I Stay or Should I Go? worksheet (Core Activity)
- Trophy Case worksheet (Reflection Activity)
- Comparing Models discussion (Synthesis Activity)

The activities and tasks included in this tool should take about 60 minutes to complete.

TIPS AND VARIATIONS

1. Motivating Activity

- Write the following statement on the board. "Young people should be paid to go to school." Ask students who agree with the statement to raise their hands. Tally the number of supportive students and write the number on the board.

• Divide the class into groups of four. Have the groups discuss the statement and reach a consensus of opinion. If students can't get past a simple "yes" answer, encourage them to think about why people get paid to work and what sorts of expectations employers have of them in return. After all groups have reached consensus, again ask students who support the opinion to raise their hands. Record the new number of supporters on the board.

• Discuss the results by asking questions such as the following: If you changed your point of view, what happened to change your mind? What were the steps of your thinking process? Were you aware of how your thinking changed, or did it just happen?

2. Core Activity

• Give students the Should I Stay or Should I Go? worksheet. Tell them you would like them to repeat the previous activity with the question listed on the worksheet. However, this time they should draw a flowchart to show their own thinking process as they discuss the issue. You may wish to list all or part of the sample flowchart from page 59 on the board to help get students started.

• Then have students find a partner in another group and compare flowcharts.

• Ask: How did your thought process differ from that of your partner? If you performed this type of decision-making activity again, how might you change your thinking process to help you reach a conclusion more efficiently? Could a flowchart help you think through difficult situations? (Mapping thoughts can help people organize and clarify their thinking.)

3. Reflection Activity

• Give students the Trophy Case worksheet. Have them work independently to map a solution to the proposed difficulty.

• If students are struggling to complete this assignment, you may want to help get them started by putting a sample answer, such as the one on page 61, on the board.

4. Synthesis Activity

• Connect the activities in this lesson to the Thumbs Up, Thumbs Down, What If … model used in the Flexible Thinking lesson. Ask students to compare and contrast these models for thinking through situations.

• Encourage students to brainstorm other tools for clarifying and organizing thoughts, planning activities, and solving problems.

Name _____ Class _____ Date _____

Should I Stay or Should I Go?

In the space below, create a flowchart that shows your thought process as you discuss the following idea.

Students should be able to decide the age at which they may leave school.

Name _____ Class _____ Date _____

Should I Stay or Should I Go?

In the space below, create a flowchart that shows your thought process as you discuss the following idea.

Students should be able to decide the age at which they may leave school.

The following sample flowchart shows one person's train of thought about the idea.

We should be able to choose when we leave school. →	Most of us would leave early. →	We need more freedom.

Our parents would hate it. ←	We could read, hang out with friends, swim, play video games, watch movies, write songs, and a million other things. ←	We could do a lot more on our own.

They'd want us to do something productive. →	Would we have to go straight to work or college? →	I think I need more skills.

I doubt I'd learn much practical stuff on my own. ←	And knowledge.

Name _____ Class _____ Date _____

Trophy Case

Suppose you are part of a group of three people who are in charge of creating a display to showcase the school's trophies and awards. Unfortunately, your partners completely disagree on how to go about the task. Review your partners' opinions, and then complete a flowchart showing how you might think through the situation and offer a compromise.

Partner A thinks: Let's do this as quickly and efficiently as possible. We don't have to create a fancy masterpiece. Let's just put a basic background in the case, then neatly put all the trophies and awards wherever they fit best.

Partner B thinks: Let's make a real statement! We can find newspaper clippings and photographs, and get special fabric and stands to display things. Maybe we could even create clay versions of our mascot to prop up the awards in different ways. I bet we can find an artist to help us add some graphic interest. Let me get a sketch pad …

Clearly these two people have different ideas. Here's what I think:

Name _____ Class _____ Date _____

Trophy Case

Suppose you are part of a group of three people who are in charge of creating a display to showcase the school's trophies and awards. Unfortunately, your partners completely disagree on how to go about the task. Review your partners' opinions, and then complete a flowchart showing how you might think through the situation and offer a compromise.

Partner A thinks: Let's do this as quickly and efficiently as possible. We don't have to create a fancy masterpiece. Let's just put a basic background in the case, then neatly put all the trophies and awards wherever they fit best.

Partner B thinks: Let's make a real statement! We can find newspaper clippings and photographs, and get special fabric and stands to display things. Maybe we could even create clay versions of our mascot to prop up the awards in different ways. I bet we can find an artist to help us add some graphic interest. Let me get a sketch pad …

Clearly these two people have different ideas. Here's what I think:

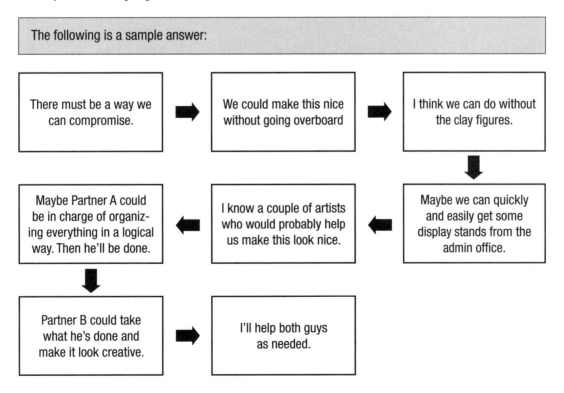

The following is a sample answer:

There must be a way we can compromise. →	We could make this nice without going overboard →	I think we can do without the clay figures.

Maybe Partner A could be in charge of organizing everything in a logical way. Then he'll be done. ← I know a couple of artists who would probably help us make this look nice. ← Maybe we can quickly and easily get some display stands from the admin office.

Partner B could take what he's done and make it look creative. → I'll help both guys as needed.

Striving for Accuracy and Precision

PURPOSE OF THIS TOOL

The Habit of Mind called Striving for Accuracy and Precision highlights the accuracy and craftsmanship needed to produce exceptional results. Striving for accuracy means reviewing the rules, criteria, and models relevant to a task and confirming that work completed exactly matches specifications. Reviewing this Habit of Mind will motivate students to take pride in their work and ensure that it is complete, correct, and faithful to the requirements of the assignment.

The resources in this tool will enable students to

- Form a general understanding of the concept of striving for accuracy and precision.
- Identify the difference between the terms *accuracy* and *precision*.
- Determine when they have used or failed to use accuracy and precision in their life.
- Apply quotations related to this Habit of Mind to their experiences.
- Define tools they have used to perform accurately and precisely.

HOW TO USE THIS TOOL

The following list of resources includes the suggested sequence for using this tool:

- Getting a Basic Idea (Introductory Discussion)
- Hitting the Target worksheet (Core Activity)
- My Terms worksheet (Core Activity)
- Accurately Quoted worksheet (Reflection Activity)
- Useful Tools worksheet (Extension Activity)

The activities and tasks included in this tool should take 30–45 minutes to complete.

TIPS AND VARIATIONS

1. Introductory Discussion

- Write "Striving for Accuracy and Precision" on the board. Let the students brainstorm a few basic definitions; record their ideas on the board. (Examples: desiring exactness, fidelity, perfection, elegance, craftsmanship, checking and rechecking, knowing when something is right.)
- Explain that the terms *accuracy* and *precision* do not mean the same thing. Ask if anyone can explain the difference. You may get one or two correct definitions, which is fine for now.

2. Core Activity

- To illustrate the difference between accuracy and precision to the entire class, give students the Hitting the Target worksheet. Explain that a dartboard is a very useful tool for describing the difference between the two concepts.
- Let students complete the worksheet on their own. Then discuss the difference between accuracy and precision as a class.
- Students are most likely to retain an understanding of these terms if they can personalize them. Distribute the My Terms worksheet and ask students to use examples that will help them apply the terms in their lives.
- When everyone is finished, call on various students to share their images and examples with the class.

3. Reflection Activity

- Give students the Accurately Quoted worksheet. Have them work in pairs to reflect on the quotes to determine their meaning.
- Then have students work independently to list one or more examples of how the quotes apply in their own lives.

4. Extension Activity

- Give students the Useful Tools worksheet. Have them think about hobbies and other activities they perform that require tools in some way.
- Then have students complete the worksheet to describe the importance of those tools.

Exploring Meanings

Name _____ Class _____ Date _____

Hitting the Target

For each dartboard shown below, indicate whether the person tossing the darts was *accurate* or *precise*. Then explain your answer. In the last row, draw a dartboard that shows high accuracy and high precision.

Example	Accurate?	Precise?	Explain

Name _____ Class _____ Date _____

Hitting the Target

For each dartboard shown below, indicate whether the person tossing the darts was *accurate* or *precise*. Then explain your answer. In the last row, draw a dartboard that shows high accuracy and high precision.

Example	Accurate?	Precise?	Explain
	X		High accuracy, low precision. The darts aren't too far from the bull's-eye. However, they are distant from one another. Whoever threw these darts did not use a precise method for doing so.
		X	Low accuracy, high precision. Because the darts are not very close to the bull's-eye, they aren't very accurate. However, whoever threw them was very precise in terms of the flight path followed.
			Low accuracy, low precision. This person did not throw accurately or precisely because there is no coherence to the dart placement.
	X	X	High accuracy, high precision. The person throwing these darts used a precise flight path to locate the darts very close together. Because all the darts hit the bull's-eye, the tosses were also very accurate.

Name _____ Class _____ Date _____

My Terms

Use the following charts to record your own definitions and visual clues for the terms *accuracy* and *precision*. Use terms and images that will be memorable to you.

Accuracy

To me, accuracy is ...	**A diagram or sketch to help me remember accuracy:**
An example to help me remember what accuracy means:	**I have been accurate when:**

My Terms

Precision

To me, precision is …	**A diagram or sketch to help me remember precision:**
An example to help me remember what precision means:	**I have been precise when:**

One example of a time when I was both accurate and precise:	**One example of a time when I was neither accurate nor precise:**

Name _____ Class _____ Date _____

My Terms

Use the following charts to record your own definitions and visual clues for the terms *accuracy* and *precision*. Use terms and images that will be memorable to you.

Accuracy

To me, accuracy is …	**A diagram or sketch to help me remember accuracy:**
To me, accuracy is getting close to or achieving my goal.	An illustration of a tennis ball hitting inside the service box of a tennis court.
An example to help me remember what accuracy means:	**I have been accurate when …**
When I play tennis, I've served accurately if I've hit the ball anywhere inside the service box.	*During my last tennis match, I served with 90% accuracy.*

My Terms

Precision

To me, precision is …	A diagram or sketch to help me remember accuracy:
To me, precision is a fine-tuned technique.	A sample answer might show proper technique for serving the ball. Encourage students to label their diagrams.
An example to help me remember what precision means:	**I have been precise when …**
My serves are precise if I'm using the intended stroke, velocity, and follow-through to hit the ball.	*My second serve is very precise. I risk on the first serve. On the second serve, I use a method that I'm sure will get the ball in given the circumstances.*

One example of a time when I was both accurate and precise:	One example of a time when I was neither accurate nor precise:
Sample answer: An illustration of a tennis ball exactly hitting the far outside line of a tennis court.	*My dad is a great tennis player. For some reason, I choke when I play with him. Last time, I was lucky to get a serve in the box, and my technique was horrible!*

Name _____ Class _____ Date _____

Accurately Quoted

Below are some quotes related to the Habit of Mind called Striving for Accuracy and Precision. Discuss the quotes with a partner. Then write an example of how each quote is true for you.

On course doesn't mean perfect. On course means that even when things don't go perfectly you are still going in the right direction.

—George B. Leonard, writer

Only the mediocre are always at their best.

—Jean Giraudoux, French novelist, playwright, and diplomat

Name _____ Class _____ Date _____

Accurately Quoted

Below are some quotes related to the Habit of Mind called Striving for Accuracy and Precision. Discuss the quotes with a partner. Then write an example of how each quote is true for you.

On course doesn't mean perfect. On course means that even when things don't go perfectly you are still going in the right direction.

—George B. Leonard, writer

Sample answer: *To me, this quote refers to the fact that as long as you are trying to do your best and are truly putting effort into your endeavors, you are on the right path. When I played Jenny Garretty in tennis, she creamed me. I didn't even win a single game. I knew Jenny was a lot more talented than I was. I just tried to learn from the experience. Then I showed up at my next practice and tried to apply what I'd seen.*

Only the mediocre are always at their best.

—Jean Giraudoux, French novelist, playwright, and diplomat

Sample answer: *To me, this quote means that if you set low standards for yourself, it's easy to accomplish your goals. But you might not accomplish much. It's only by setting high standards, pushing yourself, and being willing to fail that you accomplish something truly amazing. One of my tennis goals is to beat Jenny Garretty—that's a tough challenge!*

Name _____ Class _____ Date _____

Useful Tools

Read the following paragraphs and then answer the question that follows.

The ancient Egyptians strove for accuracy and precision when they built the pyramids. They developed the area of mathematics called geometry to ensure that their plan for the pyramids was accurate. Then they precisely followed their plan so the outcome was what they intended.

Similarly, Michelangelo designed the ceiling of the Sistine Chapel with precise sketches detailing the final outcome. As he worked on the ceiling, he was too close to it to see what he had already painted. As a result, he relied heavily on detailed plans to ensure that all parts fit together.

The Egyptians designed the tools of geometry to ensure their architecture was precise. Michelangelo used fine brushes with just a few hairs to add minuscule details that render his painting accurate to his plans.

What tools and equipment do you use to help you work precisely? Describe the items and explain how you use them.

1.

2.

3.

4.

Name _____ Class _____ Date _____

Useful Tools

Read the following paragraphs and then answer the question that follows.

The ancient Egyptians strove for accuracy and precision when they built the pyramids. They developed the area of mathematics called geometry to ensure that their plan for the pyramids was accurate. Then they precisely followed their plan so the outcome was what they intended.

Similarly, Michelangelo designed the ceiling of the Sistine Chapel with precise sketches detailing the final outcome. As he worked on the ceiling, he was too close to it to see what he had already painted. As a result, he relied heavily on detailed plans to ensure that all parts fit together.

The Egyptians designed the tools of geometry to ensure their architecture was precise. Michelangelo used fine brushes with just a few hairs to add minuscule details that render his painting accurate to his plans.

What tools and equipment do you use to help you work precisely? Describe the items and explain how you use them.

> **The following is a sample answer.**

1. My tennis racket: I just got a new racket. It has a tighter stretch and lighter frame than my old one, and it has improved my game dramatically. The strings react better with the ball—I get a better bounce off the racket with the tighter strings. The lighter frame makes it easier for me to make precise hits.

2. My tennis shoes: One time I accidentally wore my running shoes to a tennis match. They felt so strange. My tennis shoes are definitely designed to allow for the right kind of movement on the court.

3. My tennis clothing: I wear clothes that are specially designed for tennis. They wick moisture away from my skin and allow me the comfort and flexibility I need. In addition, I always have a place to store the tennis balls!

Questioning and Posing Problems

PURPOSE OF THIS TOOL

With this tool, students learn the importance of inquiring about the world around them. They learn how to pose questions about alternative points of view, ask questions to help them make causal connections and see relationships, and devise hypothetical (if/then) questions.

This Habit of Mind helps students realize that questions vary in complexity, structure, and purpose. It also reinforces the value of asking good questions in order to find solutions and expand understanding.

The resources in this tool will enable students to

- Explain the value of questioning and posing problems.
- Learn how to ask high-quality questions.
- Discuss Bloom's taxonomy.
- Use Bloom's taxonomy to create a series of interview questions.
- Determine how some good might come from problems.
- Identify and describe the qualifications of a good problem solver.

HOW TO USE THIS TOOL

The following list of resources includes the suggested sequence for using this tool:

- What Do You Think? (Introductory Discussion)
- Famous People teacher resource page (Core Activity 1)
- 20 Questions (Core Activity 2)
- Bloom's Taxonomy worksheet (Synthesis Activity)
- Man on the Moon worksheet (Synthesis Activity)
- The Best Problems discussion (Reflection Activity)
- Qualifications for Problem Solving worksheet (Extension Activity)

The activities and tasks included in this tool should take about 60 minutes to complete. You will need tape or pins and scissors. Please note that some advance preparation is needed for the first Core Activity.

TIPS AND VARIATIONS

1. Introductory Discussion

- Write "Questioning and Posing Problems" on the board. Ask students what comes to mind when they see the name of this Habit of Mind. Record their answers on the board. (Examples: a questioning attitude, developing strategies to produce needed data, finding problems to solve, wanting to know about something.)

- Explain that the starting point of all thinking may well be our ability to question. We question to gain new knowledge, to clarify information, to find and solve problems, and for many other reasons. At the root of all questioning is a particular kind of attitude. People with this attitude do not merely sit back and accept everything they see or hear. They ask questions about it. They investigate, inquire, and probe. This Habit of Mind is about being an active, perceptive thinker who doesn't take matters at face value.

2. Advance Preparation for Core Activity 1

- Cut out the names on the Famous People resource page or create your own slips of paper with the names of famous people on them.

- Write the following on the board:

> **Rules of the Game**
> - Ask only questions that can be answered with a yes or no.
> - Ask up to 20 questions—no more.
> - Keep a tally of the number of questions you ask.

3. Core Activity 1

- Tell students they are now going to take on the identity of a famous person. Tape or pin the name of a famous person to each student's back so that the student does not know who it is. Tell students that their challenge is to determine who they are by asking questions of a partner.

- Have students begin by finding a partner and silently reading each other's identities. Tell students to read the rules written on the board.

- When everyone has asked 20 questions, lead a class discussion with questions such as the following: How many of you guessed your identity? How many questions did you ask? What questions do you wish you'd asked sooner?

- Ask students to give you an example of a high-quality question versus a low-quality question. Explain that asking the right type of question is an important skill.

Exploring Meanings

4. Core Activity 2

- Give students the Bloom's Taxonomy worksheet. Explain that the worksheet shows a hierarchy of thinking developed by Benjamin Bloom in the 1950s. Knowledge, at the top of the chart, is the easiest form of thinking. Evaluation, at the bottom of the chart, is the highest-order thinking.

- Ask students whether they've ever seen this model before. (Some may have seen it, but most probably have not.) Tell them that even if they haven't seen the model before, they have been affected by it. Explain that the model is often used to create test questions and plan educational curricula. Tell students that understanding Bloom's taxonomy can help them perform better on tests.

- Have students find a partner. Distribute the Man on the Moon worksheet. Ask students to pretend it is the year 1969 and they are famous journalists who are about to interview the first man to walk on the moon. Have them work together to create a list of six questions, one based on each level of Bloom's taxonomy.

- Review students' lists as a class.

5. Reflection Activity

- Write the following quote on the board:

  A problem is your chance to do your best.
  —Duke Ellington, musician

- Ask: To what extent do you agree with this statement? Ask students to justify their answers. (You might point out that this is an example of a higher-order question.)

6. Extension Activity

- Give students the Qualifications for Problem Solving worksheet. Have them take the worksheet home so they have time to consider their answers. Suggest that they talk about it with their parents if they wish.

- The next day, have students share their answers in a class discussion.

Famous People

Dalai Lama Spiritual and political leader	**Bill Clinton** 42nd President of the U.S.	**Hillary Rodham Clinton** U.S. Secretary of State	**Barack Obama** 44th President of the U.S.
John McCain Politician	**George W. Bush** 43rd President of the U.S.	**Brad Pitt** Actor and philanthropist	**Angelina Jolie** Actor and philanthropist
Johnny Depp Actor	**Tyra Banks** Model and TV host	**Will Smith** Actor and rapper	**Bono** Singer and philanthropist
David Beckham Professional soccer player	**Nelson Mandela** Former President of South Africa; world leader	**Jon Stewart** TV show host and political satirist	**Tiger Woods** Professional golfer
Bill Gates Founder of Microsoft	**Christina Aguilera** Singer	**Jennifer López** Actress, singer, and dancer	**Lance Armstrong** Cyclist and philanthropist
Arnold Schwarzenegger Bodybuilder, actor, and politician	**Oprah Winfrey** TV host and philanthropist	**Wolfgang Amadeus Mozart** Classical music composer	**J. K. Rowling** Author of the *Harry Potter* series
Prince Charles Prince of Wales, Heir Apparent to the British Crown	**César Chávez** Labor leader, civil rights activist	**Mother Teresa** Nun and charitable worker in India	**Sammy Sosa** Professional baseball player

Name _____ Class _____ Date _____

Bloom's Taxonomy

Knowledge

Can you determine who, what, when, where, how? Can you list? Recall? Define?

⇓

Comprehension

Can you summarize? Estimate? Indentify? Discuss? Describe?

⇓

Application

Can you apply? Choose? Illustrate? Demonstrate? Interpret? Explain how one thing relates to another?

⇓

Analysis

Can you compare and contrast? Calculate? Distinguish between? Test?
Tell the most important part and explain why?

⇓

Synthesis

Can you predict? Infer? Add ideas? Rearrange? Redesign? Combine? Suggest solutions?

⇓

Evaluation

Can you justify? Evaluate? Prioritize? Rationalize? Explain?
Determine criteria for decision making? Judge?

Name _____ Class _____ Date _____

The Man on the Moon

Suppose the year is 1969. You are a well-regarded journalist who is about to be the first person to interview astronaut Neil Armstrong after his lunar landing. Read the following news report. Then use Bloom's taxonomy to write six progressively higher-order questions for the interview.

Man Arrives on the Moon!

As American astronaut Neil Armstrong set foot on the surface of the moon at 0256 GMT today, he said: "That's one small step for man, one giant leap for mankind." Twenty minutes earlier, Armstrong reported the lunar module's safe landing with these words: "Houston, Tranquility Base here. The Eagle has landed."

As television cameras installed on the Eagle recorded, Armstrong spent his first few minutes on the moon taking photographs and collecting soil samples. Fellow astronaut Edwin "Buzz" Aldrin joined Armstrong at 0315 GMT. The two astronauts jumped across the landscape and collected data before planting the American flag at 0341 GMT. They also delivered a plaque with President Nixon's signature and the following inscription: "Here men from the planet Earth first set foot upon the Moon in July 1969 AD. We came in peace for all mankind."

Interview Questions

1. Knowledge:

2. Comprehension:

3. Application:

4. Analysis:

5. Synthesis:

6. Evaluation:

Name _____ Class _____ Date _____

The Man on the Moon

Suppose the year is 1969. You are a well-regarded journalist who is about to be the first person to interview astronaut Neil Armstrong after his lunar landing. Read the following news report. Then use Bloom's taxonomy to write six progressively higher-order questions for the interview.

Man Arrives on the Moon!

As American astronaut Neil Armstrong set foot on the surface of the moon at 0256 GMT today, he said: "That's one small step for man, one giant leap for mankind." Twenty minutes earlier, Armstrong reported the lunar module's safe landing with these words: "Houston, Tranquility Base here. The Eagle has landed."

As television cameras installed on the Eagle recorded, Armstrong spent his first few minutes on the moon taking photographs and collecting soil samples. Fellow astronaut Edwin "Buzz" Aldrin joined Armstrong at 0315 GMT. The two astronauts jumped across the landscape and collected data before planting the American flag at 0341 GMT. They also delivered a plaque with President Nixon's signature and the following inscription: "Here men from the planet Earth first set foot upon the Moon in July 1969 AD. We came in peace for all mankind."

The following is a sample set of answers.

Interview Questions

1. Knowledge: *What happened at 2:56 today?*

2. Comprehension: *Tell us about what you saw and did as you walked on the moon.*

3. Application: *What skills did you need to have to make the journey through space and onto the moon?*

The Man on the Moon

4. Analysis: *You are a remarkable man who has achieved a great deal in your life. How does this event compare to flying planes in the war, getting married, and having children?*

5. Synthesis: *What did you mean by "one giant leap for mankind"? Tell us how you think this achievement will affect us.*

6. Evaluation: *How would you evaluate your entire experience? Was it worth the time and expense?*

Exploring Meanings

Name _____ Class _____ Date _____

Qualifications for Problem Solving

Answer the following questions to describe some of the characteristics of a good problem solver.

1. Name someone you know who is a good problem solver.

2. What makes this person good at solving problems?

3. What qualities are necessary for a person to be a good problem solver?

4. What skills are needed for a person to be a good problem solver?

5. What five Habits of Mind are most useful when solving problems? List the habits in order of usefulness and explain each choice.

Exploring Meanings

Name _____ Class _____ Date _____

Qualifications for Problem Solving

Answer the following questions to describe some of the characteristics of a good problem solver.

> The following are sample answers. You may wish to let students take this worksheet home to think about their answers.

1. Name someone you know who is a good problem solver.

   My mother

2. What makes this person good at solving problems?

   She always seems to know what to do, no matter what sort of crisis arises.

3. What qualities are necessary for a person to be a good problem solver?
   - *listening with empathy*
   - *ability to think flexibly*
   - *ability to find humor*
   - *calm demeanor*

4. What skills are needed for a person to be a good problem solver?
   - *creative thinking*
   - *critical thinking*
   - *ability to decide what the right thing is in any situation*
   - *metacognition*

Exploring Meanings

Exploring Meanings

5. What five Habits of Mind are most useful when solving problems? List the habits in order of usefulness and explain each choice.

- *Gathering Data Through All Senses The first thing you have to do is figure out what is going on by talking to people and gathering facts.*
- *Questioning: Ask good questions to make sure you understand the issues. Sometimes asking the right questions can solve the problem.*
- *Applying Past Knowledge to New Situations: Ask yourself if you've ever had a situation like this that you could learn from.*
- *Thinking Flexibly: Think outside the box to find solutions.*
- *Finding Humor: Reduce stress and induce creativity with humor.*

Applying Past Knowledge to New Situations

PURPOSE OF THIS TOOL

With this tool, students learn the importance of drawing forth experience from the past when dealing with new situations. They use their past experiences as sources of data to support, theories to explain, and processes to solve new challenges. With this Habit of Mind, students abstract meaning from one experience and apply it in a new situation.

The resources in this tool will enable students to

- Discuss how a person learns from past knowledge.
- Explore how a historical figure might have learned from his or her mistakes.
- Relate their experiences of learning from mistakes to the experiences of the historical figure.
- Give examples of how they have applied previously learned skills and knowledge.

HOW TO USE THIS TOOL

The following list of resources includes the suggested sequence for using this tool:

- No Learning Is Wasted (Introductory Discussion)
- No Mistakes worksheet (Core Activity)
- Transferring Knowledge worksheet (Reflection Activity)

The activities and tasks included in this tool should take 30–45 minutes to complete.

TIP AND VARIATIONS

1. Introductory Discussion

- Write the following quotation on the board:

Nothing we learn in this world is ever wasted.

        —Eleanor Roosevelt, former first lady and politician

- Generate discussion about the quote. Steer students to an understanding of the fact that throughout our lives we have opportunities to use knowledge and skills we have developed over time. Tell students that every day at school their knowledge broadens as they add to what they already know. Explain that they draw upon what was learned in a previous lesson, in a previous topic, or even at a previous school. For example, students may have learned in middle school that Abraham Lincoln was the U.S. president during the Civil War. In high school, they may explore how Lincoln's actions as a civil rights advocate shaped the future of the United States. The basic initial knowledge provides a framework for new growth.

• Ask: Is school the only place we learn? (No. We can learn anyplace, anytime.) Point out that we can also learn from our mistakes, even if it is difficult to get over them. However, if we can learn from mistakes and ensure they don't happen again, we become stronger. You might wish to share a simple example and ask students to share examples too.

2. Core Activity

• Give students the No Mistakes worksheet. Have them work in pairs to discuss the quote.
• Then have students respond independently to the questions on the worksheet.

3. Reflection Activity

• Explain to students that there are two ways to think about this past knowledge: we can consider it in terms of facts and figures we learn or in terms of skills we obtain.
• Give students the Transferring Knowledge worksheet. Have them reflect on how they have applied skills and knowledge learned.

Name _____ Class _____ Date _____

No Mistakes

Read the following quote and answer the questions that follow.

I've never made a mistake. I've only learned from experience.

—Thomas A. Edison, inventor

1. What did Edison mean?

2. Do you agree or disagree with the quote? Justify your response.

Name _____ Class _____ Date _____

No Mistakes

Read the following quote and answer the questions that follow.

I've never made a mistake. I've only learned from experience.

—Thomas A. Edison, inventor

> The following are sample answers. You may wish to have students work in groups to complete this exercise.

1. What did Edison mean?

It seems that Edison viewed his pursuits as part of a process. When he was trying to invent something, he would try various methods. When one failed, he did not see this is a mistake or a personal failure. He saw the results as information that would lead him closer to his goal. So as he "failed," he learned.

2. Do you agree or disagree with the quote? Justify your response.

Yes, I agree. At first I thought Edison was probably different from most of us in that he may have been focused and working in a productive way toward a goal most of the time. If that were the case, then any time he wasn't able to accomplish what he was trying to do, he would still learn from something productive. I didn't think that really applied to me because I'm not focused and on target all the time. Sometimes I simply don't try very hard. But even then, I think I learn something. I gain the experience of what happens when you don't try! So, yes, I agree with the statement.

Name _____ Class _____ Date _____

Transferring Knowledge

Things you learn at school are useful to you outside of school. Complete the following statements to describe knowledge you have gained or a skill you were taught at school that you have used, unprompted, outside of school.

1. Some knowledge I transferred was . . .

2. I could use this knowledge again when . . .

3. A skill I transferred was . . .

4. I could use this skill again when . . .

Name _____ Class _____ Date _____

Transferring Knowledge

Things you learn at school are useful to you outside of school. Complete the following statements to describe knowledge you have gained or a skill you were taught at school that you have used, unprompted, outside of school.

Share the following sample answers with students to help them get started.

1. Some knowledge I transferred was ...

In my video game production class, we learned how to manage a big project. When my mom asked me to take care of my siblings for the week while my parents were away, I used every bit of that project management information!

2. I could use this knowledge again when ...

I need to handle multiple tasks at one time.

3. A skill I transferred was ...

I used skills of time management, organization and planning, goal setting, problem solving, and budget management.

4. I could use this skill again when ...

I need to manage money, time, or problems.

Thinking and Communicating with Clarity and Precision

PURPOSE OF THIS TOOL

Thinking and Communicating with Clarity and Precision describes effective thinking as the process of simultaneously enriching the complexity and specificity of language. This Habit of Mind stresses the importance of using precise language, clearly defined terms, correct names, and universal labels and analogies to communicate accurately in both written and oral forms.

With this tool, students learn to avoid vague and imprecise language and start supporting their statements with explanations, comparisons, quantification, and evidence.

The resources in this tool will enable students to

- Repeat facts from an earlier communication.
- Rely on precise communication and work around hindrances to organize a group of people.
- Identify effective and ineffective means for thinking and communicating with clarity and precision.
- Apply effective thinking, communication, and teamwork strategies to make pudding.
- Describe what it means to think and communicate with clarity and precision.

HOW TO USE THIS TOOL

The following list of resources includes the suggested sequence for using this tool:

- I Had Dinner (Motivating Activity)
- A Suit Challenge worksheet (Core Activity)
- Pudding Making Contest (Reflection Activity)

The activities and tasks included in this tool should take 45–60 minutes to complete. You will need the following materials:

- For the entire class, a deck of traditional western cards and a watch or clock.
- For every group of four students,

box of instant pudding	measuring cup
medium bowl	wire whisk
spoon	serving cups or bowls
2 cups milk	disposable spoons
storage space in a large, portable cooler or refrigerator	

Note: See the tip for the Reflection Activity about using fewer than the listed number of some materials to make the challenge more complicated.

TIPS AND VARIATIONS

1. Motivating Activity

* Have students find a partner. Partners will be designated as A and B.
* Give partner A two minutes to describe what she did after school yesterday, from the last school bell to the time she went to bed. Tell students to be very detailed and specific. For example, they should not simply say, "I had dinner," but say, "I had dinner with my brother Joe and my dad, Rick. My dad made the meal. We had spaghetti with meat sauce, salad with balsamic dressing, garlic bread, and French-style green beans. I had a glass of water to drink. We talked about politics, mostly about how frustrated my father is with our current city council. I disagreed with my brother that our mayor is doing a poor job, because I think the mayor's been tough on crime and effective in bringing new business to town. My brother thinks our mayor is too easy on large corporations, so small businesses and the environment are suffering."
* Give partner B two minutes to do likewise.
* Ask partner B to repeat to partner A the events of partner A's prior evening. Then direct the partners to switch, so partner A repeats the events of partner B's prior evening to partner B. Again, allow two minutes for each of these conversations.
* When the activity is finished, discuss with the class what happened. Ask questions such as the following: How well did you recollect your partner's activities? Did you need the full two minutes? What happened? What types of things were easier to remember? What details did your partner leave out?
* Conclude the discussion with this question: Which was easier to remember—vague language or specific examples? Explain that this activity serves as an introduction to the Habit of Mind called Thinking and Communicating with Clarity and Precision.

2. Core Activity

* Write the following information on the board:

Rules
Don't show your card to anyone.
Don't tell anyone what card you hold.
No rhyming.
Don't say what the card is not.

Use only words. No pictures or gestures.

Talk to only one person at a time.

Ask only yes/no questions.

Don't name the suit of the card you hold.

• Give everyone in the class a playing card from a traditional western deck of 52 cards. (Be careful not to pass out Jokers or instruction cards.) Tell students to look at the card but not reveal it to anyone else. Remind students that there are four suits in a traditional deck of cards: spades, hearts, diamonds, and clubs. You may wish to list them on the board.

• Challenge students to find all students who are holding a card in the same suit as theirs, and to organize themselves together in one group so that there will be four groups of students—one each for spades, hearts, diamonds, and clubs. You probably don't have 52 students in your class, so students won't know exactly how many cards in the suit constitute the whole group. They will need to talk to almost everyone.

• Students should quickly learn that they need to use very specific language to describe their card. They will also quickly think about their situation and develop strategies for identifying and grouping students with the same suit. They may find one question that works well—such as, "Does your card have three circular areas coming out of a central area?" or "Is the name of the symbol on your card the same word used to describe a popular gemstone for wedding rings?"—and then ask that question of every student. Do not guide or direct the students. Let them investigate and communicate poorly at first. The students who think and communicate well will quickly become leaders and the other students will follow them around until the groups are settled.

• When all students are in four groups, have them turn over their cards.

• Give students the worksheet A Suit Challenge. Have them work alone to record communication techniques that worked well and those that did not work so well.

• Conclude with a class discussion. Record effective techniques and not-so-effective techniques on the board. Leave them posted for reference.

3. Synthesis Activity

• Give students an opportunity to apply what they learned in this lesson through a tasty contest. Explain that the challenge is to work together to make pudding. Whoever finishes first gets to eat first.

• Divide the class into groups of four. Have each group pick a lead chef, an assistant chef, a materials gatherer, and a cleaner.

• Explain that the lead chef is going to run the show and is the only one who may talk. All other members of the group must remain completely silent. No one but the lead chef may look at the instructions on the box. Each person is to complete only tasks appropriate to his role, and no one may complete a task unless requested to by the lead chef. Suggest that the four lead chefs take another look at and be prepared to apply the effective communication techniques on the board from the previous class discussion activity.

• Have the ingredients and materials in a central place at the front of the room. To make this exercise more challenging, you might wish to have fewer than the total required materials, such as fewer whisks or measuring cups, to force lead chefs to communicate with other chefs.

Note: Make sure you have a cooler large enough for at least one bowl of pudding at a time to settle for five minutes.

• Give the signal to begin, and start timing. Add a time penalty of one minute to any group that disobeys the rules. The group that finishes first gets to eat first! While students are enjoying their pudding, ask them to summarize their thoughts about the Habit of Mind of Thinking and Communicating with Clarity and Precision.

Exploring Meanings

Name _____ Class _____ Date _____

A Suit Challenge

List what you learned in the game about effective and not-so-effective ways of thinking and communicating with clarity and precision.

Effective Thinking and Communication Techniques	Not-So-Effective Thinking and Communication Techniques

Gathering Data Through All Senses

PURPOSE OF THIS TOOL

This Habit of Mind relates to getting information into the brain through sensory pathways: gustatory, olfactory, tactile, kinesthetic, auditory, and visual. Those whose sensory pathways are open and alert absorb more information from the environment than those whose pathways are oblivious to sensory stimuli. In this lesson, students learn to explore the textures, rhythms, patterns, sounds, and colors around them.

The resources in this tool will enable students to

- Discuss the six senses.
- Define the term *kinesthesia*.
- Link the sensory pathways to a sense and provide an example of each.
- Use imagination and understanding of the senses to "explore" a distant land.
- Reflect on why intelligent people must rely on the senses to gather data.
- Synthesize their thoughts in an essay.

HOW TO USE THIS TOOL

The following list of resources includes the suggested sequence for using this tool:

- Six Senses (Introductory Discussion)
- Sensory Pathways worksheet (Vocabulary Activity)
- Safari Field Trip worksheet (Core Activity)
- The Blind Men and the Elephant poem (Reflection Activity)
- All in a Word worksheet (Extension Activity)

The activities and tasks included in this tool should take about 60 minutes to complete.

TIPS AND VARIATIONS

1. Introductory Discussion

- Ask students to identify the senses. List taste, touch, smell, hearing, and sight on the board as students identify each.
- Explain that these are the most familiar senses, but in terms of improving our learning there is another very important sense called kinesthesia. Ask students if they know what the word *kinesthesia* means.

• Have students close their eyes. Then ask whether they have a sense of where their arms and legs are. Have them move an arm or a leg. Tell them to open their eyes again. Explain that kinesthesia, or kinesthesis, explains why even with the eyes closed we are aware of the position of our arms and legs and can perceive the active or passive movement of a limb and its direction. The term *kinesthesis* literally means "feeling of motion."

• Explain that the first five senses all concern our relationship to the world around us. Kinesthesia, however, is an internal sense. It speaks to how we sense our own movements and our position in relation to things around us. It also accounts for muscle memory and hand-eye coordination.

• Tell students that in this lesson they will learn about gathering data through all the senses using sensory pathways.

2. Vocabulary Activity

• Have students work independently or in pairs to complete the Sensory Pathways worksheet. This worksheet will help students refine their understanding of terms and concepts related to the senses.

• Ask students to form groups of four to compare and contrast answers.

3. Core Activity

• Tell students to close their eyes. As you walk around and distribute the Safari Field Trip worksheet, describe an experience that is rich with input for the senses. Don't list specific sensory images, just set the scene for students' senses to engage. Example:

> You and your closest friends or family are in Kenya, Africa. You are here for a safari. It is day 3 at a huge natural area called a safari park. What do you see? What do you hear? What do you smell? Imagine riding along in a jeep. Sometimes you get out and explore. You touch various items in your environment that you have never seen up close before. You hear birds and other animals. You take in the unique sights of the vast landscape. At one point you stop in a small village to have lunch. What do you smell cooking in the café as you enter? After lunch, you walk into the village center. Here a market is in full swing. Again, what do you hear? What exotic fragrances do you smell? How do you feel? As night falls, you are invited to dance in a tribal ceremony. Again, what do you hear, smell, see, and feel? At the end of this long day, you lie down in a small bed in a canvas hut.

• Tell students to open their eyes and begin recording their sensory memories of this "trip" on the worksheet they have in front of them.

• After students have finished recording details of their safari adventure, recap the experience with words such as the following:

> When you are in a new and exciting place like Kenya, it is easy to learn through your senses. In fact, your senses will be essential for you to make the most out of your safari experience. Generally, paying attention with all our senses is a simple and very effective way to learn. Whether you are in a classroom, in a sports arena, or exploring a new city, your senses can be used together to gather information and support your learning.

4. Reflection Activity

• Have students work in small groups to read and discuss the poem "The Blind Men and the Elephant."

• To stimulate discussion, write the following sentence on the board: How and why do intelligent people rely on their senses to better understand the world?

5. Extension Activity

• Allow students an opportunity to summarize their thoughts about this Habit of Mind. Give them the All in a Word worksheet and ask them to record their thoughts in an essay inspired by the saying.

• Student essays should demonstrate higher-order thinking. Students should be able to describe how appreciating and making good use of the senses helps people gather data effectively and efficiently, as well as learn more and get more out of experiences.

Name _____ Class _____ Date _____

Sensory Pathways

Complete the chart below by naming the type of sense for each pathway and then giving an example of how we use each sense to learn.

Sensory Pathway	Type of Sense	Example of How We Learn Through This Sense
Olfactory		
Gustatory		
Auditory		
Visual		
Tactile		
Kinesthetic		

Name _____ Class _____ Date _____

Sensory Pathways

Complete the chart below by naming the type of sense for each pathway and then giving an example of how we use each sense to learn.

The following are sample answers.

Sensory Pathway	Type of Sense	Example of How We Learn Through This Sense
Olfactory	Smell	We can tell if milk has soured before drinking it.
Gustatory	Taste	We learn about new places when we taste local food.
Auditory	Sound	We can hear the words of our teachers, which help us to learn.
Visual	Sight	We can watch a TV documentary and add to our knowledge.
Tactile	Touch	We can examine the texture of a leaf to help us identify a plant.
Kinesthetic	Movement	We can refine our movement to excel in a sport.

Name _____ Class _____ Date _____

Safari Field Trip

Record sensory details of the imaginary trip you took to Africa.

Sight	Hearing	Touch
Taste	**Smell**	**Kinesthesia**

Name _____ Class _____ Date _____

Safari Field Trip

Record sensory details of the imaginary trip you took to Africa.

> You may wish to walk around the class while students are working on this activity. If students struggle to come up with images or recollections from this thought exercise, take them back to a specific place—like the safari park or the village café or market. Ask: What do you see, hear, taste, touch, smell? How does your body feel? The following are sample answers.

Sight	Hearing	Touch
This place is immense. I see a large group of lions, lionesses, and cubs.	I hear a bird call I don't recognize.	The safari grass feels really dry on my legs as I walk through it.
There are vultures overhead.	There are also many strange insects buzzing around here.	There are many ways to get scratched or stung here at the park.
The vegetation here looks dry. I see a lot of yellowish-colored grass.	Our truck rumbles as it crosses the landscape.	I got to pet an ostrich. Wow! Its feathers were tougher than I'd expected.
The earth here is red.	Our guide has an interesting accent.	The vinyl seats in the jeep are hot!
	The drums and voices at the campfire were rhythmic and beautiful.	
Taste	**Smell**	**Kinesthesia**
We drank some guava juice that was surprisingly good.	The closer we got to wild animals like the lions, the more I could smell them. They smell like my dogs after they haven't had a bath in a really long time.	As we move through the park in the jeep, I feel my legs and arms getting jostled and shaken.
The food in the café was strange but really yummy.	The market smelled like flowers and fish.	Dancing was a bizarre experience. For a while there I felt like I could feel my limbs, but I couldn't see them.
I think I might've eaten some kind of snake. It tasted like chicken.	Nothing smells quite like a campfire, especially here in Africa.	By the end of the day, I was so tired every muscle and bone in my body ached.

The Blind Men and the Elephant

by John Godfrey Saxe (as cited in Linton, 1878)

It was six men of Indostan,
To learning much inclined,
Who went to see the Elephant
(Though all of them were blind),
That each by observation
Might satisfy his mind.

The First approach'd the Elephant,
And happening to fall
Against his broad and sturdy side,
At once began to bawl:
"God bless me! But the Elephant
Is very like a wall!"

The Second, feeling of the tusk,
Cried, "Ho! What have we here
So very round and smooth and sharp?
To me 'tis mighty clear,
This wonder of an Elephant
Is very like a spear!"

The Third approach'd the animal,
And happening to take
The squirming trunk within his hands,
Thus boldly up and spake:
"I see," quoth he, "the Elephant
Is very like a snake!"

The Fourth reached out an eager hand,
And felt about the knee:
"What most this wondrous beast is like
Is mighty plain," quoth he,
"'Tis clear enough the Elephant
Is very like a tree!"

ASCD
□ 103

The Fifth, who chanced to touch the ear,
Said, "E'en the blindest man
Can tell what this resembles most;
Deny the fact who can,
This marvel of an Elephant
Is very like a fan!"

The Sixth no sooner had begun
About the beast to grope,
Then, seizing on the swinging tail
That fell within his scope,
"I see," quoth he, "the Elephant
Is very like a rope!"

And so these men of Indostan
Disputed loud and long,
Each in his own opinion
Exceeding stiff and strong,
Though each was partly in the right,
And all were in the wrong!

MORAL:
So, oft in theologic wars
The disputants, I ween,
Rail on in utter ignorance
Of what each other mean;
And prate about an Elephant
Not one of them has seen!

Name _____ Class _____ Date _____

All in a Word

Read the saying below and think about everything else you've learned in this lesson.

To know a taste it must be tasted, to know a dance it must be moved, to know a game it must be played, to know a role it must be acted, to know a goal it must be envisioned.

Now summarize your thoughts about the Gathering Data Through All Senses Habit of Mind in an essay. Limit your essay to 500 words.

Creating, Imagining, and Innovating

PURPOSE OF THIS TOOL

This Habit of Mind speaks to the inherent ability of all human beings to generate new, original, and clever ideas, solutions, and techniques. When this habit is well developed, a person is adept at solving problems because he or she can view a situation from many angles and offer numerous alternative possibilities. Such a person can also jump into new roles, using analogies, vision, and perspective to take charge of each new role.

People who are good at creating, imagining, and innovating are not afraid to take risks. They can push the boundaries of what is considered the norm. With this tool, students are encouraged to eliminate "can't" from their vocabulary and believe in their own creative potential.

The resources in this tool will enable students to

- Define and differentiate the terms *creating, imagining,* and *innovating.*
- Brainstorm an idea for a product they would like to invent.
- Review several products to study their positive aspects.
- Work with a team to design a product to meet specific criteria.
- Plan, sketch, and finalize a design for a unique product.
- Evaluate the product design.
- Discuss the creative process.
- Let a quotation about creativity inspire them to create.

HOW TO USE THIS TOOL

The following list of resources includes the suggested sequence for using this tool:
- Defining Terms discussion (Vocabulary Activity)
- Whirling Sycamore Seeds worksheet (Motivating Activity)
- Comparing, Planning, Sketching, and Checking worksheets (Core Activity)
- How It Feels to Be Creative discussion (Reflection Activity)
- Looking Afresh worksheet (Extension Activity)

The activities and tasks included in this tool should take three to four class periods of approximately 60 minutes each to complete. You will need the following materials:
- sketch paper
- color pencils
- erasers
- rulers

TIPS AND VARIATIONS

1. Vocabulary Activity

- Write the words *creating*, *imagining*, and *innovating* on the board, leaving room to write beside each term. Tell students that they are going to explore the Habit of Mind that encompasses these three concepts.
- Ask students to define the term *creating*. Write their answers next to the term on the board (e.g., making something or saying something that wasn't present before; coming up with new ideas and novel ways of doing things). Point out that the word comes from the Latin word *creatus*, which translates as "to have grown."
- Ask students to define the term *innovating*. (This term takes the concept of creating one step further. It means creating something new and novel that is also useful.)
- Ask students to define the term *imagining* (allowing one's mind to wander to follow and originate creative thoughts, forming new ideas, images, and pictures). Explain that when imagining, the mind makes subconscious leaps and follows patterns that are unique to the person imagining. Imagining is an activity that does not result in an actual product.
- Point out that the term *creativity* encompasses all three terms that have just been defined and discussed. Stress that being able to think creatively, or "outside the box," and being able to think of original ideas are valuable skills in all walks of life. Reassure students that everyone can be creative. It just takes an understanding of the thinking involved, practice, and self-review.

2. Motivating Activity

- Give students an opportunity to think of an innovative idea. Hand out the Whirling Sycamore Seeds worksheet and let students brainstorm individually. Encourage them to be imaginative. You may wish to work with students who have trouble coming up with an idea, or suggest they pair up with a friend. If they still have trouble, suggest they think about a time when they struggled with technology, cooking, riding a bike, or any number of other simple situations, and tell them to think of a way to make that process simpler. Also encourage students to think of objects in nature that have fascinated them in the past and how the unusual or inspiring aspects of those natural objects might be applied to human use.
- If students have practical ideas that can be easily constructed in the classroom, encourage them to use this lesson's worksheets to design their invention. If students don't have a good idea of their own, suggest they design a game. If time and facilities are limited, you may wish to restrict students to creating a board game. If you have

Exploring Meanings

the appropriate programs, students may prefer to create a simple video game. You may have enough workable ideas to divide the class into groups and have each group work on an invention idea.

3. Core Activity

• Give students the Comparing worksheet. Have them work in small groups to complete it. They should provide examples of products in a category similar to the one they are creating.

• Lead a class discussion about what students like in that category of product. Then tell students they are actually going to design and build a product.

• Divide the class into groups, or production teams, and give each team the Planning worksheet to help guide their ideas. Encourage creativity, and let students follow ideas that occur to them. You may wish to put the following information on the board to direct students' ideas and planning.

Things to Keep in Mind

Remember the kinds of things people like in similar products.

Make your product really different and innovative.

Your product should have a central purpose.

Does your product need rules or safety accommodations?

What reward do people get from using your product?

Your product should be better than existing products!

• When students have a working idea, give them the Sketching worksheet and let them begin sketching some initial ideas for their game or product. Encourage students to sketch out several ideas here. If some students are concerned that they can't draw, assure them that it doesn't have to be perfect. Suggest that students label the various parts of their design and add a caption if an explanation is needed. Encourage them to meet after school to further think about and sketch their plan.

• The next class period, have students use the Checking worksheet to evaluate their product designs.

• Lead a class discussion about this project so far.

• Have students work together on their own time to finish creating their products. Allow one or more days for students to try out and evaluate one another's products.

4. Reflection Activity

• Have a class discussion about the process of coming up with an original idea, sketching out some ideas, thinking about those plans, and revising as necessary. Ask questions such as the following: Did you enjoy this process? Was it difficult? What helped you? What hindered you? Did you find that being in a certain environment was useful? Did you create better when you were alone, or when you had music on, or when there was some other circumstance present?

5. Extension Activity

• Conclude the lesson by giving students the Looking Afresh worksheet. Have them plan and create a piece of art, a poem, or a short essay in response to the quotation.
• If students do not feel inspired by the quote, suggest they find another and create something in response to that quotation.

Name _____ Class _____ Date _____

Whirling Sycamore Seeds

Read the following passage about Leonardo da Vinci. Then read on to think about your own "whirling sycamore seed."

> Leonardo da Vinci (1452–1519) may well be one of the most creative people who ever lived. As a child, he loved to observe birds in flight and falling objects. One such object that fascinated da Vinci was the sycamore seed. He watched in fascination as the seed gently whirled its way to the ground. Da Vinci took his observations and imagined how humans might apply similar concepts. Human flight was to da Vinci a great engineering dream. He sketched ideas for objects we recognize today as parachutes, gliders, airplanes, and helicopters. In fact, his helicopter sketches may have been based on his observations of sycamore seeds. Unfortunately, the technology of the time prevented da Vinci from obtaining materials that were both strong enough and lightweight enough to make his dream a reality. In fact, the lightweight engine didn't become available until five centuries later. Nonetheless, da Vinci's imagination has inspired some of the greatest inventions of all time.

Brainstorm ideas for something you would love to see invented. Then pick one idea and create sketches and a written description of your innovation.

Name _____ Class _____ Date _____

Comparing

At the top of columns 2–4 of the following chart, list three features of a product you really like, one per column. In column 1, list several existing products that are similar to your invention. Then compare the products based on the three features you listed.

Product Name:	Feature 1:	Feature 2:	Feature 3:

Exploring Meanings

Name _____ Class _____ Date _____

Planning

Use this worksheet to help you plan a terrific product.

Our product is designed for the following type of person:

The basic idea of this product is this:

It's going to look like this:

We need to keep these things in mind:

Additional thoughts:

Name _____ Class _____ Date _____

Sketching

Use this space to sketch an overall plan for your product. Be sure to use pencil and have an eraser handy so you can revise your designs as you think about them.

Name _____ Class _____ Date _____

Checking

Use the following questions to evaluate your idea so far.

1. Is my idea practical?

2. Can this product be easily made?

3. Is my idea as simple as possible?

4. Is the product appropriate for my intended audience?

5. Is my idea original?

6. Will the product be easy to create or will it be complicated and expensive?

7. Will people want to use this product?

8. Can I do anything to make my product better?

Name _____ Class _____ Date _____

Looking Afresh

Read the following quotation. Then allow the words to inspire you to create something. You may wish to write a poem or an essay. Or perhaps you could create a sculpture or a painting.

> *Creativity, it has been said, consists largely of rearranging what we know in order to find out what we do not know. Hence, to think creatively, we must be able to look afresh at what we normally take for granted.*

> —George Kneller, philosopher

Use this space to plan your idea. For example, you could create an outline for your story or sketch your artwork.

Responding with Wonderment and Awe

PURPOSE OF THIS TOOL

This Habit of Mind recognizes the "I can" and "I enjoy" attitude of intelligent people. It relates to the creative and passionate force that drives individuals to enjoy solving challenges and problems. As students develop this habit, they learn to cultivate and appreciate their curious nature. They learn to enjoy communing with the world around them, feel charmed by natural forces, and appreciate the logical simplicity of mathematics.

This tool gets students started on the path of being passionate lifelong inquirers. Art Costa says that this Habit of Mind is "caught, not taught." With this tool, you can help inspire kids and teach them how to be open to inspiration.

The resources in this tool will enable students to

- Discuss what it means to respond to something with wonderment and awe.
- List examples of things in life that have amazed them.
- Discuss how a person can be open to experiencing wonderment and awe.
- Reflect on the meaning of several quotations and their relevance to life.
- Take time to carefully observe the many little things happening around them as they walk or sit in a park.

HOW TO USE THIS TOOL

The following list of resources includes the suggested sequence for using this tool:

- The "Wow" Factor (Introductory Discussion)
- Eureka! worksheet (Core Activity)
- Wonderful Quotes worksheet (Reflection Activity)
- Observation Walk (Extension Activity)

The activities and tasks included in this tool should take 30–45 minutes to complete.

TIPS AND VARIATIONS

1. Introductory Discussion

- Write the phrase *Responding with Wonderment and Awe* on the board. Ask: What does this mean? (Put simply, it relates to the "Wow" factor.) Encourage students to think about times when they stood back in amazement and fascination about something they were seeing, hearing, feeling, or doing. Explain that this Habit of Mind is about those times when people realize that learning can be fun and inspiring and take them to new places. People who have this as a well-developed Habit of Mind appreciate the wonders of the world, like the challenge of solving problems, and enjoy discovering things for themselves.

• Write the following quote on the board:

> *I have no special gift. I am only passionately curious.*
>
> —Albert Einstein, scientist

Tell students that being open to ideas and curious is an essential part of this Habit of Mind.

2. Core Activity

• Give students the Eureka! worksheet. Have them work in small groups to discuss the questions.
• Put pairs together into groups of four to compare and contrast ideas.
• Lead a class discussion on the ideas that have arisen.

3. Reflection Activity

• Have students choose a partner. Give them the Wonderful Quotes worksheet, and have them discuss each quotation and to what extent they subscribe to the notion described.
• Circulate as the partners discuss, to ensure that they justify their opinions.

4. Extension Activity

• Encourage students to take an "observation walk" with a pad of paper and pen. Tell them that along their walk they should pay attention to every detail they see, write each down, sketch it, or simply enjoy and remember what they observe. Caution them not to linger in any one place too long but to keep walking. Suggest they pick a public place, such as a park or a mall, or a private place, such as their own backyard. Encourage them to sit and record everything they see for a period of time. Tell them they may be amazed at how much can happen and how rich the experience can be. Read the following entry from one student's observation walk as an example.

> *There's that yellow tabby again. I wonder who she belongs to. She looks like a miniature version of a large, wild cat like I've seen at the zoo the way she stalks like that. I never noticed that house had a purple door. And it has new windows. There are six different types of trees in this yard. The house next door has two stories. Most*

of the houses in the neighborhood are one story. I wonder what it's like to be on the second story, looking down on everyone else's rooftops.

• Tell students that the observation walk is a great tool for opening up the mind. It's also a very good technique for improving mood because it focuses a person's attention on only what is in front of her so she can't think about what may have caused her bad mood. An observation walk helps a person stay very present in the moment, where everything is OK—birds are singing, cats are prowling, the clouds move along in the sky.

Exploring Meanings

Name _____ Class _____ Date _____

Eureka!

The following are just a few of countless "Eureka!" moments. Read through the examples and then answer the questions that follow.

- An astrophysicist discovers a new planet.
- Sir Isaac Newton understands the concept of gravity via a falling apple.
- A Swiss mountaineer takes his dog for a walk and invents Velcro.
- Chocolate fudge inspires the design of a liquid-metal character in the science fiction movie *The Terminator*.
- Thomas Edison invents the lightbulb.

Questions

1. When was the last "Eureka!" moment you experienced? (Such moments can happen anytime—over big and small events.)

2. When have you been amazed or in awe of something?

3. How might a person keep open to amazement?

Name _____ Class _____ Date _____

Eureka!

The following are just a few of countless "Eureka!" moments. Read through the examples, and then answer the questions that follow.

- An astrophysicist discovers a new planet.
- Sir Isaac Newton understands the concept of gravity via a falling apple.
- A Swiss mountaineer takes his dog for a walk and invents Velcro.
- Chocolate fudge inspires the design of a liquid-metal character in the science fiction movie *The Terminator*.
- Thomas Edison invents the lightbulb.

> Encourage students to discuss these questions in small groups. You may wish to get them started with one or more of the following sample answers.

Questions

1. When was the last "Eureka!" moment you experienced? (Such moments can happen anytime—over big and small events.)

I love running on the trail. I'm not really competitive, but I've been frustrated with my slow pace and no matter what I do, it doesn't seem to be getting any faster. Then I got a portable music player, and BAM! I run so much faster now!

2. When have you been amazed or in awe of something?

Last week Mom and I planted a really neat passion flower vine. It has large purple and green flowers that look like something out of a sci-fi movie. I really can't believe nature came up with those. The guy at the nursery warned us that there is a particular variety of caterpillar that loves the vine. Yesterday I noticed a bunch of small, orange butterflies surrounding the vine. When I inspected closely, I could see that a bunch of leaves had been eaten, and there were 10 or so caterpillars on the vine. Those weren't there when we planted the vine. Where did they come from? How did they know we were planting that particular vine? How did the butterflies hatch so soon? Or were they visitors? It's all very amazing to me.

Eureka!

3. How might a person keep open to amazement?

When I'm in a bad mood I've noticed that I'm not open to anything. On the other hand, if I tell myself to be open, I can often get out of my bad mood by noticing something amazing. I think it takes practice.

Exploring Meanings

Name _____ Class _____ Date _____

Wonderful Quotes

Choose one or more of the quotes below. Explain what each quote means to you. Then decide whether you agree 100 percent, 1 percent, or somewhere in between. Justify your thoughts.

You can do anything if you have enthusiasm. Enthusiasm is the yeast that makes your hopes rise to the stars. With it, there is accomplishment. Without it there are only alibis.

—Henry Ford, car manufacturer

Wonder, rather than doubt, is the root of knowledge.

—Abraham Joshua Heschell, rabbi and civil rights activist

One thing life has taught me: If you are interested, you never have to look for new interests. They come to you. When you are genuinely interested in one thing, it will always lead to something else.

—Eleanor Roosevelt, former first lady and politician

Taking Responsible Risks

PURPOSE OF THIS TOOL

As students study this Habit of Mind, they learn that flexible people frequently go beyond established limits and put themselves in situations where the outcome is not known. They accept confusion, uncertainty, and the risk of failure as necessary, challenging, and rewarding. But when flexible people take risks, their risks are educated.

In this tool, students learn that there is a responsible way to take risks. They gain knowledge that allows them to make educated decisions about when and how to risk.

The resources in this tool will enable students to

- Think about the value of taking risks.
- Think about the perils of taking risks.
- Learn how to classify different types of risks.
- Learn how to evaluate personal risks.

HOW TO USE THIS TOOL

The following list of resources includes the suggested sequence for using this tool:

- Where Would We Be? (Introductory Discussion)
- Types of Risk worksheet (Core Activity)
- To Risk or Not to Risk? worksheet (Reflection Activity)

The activities and tasks included in this tool should take 30–45 minutes to complete.

TIPS AND VARIATIONS

1. Introductory Discussion

- Introduce this Habit of Mind by asking students questions such as the following: What would the world be like if no one took risks? How different would the world be if Christopher Columbus had never risked his life to sail away and find new lands? Where would we be if Martin Luther King Jr. and Mahatma Gandhi had not risked their lives and reputations to speak out for civil rights and the right to peaceful protest? Would a man have walked across the surface of the moon without taking a risk? Do you take risks in your life? (We may not be walking on the surface of the moon, but everyone is faced with risks throughout their lives.)
- Shift the discussion by asking these questions: What happens if we avoid risks altogether? (We may miss out on opportunities to grow our experiences and talents.)

Exploring Meanings

What happens if we rush into risks without thinking through the consequences for ourselves and others? (Any number of things could go wrong—e.g., we could be hurt, or we could hurt someone else.) Point out that risks may be significant, so we must calculate what we may gain against what we might lose. Tell students that as they learn about this Habit of Mind, they will become more adept at measuring risks and knowing how to take a responsible risk.

2. Core Activity

- Tell students that knowing how to take a responsible risk helps us handle new and unexpected situations. We need not fear change or the unknown if we know how to behave intelligently when these situations arise.
- Hand out the Types of Risk worksheet. Tell students that being able to identify a responsible risk is a habit that will be useful now and throughout their life. Allow students to work in pairs to complete the worksheet if they wish. Some students may be more comfortable completing the worksheet on their own.
- When everyone is finished, call for a few examples from each category. Ask: Do some categories of risk overlap? Can you think of other categories?

3. Reflection Activity

- Give students the To Risk or Not to Risk? worksheet. Then give them a scenario to analyze, such as the following:

  Suppose you have been invited to spend a month with a friend in a foreign country this summer. Your friend has told his parents that this is an opportunity to learn a foreign language and it is a supervised educational trip. However, you know that the extent of the supervised educational portion of the trip is a one-hour language class on the first day. You know you could have a lot of fun and this will be a grand adventure. Should you ask for permission to join the trip?

- Discuss students' answers as a class.

Note: Keep copies of this form handy in the classroom. When students come to you with issues or if students want to be adventuresome in some way, suggest they use this form to analyze the situation.

Name _____ Class _____ Date _____

Types of Risk

Add two or three examples to each category or risk below.

Academic *This type of risk involves your studies and learning.*	**Physical** *This type of risk involves your physical well-being.*
Should I study for every exam or just for the ones I am not confident about? Should I study only the subjects I think will get me into the best college program, or should I take the ones I enjoy the most?	Should I try bungee jumping even though it looks so dangerous? I'm not very athletic, but I'd like to try out for the basketball team.
Social *This type of risk affects how you relate to others.*	**Emotional** *This type of risk involves your emotional well-being.*
All my friends think smoking is cool, but all I can think about is bad breath, smelly clothes, and disease. Should I say what I think or keep my opinions to myself? Should I try harder to fit in and make more friends at school?	Should I talk to the person I like even though I don't know if she likes me? A person I have admired has asked me out. I would like to go but have a feeling he will not find me interesting. Should I cancel?

Name _____ Class _____ Date _____

To Risk or Not to Risk?

Ask yourself the following questions when you are calculating whether it is responsible or unwise to take a risk.

What good things could result from this decision?	What bad things could result from this decision?	What unlikely or unexpected things could result from this decision?

Explain the most likely outcome.

In light of these questions, is it responsible to take this risk? Yes / No / Maybe

Finding Humor

PURPOSE OF THIS TOOL

The ability to find humor in a situation has many positive physiological benefits, such as stress release and decreased blood pressure. In addition, this Habit of Mind can provoke creative and higher-order thinking, allowing a person to see powerful visual imagery and make analogies.

People who find ways to infuse humor into situations have the ability to perceive situations from an original and often interesting vantage point. Some students find humor in all the wrong places, such as human differences, ineptitude, injurious behavior, vulgarity, violence, and profanity. With this tool, students distinguish between situations that require compassion and those that are truly funny.

The resources in this tool will enable students to

- Share jokes with the class.
- Identify multiple benefits of using humor.
- Practice finding humor by creating a short skit and producing it for the class.

HOW TO USE THIS TOOL

The following list of resources includes the suggested sequence for using this tool:

- Sharing Jokes discussion (Motivating Activity)
- Why Should We Laugh? worksheet (Core Activity)
- An Opportunity to Play worksheet (Reflection Activity)

The activities and tasks included in this tool should take two 60-minute class periods to complete.

TIPS AND VARIATIONS

1. Motivating Activity

- Ask students if they know any good, clean jokes. For example, a six-year-old came up with the following: "Where do bees wait? At the buzz stop!"
- If a student shares an inappropriate joke, have a discussion about finding humor in the wrong places. To avoid this problem, come to class with several jokes to share.

2. Core Activity

• Tell students that one very important characteristic of intelligent people is their ability to find humor in ordinary and even difficult situations. Ask: Why might finding humor be an important Habit of Mind? Write student responses on the board. Examples:

> Shows the ability to laugh at oneself and with others.
>
> Lifts spirits and creates resilience.
>
> Reduces stress, tension, and conflict.
>
> Helps us deal with the unfamiliar.
>
> Allows us to see things in a new way.
>
> Helps people bond and enjoy experiences together.

• Give students the Why Should I Laugh? worksheet and have them work in pairs to complete this simple matching activity. Accept all reasonable answers. Students may wish to assign more than one statement to a quote.

• Ask students about what Finding Humor is **not**. Make sure they understand that a person doesn't have to crack jokes, tell riddles, or be a joker to exemplify this Habit of Mind. Point out that this habit isn't about being the funniest person in the class or entertaining others.

• Tell students that it has been said that finding humor is a habit that is "caught, not taught." Ask: What does this expression mean? (We can catch a moment to practice this habit. We don't need to be taught exactly how and when it is appropriate.)

• Reassure students that as they become familiar with this habit, they will become aware of occasions when finding humor is a good thing to do and even when it is the intelligent thing to do.

3. Extension Activity

• Divide the class into groups of four or five students.

• Distribute the worksheet An Opportunity to Play. Have groups choose one of the quotes as inspiration for a short skit. Students should write, direct, and produce these skits for the class. Skits should last no longer than four minutes and should clearly demonstrate the Finding Humor Habit of Mind. Encourage students to have fun with this assignment!

Name _____ Class _____ Date _____

Why Should We Laugh?

Match each quote below with the statement about finding humor that best fits.

QUOTE	QUOTE
Laughter is the shortest distance between two people. —Victor Borge, Danish entertainer and pianist	Finding humor in a situation can lift our spirits and help us develop resilience.
You can increase your brain power three- to fivefold simply by laughing and having fun before working on a problem. —Doug Hall, author and inventor	Finding humor in a situation can reduce stress, tension, and conflict.
People are at their most mindful when they are at play. If we find ways of enjoying our work—blurring the lines between work and play—the gains will be greater. —Ellen Langer, professor, Harvard University	Finding humor in a situation can help us cope with unfamiliar circumstances.
At the height of laughter, the universe is flung into a kaleidoscope of new possibilities. —Jean Houston, writer and spiritualist	
If you can laugh at it, you can live with it. —Erma Bombeck, writer	Finding humor can allow us to see things in a new way.
A person without a sense of humor is like a wagon without springs. It's jolted by every pebble on the road. —Henry Ward Beecher, clergyman and abolitionist	Finding humor can help people bond and enjoy experiences together.

Name _____ Class _____ Date _____

An Opportunity to Play

Use one of the quotes below as inspiration to write a short skit. Use the quote in the skit somewhere and be sure the skit demonstrates the Finding Humor Habit of Mind. The skit should be no longer than four minutes.

Fun is about as good a habit as there is.
> —Jimmy Buffett, singer and songwriter

Laughter is an instant vacation.
> —Milton Berle, comedian

You grow up the day you have your first real laugh at yourself.
> —Ethel Barrymore, actress

Humor is a rubber sword—it allows you to make a point without drawing blood.
> —Mary Hirsch, writer and humorist

Thinking Interdependently

PURPOSE OF THIS TOOL

This Habit of Mind relates to the fact that human beings are by nature social. Individuals who have developed this Habit of Mind understand that people can often accomplish a lot more intellectually and physically by working together than they can by working alone. With complex problems, many people bring many sources of experience and data. They also bring alternative points of view and ideas.

As students develop this Habit of Mind, they learn to try out and justify ideas on others. They also develop a willingness to be open to feedback, and they become motivated to help others via constructive critiques. With this tool, students learn that listening, consensus seeking, giving up one idea to work on someone else's idea, developing empathy and compassion, leading, and supporting are all behaviors of cooperative human beings.

The resources in this tool will enable students to

- Describe the value of working together.
- Use the words of a world leader to consider the value of working interdependently.
- Draft plans for their vision of an ideal school.
- Share ideas with a partner and then a group.
- Give others feedback on their ideas.
- Evaluate effective feedback techniques.
- Describe skills and habits useful for working in groups.

HOW TO USE THIS TOOL

The following list of resources includes the suggested sequence for using this tool:

- A Problem Shared (Introductory Discussion)
- The Touchstone of Reality worksheet (Motivating Activity)
- An Ideal School worksheet (Core Activity)
- Feedback worksheet (Reflection Activity)
- Sharing Habits worksheet (Extension Activity)

The activities and tasks included in this tool should take 60–75 minutes to complete. You will need to supply color pens or pencils.

TIPS AND VARIATIONS

1. Introductory Discussion

- Write the old saying "A problem shared is a problem halved" on the board. Ask students if they think this saying is true. Students may enter into a lively discussion about the pros and cons of sharing problems. Steer the conversation toward facing challenges together. Explain that when we face a challenge, make a decision, or solve a problem, we often benefit from asking others for their thoughts. One person working alone doesn't have a chance to compare, elaborate, or externally evaluate his or her own idea. Outcomes are often better when "great minds think alike."

- Read the following quotation aloud:

> I refuse to accept the view that mankind is so tragically bound to the starless midnight of racism and war that the bright daybreak of peace and brotherhood can never become reality. I believe that unarmed truth and unconditional love will have the final word.

> —Martin Luther King Jr., civil rights leader and pastor

- Ask: How might this quote be relevant to the Habit of Mind of Thinking Interdependently? (In addition to working with partners and teams in the classroom, family members at home, or coworkers on the job, we increasingly work with people in other cities or perhaps on the other side of the world. Often, people we work with come from a different culture or have habits very different from our own. We must be open to thinking together with a wide variety of people and recognizing different ways people can contribute.)

- Explain that in our modern, technological world, we must find new technologies and media for communication that will allow us to share ideas and benefit from collaborative thinking and learning.

2. Motivating Activity

- Give students the worksheet The Touchstone of Reality. Have them work in small groups to decipher the meaning of the quotation and provide examples. You may wish to let students work together, but give each student a worksheet so that they all can write their own specific definitions and examples.

3. Core Activity (Think-Pair-Share)

- Give students the worksheet An Ideal School. Allow them five minutes to describe what their ideal school would look like outside and inside, how it would be structured, and what the school philosophy or basic approach to learning would be. Then give them five minutes to draw rough sketches of their ideal school, highlighting important new features.

• Have students choose a partner. Allow five minutes for the partners to explain their ideas and listen to feedback. Remind students to listen to their partners' ideas with understanding and empathy. Explain that it is important to respect the ideas and feelings of classmates. Challenge students to find constructive words for delivering feedback.

• Encourage students to use a different color pen to make changes to their initial plans if they wish to in response to the feedback they receive from their partner.

• Have each set of partners join another pair. Again, ask students to explain their ideas and listen to feedback. Have many colors of pens available so that students can choose a different color of pen to alter their plans based on new ideas and feedback they hear.

4. Reflection Activity

• Give students the Feedback worksheet and allow them a few minutes to record their thoughts.

• Discuss as a class how students felt about this activity and what they learned.

5. Extension Activity

• Give students the Sharing Habits worksheet to determine and justify other Habits of Mind that could be useful for working with a group.

• Encourage students to share and explain their ideas.

Name _____ Class _____ Date _____

The Touchstone of Reality

Read the quote below. What did Gandhi mean by these words? Rewrite the quote in your own words and then list several examples that illustrate Gandhi's message.

> *Interdependence is and ought to be as much the ideal of man as self-sufficiency. Man is a social being. Without interrelation with society he cannot realize his oneness with the universe or suppress his egotism. His social interdependence enables him to test his faith and to prove himself on the touchstone of reality.*
>
> —Mahatma Gandhi, campaigner for independence
> for India through peaceful protest

I think Gandhi meant the following:

Here are three examples of Gandhi's message:

Exploring Meanings

Name _____ Class _____ Date _____

The Touchstone of Reality

Read the quote below. What did Gandhi mean by these words? Rewrite the quote in your own words and then list several examples that illustrate Gandhi's message.

> *Interdependence is and ought to be as much the ideal of man as self-sufficiency. Man is a social being. Without interrelation with society he cannot realize his oneness with the universe or suppress his egotism. His social interdependence enables him to test his faith and to prove himself on the touchstone of reality.*
>
> —Mahatma Gandhi, campaigner for independence
> for India through peaceful protest

> **Share the following sample answers with students to help them get started.**

I think Gandhi meant the following:

People should be as concerned about working with other people as they are about being independent. We are social by nature. If we do not interact with our society, we cannot realize how similar we are. As a result, we will become egotistical, thinking we are better than some people who are different from us. By understanding and valuing our connection to society, we can be better people and make the most of our time on this planet.

Here are three examples of Gandhi's message:

1. I heard about a guy who was held captive as a prisoner of war. He was chained together with other people, so it was difficult doing even the most basic things. One day one of the prisoners asked the guard when they would be released. The guard said, "When you are free, I will be free," and he glumly looked at his hands as if he, too, were chained to them.

2. I joined a community gardening group. The point of the group is to train people on how to create gardens that require little water or fertilizer but still look beautiful. Having the group makes the challenge of honoring the environment a little easier.

3. A friend of mine is a hurricane survivor. The storm brought her together with people she might not have met otherwise. When everyone lost their homes, their jobs, their schools, and so many other resources, she realized they all had the same fears and concerns. Friends she made there are now my friends, too.

 □ 135

Name _____ Class _____ Date _____

Exploring Meanings

An Ideal School

Describe what your ideal school would look like outside and inside. How would it be structured? What would the school philosophy or basic approach to learning be?

Draw rough sketches of the school, highlighting important new features.

Name _____ Class _____ Date _____

Feedback

Answer the following questions to evaluate your experience of sharing your ideas with a group.

Changing Ideas: Did you change your ideas in light of the feedback given? Explain.

Sharing Your Ideas: What was useful about sharing your thoughts with others?

How could you improve your style of giving feedback?

Receiving Feedback: Without using names, did you notice any strategies of offering feedback that were not comfortable for you? Describe those techniques.

Describe more productive alternatives to those techniques.

Thinking Interdependently: What advice would you give a team of people who are about to embark on a project together?

What qualities will they need to develop?

What skills will they need to develop?

Name _____ Class _____ Date _____

Sharing Habits

Select at least three Habits of Mind you think would be useful to have when working with groups. Explain why you think each is important. Then rank the habits in order of importance.

Helpful Habits of Mind for Group Activities	How This Habit of Mind Will Help	Rank
Persisting		
Managing Impulsivity		
Listening with Understanding and Empathy		
Thinking Flexibly		
Thinking About Thinking (Metacognition)		
Striving for Accuracy and Precision		
Questioning and Posing Problems		
Applying Past Knowledge to New Situations		
Thinking and Communicating with Clarity and Precision		
Gathering Data Through All Senses		
Creating, Imagining, and Innovating		
Responding with Wonderment and Awe		

Exploring Meanings

Sharing Habits

Helpful Habits of Mind for Group Activities	How This Habit of Mind Will Help	Rank
Taking Responsible Risks		
Finding Humor		
Thinking Interdependently		
Learning Continuously		

Exploring Meanings

Learning Continuously

PURPOSE OF THIS TOOL

This Habit of Mind relates to the importance of staying in a continuous learning mode. People with this habit regularly look for ways to improve, grow, learn, and otherwise modify and improve themselves. They look upon problems and complicated circumstances as opportunities to grow and learn. Many people confront learning opportunities with fear. With this tool, students can begin to look upon challenges with wonder and intrigue.

The resources in this tool will enable students to

- List skills they learned in the last year.
- Self-evaluate their willingness to learn.
- Reflect on quotations about learning.
- Provide personal examples of learning experiences.
- Write a short story or comic strip that incorporates all 16 Habits of Mind in some way.

HOW TO USE THIS TOOL

The following list of resources includes the suggested sequence for using this tool:

- Changing Times (Introductory Discussion)
- New Skills worksheet (Motivating Activity)
- Learning Self-Evaluation worksheet (Core Activity)
- Considering Quotations worksheet (Reflection Activity)
- Using the Habits of Mind (Extension Activity)

The activities and tasks included in this tool should take 60–90 minutes to complete. You will need the following materials:

- color pencils and markers
- paper
- other art materials students could use to create a comic strip (optional)

TIPS AND VARIATIONS

1. Introductory Discussion

- Tell students that there was a time when they could have left school with a fistful of qualifications and never have to worry much about further learning. Ask: Is that still true today? (The world has changed and an ever-expanding list of qualifications is needed to help people live and survive during our technological era.)

• Tell students it has been said that the knowledge and understanding the students of today will need in their later lives has yet to be considered. Ask: Do you agree or disagree? Why? Mention an example from your own life, such as the rapid change during your lifetime of information technology; for example, if mobile phones, laptop computers, or MP3 players were not available when you were a child, mention them.

• Remind students that technology can produce rapid and dramatic changes in a short period of time, so we must be able to learn quickly and effectively. This requires having an open mind in which we do not feel threatened by learning new things but embrace change with determination and competence to learn. That is what this final Habit of Mind is all about.

2. Motivating Activity

• Give students a copy of the New Skills worksheet. Have them list at least three examples of new skills they have learned in the past year.

• Discuss student responses.

3. Core Activity

• Give students the Learning Self-Evaluation worksheet. Encourage them to think carefully about each statement and to be honest in their responses.

• You might want to have a one-on-one conversation with students about their answers to these questions. Together, you can discuss the importance of remaining open to continuous learning. You may also want to explore obstacles to doing so.

4. Reflection Activity

• Have the students arrange themselves in pairs.

• Give each student a copy of the Considering Quotations worksheet. Have the partners discuss the quotes, then independently write an example of how each quote is true for them. If time permits, have students write their own inspirational quote about learning.

5. Extension Activity

• Have students write a short story or create a comic strip that illuminates all 16 Habits of Mind. For example, the story or comic strip might be about how an alien comes to Earth and has to learn how to cope with the odd things he sees. Encourage students to have fun and be creative.

• Suggest that students put their ideas together in the form of booklets that they can keep as reminders of the Habits of Mind. Another idea is to add the students' stories or comic strips to the school Web site or handbook to introduce future students and their parents to the Habits of Mind.

Name _____ Class _____ Date _____

New Skills

Brainstorm a list of new skills you have learned in the past year or so. Consider things you've learned at school and beyond.

New skill	How did you feel about learning this skill?
1.	
2.	
3.	

Name _____ Class _____ Date _____

New Skills

Brainstorm a list of new skills you have learned in the past year or so. Consider things you've learned at school and beyond.

Share the following sample answers with students to help them get started.

New skill	How did you feel about learning this skill?
1. I learned how to compete in mountain biking competitions.	I felt overwhelmed and underqualified at first, but it was exciting—even when I fell a couple of times.
2. I learned how to play the violin.	I feel like I was born to play the violin! It's a very natural and easy thing for me to do.
3. I learned why we are required to take Driver's Education classes.	Ugggh. I got in a lot of trouble when I "borrowed" my parents' car, drove without a license, and backed into my neighbor's stone mailbox!

Name _____ Class _____ Date _____

Learning Self-Evaluation

Check the statements below that are true about you.

_____ I like learning new skills.

_____ I like learning new skills only if they are related to something I'm interested in, such as sports or music.

_____ I like learning new skills only if I can immediately see how they will help me.

_____ I like learning new skills if I can use them to help other people.

_____ I like learning about new technologies, such as the latest video games and cell phones.

_____ I like learning new skills if the person showing me demonstrates them first.

_____ I like learning new skills only if I get a chance to practice before I have to use them.

_____ I like learning new skills only if I absolutely need to have those skills.

Name _____ Class _____ Date _____

Considering Quotations

Below are some quotes that relate to the Learning Continuously Habit of Mind. Provide an example of how each quote is relevant in your life.

Education is a progressive discovery of our own ignorance.
> —Will Durant, historian and philosopher

Learn as if you were going to live forever. Live as if you were going to die tomorrow.
> —Mahatma Gandhi, campaigner for independence
> for India through peaceful protest

The illiterate of the 21st century will not be those who cannot read and write, but those who cannot learn, unlearn, and relearn.
> —Alvin Toffler, writer and futurist

Name _____ Class _____ Date _____

Considering Quotations

Below are some quotes that relate to the Learning Continuously Habit of Mind. Provide an example of how each quote is relevant in your life.

> The following are sample answers. You may wish to share one or two to get students started. If students finish quickly, encourage them to come up with their own inspirational quote about learning.

Education is a progressive discovery of our own ignorance.

—Will Durant, historian and philosopher

I have been humiliated when I thought I understood everything about a topic and then had someone show me otherwise. I thought I was a pretty good chess player, but my cousin blew me away the other day. Now I know stuff about chess I didn't know I needed to know!

Learn as if you were going to live forever. Live as if you were going to die tomorrow.

—Mahatma Gandhi, campaigner for independence
for India through peaceful protest

I hate feeling stagnant. So if I have the attitude that I am going to live forever, then I am always motivated to learn. Living as if I am going to die tomorrow reminds me to take responsible risks. I think I'll ask my mom to teach me to cook.

The illiterate of the 21st century will not be those who cannot read and write, but those who cannot learn, unlearn, and relearn.

—Alvin Toffler, writer and futurist

It seems like just when I get a video game down, it's finished. Then I buy a new one that has a completely different set of strategies. If I try the old strategies, I fail. It's only when I figure out the new ones that I succeed. But then, it's over and time to start all over! I guess I'll be able to apply this in the "real" world.

Expanding Capacities

We don't learn from our experiences; we learn from our capacity for experience.

—Buddha

This section builds upon the foundation established in the Exploring Meanings section. Teachers and students should now be familiar with all 16 Habits of Mind and have an understanding of what each one means. At this stage, however, students aren't expected to be able to recall all of the habits by memory. In addition, they haven't really assessed themselves in relation to the habits.

Expanding capacities with the Habits of Mind occurs when learners realize that they need to call upon a particular habit and consider the different ways they can use it. With the tools in this section, students will become able to select and deploy habits as appropriate, use different strategies to employ the habits, and see changes in their own lives and learning experiences because of an application of the habits.

As students learn and practice the Habits of Mind, they become more skillful. They develop a large repertoire of strategies that they can call upon....

Learners begin to develop internal, metacognitive strategies and "self-talk" about using the Habits of Mind when confronted with problems, decisions, and ambiguous situations.... Persistence, for example, is not just a word. Rather, it is found to be a composite of numerous skills and strategies. Learners employ techniques that help them stay with a task in the face of uncertainty. When it is difficult to complete a task, learners develop new ways of encouraging themselves to stick with it. (Costa & Kallick, 2008, p. 61)

CONTENTS

TITLE OF TOOL

Expanding Capacities

Persisting

PURPOSE OF THIS TOOL

This tool gives students opportunities to find examples of persisting in the world around them. They think about people and fictional characters they know who persist, and they create a skit showing one person helping another to persist. They also assume the identity of advertising executives and create a plan for marketing the concept of persisting to a nationwide audience. As students further apply the concept of persisting, they form a deeper understanding and begin to make it a true Habit of Mind.

The resources in this tool will enable students to

- Discuss examples of people they know and fictional characters who persisted.
- Describe how persisting looks, feels, and sounds.
- Define *persisting*.
- Create a skit showing one person encouraging another to persist.
- Create a plan for marketing the idea of persisting to a nationwide audience.
- Regularly assess their ability to persist.

HOW TO USE THIS TOOL

The following list of resources includes the suggested sequence for using this tool:

- Investigating Persistence worksheet (Introductory Activity)
- Persisting skit (Core Activity 1)
- Marketing Persistence worksheet (Core Activity 2)
- Persistence Rubric worksheet (Reflection Activity)

The activities and tasks included in this tool should take about 90 minutes to complete. You will need to have color pencils available.

TIPS AND VARIATIONS

1. Introductory Activity

- Begin a discussion of examples of persisting by asking questions such as the following: Where have you seen people persist? What movies or books feature characters that persist? Who in your own life has shown persistence? Remind students that thinking about what something sounds like, looks like, feels like, and personally means to them is a great way to integrate it.

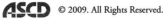

Expanding Capacities

• Give students the Investigating Persistence worksheet and have them answer the questions. You may wish to have students work with a partner.

2. Core Activity 1

• Divide the class into groups of three or four students. In groups of four, one student will be the director, another the writer, and the other two the actors. In groups of only three students, one will be the writer-director and two will be actors. Remind everyone to work together as a team.

• Ask each group to write and act out a three-minute skit in which two friends are discussing something they find difficult because it is not personally interesting or challenging. The topic may be school-related or perhaps concern an extracurricular activity or responsibility. One person could explain what the issue is and why she wants to quit. The other person could provide useful strategies to help the friend persist and achieve a goal.

• Have students perform the skit for the class. Afterward, discuss as a class the quality of the advice. Offer additional strategies if appropriate.

3. Core Activity 2

• Tell students that to solidify a personal understanding of what the Habit of Mind of Persisting means to them so that they can develop it further, they are going to pretend to be advertising executives. Their job is to pitch an idea to a representative of the Department of Health and Human Services, who wants to launch a nationwide advertising campaign to promote persisting as an important intelligent behavior for everyone.

• Distribute the Marketing Persistence worksheet to help students flesh out their ideas.

4. Reflection Activity

• Tell students that they can better develop this Habit of Mind by thinking each day about how they can integrate it into their lives. Ask them to think about questions such as these: Do you have a big test or class project coming up? Do you have responsibilities at home to consider? Then tell students to think about how they can apply Persisting to help them. Assure them that soon this habit will become a natural state of mind that they can apply without having to stop and think about it. This process is called habituation.

• To help students assess their persisting abilities at any given time, give them the Persistence Rubric worksheet. Encourage them to keep the rubric handy and to revisit it frequently. Say that they should see improvement over time.

Expanding Capacities

Name _____ Class _____ Date _____

Investigating Persistence

Sounds Like: When you are persisting, you might say to a friend …   1.   2.   3.
Looks Like: When you see a friend persisting, he or she may be …   1.   2.   3.
Feels Like: When you are persisting, you may think to yourself …   1.   2.   3.
Meaning to Me: Define *persisting* with words or a picture.

Name _____ Class _____ Date _____

Investigating Persistence

Share the following sample answers with students to help them get started.

Expanding Capacities

Sounds Like: When you are persisting, you might say to a friend …

1. *Hang in there.*

2. *It may not be easy now, but you will be very glad you persisted.*

3. *Keep your eyes on the prize!*

Looks Like: When you see a friend persisting, he or she may be …

1. *… trying a new strategy.*

2. *… reminding himself or herself what there is to gain.*

3. *… working hard for something he or she believes in.*

Feels Like: When you are persisting, you may think to yourself …

1. *I want to give up, but I want to achieve this even more.*

2. *I will be proud of myself when I am finished.*

3. *Perhaps I would be more successful with a different strategy.*

Meaning to Me: Define *persisting* with words or a picture.

Persisting means continuing even when challenges slow you down.

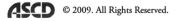

Name _____ Class _____ Date _____

Marketing Persistence

Complete the following tasks to summarize your plans for a national advertising campaign promoting the Habit of Mind of Persisting.

The logo I propose for this Habit of Mind is:	The rap song or jingle I propose for this Habit of Mind is:
The person I recommend to be spokesperson for this Habit of Mind is: **Draw or add a picture of him or her if possible.**	**My other ideas for marketing the Habit of Mind of Persisting are:**

Name _____ Class _____ Date _____

Persistence Rubric

Use the following rubric to reflect on your persisting abilities at any point in time. Add your own statements to the chart to further assess your abilities.

How regularly do you ...	Always	Usually	Sometimes	Seldom or Never
... stick to a challenge even when the answer isn't immediately obvious?				
... follow methods and processes to solve a problem?				
... find alternative ways to approach a problem when stuck?				
... find ways to bring your attention back when drifting off task?				
... keep focused on the end result even if you're not enjoying the task?				
... avoid distractions?				
... value the quality of your work or the end product?				
... independently work through problems or challenges?				

Expanding Capacities

Managing Impulsivity

PURPOSE OF THIS TOOL

In this tool, students observe behavior that is impulsive as well as behavior that involves managing impulses. They learn how to take note of this behavior, learning from the good and communicating effectively about the not-so-good. They also have opportunities to self-reflect and outline a plan for better managing their own impulsive urges. As students further apply this habit, they form a deeper understanding of it and begin to make it a true Habit of Mind.

The resources in this tool will enable students to

- Identify and describe impulsive behavior.
- Recommend methods for improving impulsive behavior.
- Communicate with a friend about managing impulsive actions.
- Analyze the behavior of someone who does a good job managing impulses.
- Identify ways to improve and monitor their own impulsive behavior.

HOW TO USE THIS TOOL

The following list of resources includes the suggested sequence for using this tool:

- Managing My Impulsivity worksheet (Motivating Activity)
- I've Gotta Tell Ya ... worksheet (Core Activity)
- Master of the Impulses worksheet (Reflection Activity)
- Create a Rubric (Extension Activity)

The activities and tasks included in this tool should take about 45–60 minutes to complete.

TIPS AND VARIATIONS

1. Motivating Activity

- Distribute the Managing My Impulsivity worksheet. Have students work in groups of three to explain the meaning of each quote in their own words, rank-order the quotes according to which they like most, and explain their rankings.
- Ask each group to write their own saying that encapsulates the meaning of this Habit of Mind for them. Have a representative of each group write the group's ideas on the board for all to see. Lead a discussion looking for similarities among the various groups' sayings.

2. Core Activity

- Distribute the worksheet I've Gotta Tell Ya . . . . Have students finish the letter started in the worksheet.
- Let students work together in pairs or small groups to discuss their letters.

3. Reflection Activity

- Tell students to think about someone they know who is good at managing impulses. Then give them the Master of Impulses worksheet to complete.
- Call on volunteers to share their responses with the class.

4. Extension Activity

- Have students work in pairs to design a rubric to measure their improvement in managing impulsivity. You may wish to show them a sample rubric, such as the one in Appendix B, to help them get started.
- When students are finished, post the rubrics on the wall and let everyone have a look. You can combine ideas to create a class rubric for managing impulses, if you wish.

Expanding Capacities

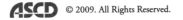

Name _____ Class _____ Date _____

Managing My Impulsivity

In your group, discuss the meaning of each of the quotes below and write your answers in the spaces provided. Next, decide which quotes your group prefers—that is, which make the most sense for the group—and indicate your ranking beside each quote, using 1 for your favorite, 2 for your second-favorite, and so on. Finally, create your group's own saying that explains what Managing Impulsivity means to you; write your quote at the bottom of the page and have a group representative write it on the board for comparison with sayings of other groups.

I count him braver who overcomes his desires than him who conquers his enemies; the hardest victory is the victory over self.

—Aristotle, ancient Greek philosopher

Before you start up a ladder, count the rungs.
—Yiddish proverb

Remember not only to say the right thing in the right place, but far more difficult still, to leave unsaid the wrong thing at the tempting moment.
—Benjamin Franklin, U.S. founding father and statesman

Look twice before you leap.
—Charlotte Bronte, British writer

Caution is the eldest child of wisdom.
—Victor Hugo, French author

Your group's own saying about Managing Impulsivity:

Expanding Capacities

Name _____ Class _____ Date _____

I've Gotta Tell Ya . . .

Finish the letter below. Keep in mind the need to balance urges to be impulsive and the need for some impulsivity in one's life.

Dear Drake,

    You have been a good friend of mine for many years. I value your friendship. Because you mean a lot to me, I feel the need to write to you about an important issue. Yesterday you made an executive decision to spend the orchestra's money on an impromptu ice cream social for the entire school. The ice cream was fantastic and I had a wonderful time, but . . .

Expanding Capacities

Name _____ Class _____ Date _____

I've Gotta Tell Ya . . .

Finish the letter below. Keep in mind the need to balance urges to be impulsive and the need for some impulsivity in one's life.

> Students should finish the letter by asking Drake to not make big decisions about orchestra money without consulting the entire orchestra, or at least forming a planning commission. Then, students could perhaps offer examples of when being impulsive might be appropriate. See the sample answer below.

Dear Drake,

   You have been a good friend of mine for many years. I value your friendship. Because you mean a lot to me, I feel the need to write to you about an important issue. Yesterday you made an executive decision to spend the orchestra's money on an impromptu ice cream social for the entire school. The ice cream was fantastic and I had a wonderful time, but . . .

   most of the orchestra members are a little unhappy with you right now. We had talked in the past about using that money for our trip to the state finals. We didn't make it to the finals, but we could have gone to see the competition. It would have been nice to get out of town. Or we could have had our own little competition at the beach! Lots of us had ideas, and we're a little bummed that you made the decision alone. We love it when you impulsively encourage a recital in the middle of the lunchroom or when you bring in sheet music for the latest video game sensation. I think it's amazing that you were able to get everything together so quickly and on your own for the surprise social yesterday. It looked and tasted really good! You are wonderfully creative. But spending our money on the whole school without any planning or checking with us was not the kind of impulsiveness we like. Check with us next time, OK?

Sincerely,

Joe Student

Expanding Capacities

Name _____ Class _____ Date _____

Master of the Impulses

Think of someone you know who does a good job managing his or her impulsivity. Then answer the questions below.

1. A person who does a good job managing his or her impulsivity is:

2. Why is this person good at managing impulsivity? Explain.

3. What could you learn from this person to become a better manager of your impulses?

4. What strategy could you use to monitor your improvement in managing your impulses?

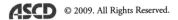

Expanding Capacities

Name _____ Class _____ Date _____

Master of the Impulses

Think of someone you know who does a good job managing his or her impulsivity. Then answer the questions below.

> Share the following sample answers with students to help them get started.

1. A person who does a good job managing his or her impulsivity is:

   Randall, a classmate in my programming class

2. Why is this person good at managing impulsivity? Explain.

   He's very calm. Sometimes people in the class get really stressed out. They blame people, they hit things, they ask for new deadlines or easier goals. I do these things sometimes when I'm working on a tight deadline to finish a big programming assignment. Randall just takes everything in stride. He's very calm. He never loses his temper. He's levelheaded and reassuring. He has got to be one of the most patient people I know.

3. What could you learn from this person to become a better manager of your impulses?

   What I have learned from Randall is that it doesn't do any good to get all worked up. In fact, I think people make bad decisions when they are upset and complaining. I can learn to take a deep breath and just relax and keep going. Eventually everything gets done. It always does. Randall has taught me to spend more time managing my impulses to ask for a new deadline or try to get my teammates to work faster. Instead, I just need to concentrate on getting it done and keep my teacher updated in a calm way.

4. What strategy could you use to monitor your improvement in managing your impulses?

   I could ask Randall to give me some pointers and keep me honest. I could also create a rubric and evaluate myself regularly.

Listening with Understanding and Empathy

PURPOSE OF THIS TOOL

This tool allows students to identify examples of effective and ineffective listening skills. They get an opportunity to practice using effective listening skills. In addition, they take time to evaluate their own personal listening behaviors and develop an action plan for improvement. As students further apply the concept of listening with understanding and empathy, they form a deeper understanding and begin to make it a true Habit of Mind.

The resources in this tool will enable students to

- Role-play a difficult situation, with one person in the listening role.
- Make observations and discuss effective and ineffective listening techniques.
- Apply effective learning behavior.
- Evaluate their listening skills and create an action plan for improvement.

HOW TO USE THIS TOOL

The following list of resources includes the suggested sequence for using this tool:

- Observation Chart worksheet (Core Activity 1)
- Good, Not-So-Good (Group Discussion)
- Trying It (Core Activity 2)
- Listening Skills to Apply worksheet (Synthesis Activity)

The activities and tasks included in this tool should take about 45–60 minutes to complete.

TIPS AND VARIATIONS

1. Core Activity 1

- Call for two volunteers to role-play a situation. Let them choose one of the following fictional scenarios or come up with a similar situation:

    A mother (or father) is angry because her child is being picked on at school and it would seem that school administrators and teachers have not taken any action.

    A customer is angry because he or she has to take a faulty CD player back to the store for the third time.

Expanding Capacities

A patient is complaining that he is very ill and needs to get treatment from a specialist right away. The person at the appointment desk says there are no appointments available for one month.

- Have the duo determine who will be listening and who will be speaking. Tell the listener to show good and bad examples of listening with understanding and empathy.
- Encourage the class to be an observant audience. Students should look for specific signs of poor listening and record their observations. Give students the Observation Chart worksheet to keep track of their thoughts.
- Facilitate a class discussion about the good and poor listening skills demonstrated. On the board, track student comments via a three-column chart (Good Skill, Not-So-Good Skill, Suggestions for Improvement). For each not-so-good skill, encourage students to brainstorm suggestions for how to improve listening to show understanding and empathy.
- After the discussion, call for a show of hands to determine whether the listener showed, on balance, understanding and empathy.

2. Core Activity 2

- Have students find a partner. Ask each pair to take the same scenario and employ the skills and tactics of a good listener. Students should show that they understand and feel empathy as they listen.
- Make sure both partners have an opportunity to be listener and speaker.

3. Reflection Activity

- Stimulate a class discussion about what it was like for students to be effective listeners. Also encourage students to talk about how it felt to be the speaker to an effective listener.
- To help students synthesize and apply what they learned, give them the Listening Skills to Apply worksheet to complete.

Name _____ Class _____ Date _____

Observation Chart

Use this chart to observe and reflect on the behavior of one person listening to another. Add additional behaviors in the blank spaces provided if you wish.

Listening Behavior	Observation	Suggestion for Improvement
Eye contact		
Body language/posture		
Facial expression		
Paraphrasing		
Clarifying with questions		
Confirming nods or other gestures		
Timing		

Name _____ Class _____ Date _____

Observation Chart

Use this chart to observe and reflect on the behavior of one person listening to another. Add additional behaviors in the blank spaces provided if you wish.

Share the following sample answers with students to help them get started.

Listening Behavior	Observation	Suggestion for Improvement
Eye contact	The listener looked at the speaker 2 out of about 10 opportunities.	Maintain more eye contact.
Body language/posture	The listener didn't move his head or body toward the speaker very often.	Have a more open and receptive manner; turn your head toward the speaker.
Facial expression	I didn't see the listener smile or maintain a friendly look until the very end.	Use more positive, reassuring facial expressions.
Paraphrasing	The listener paraphrased one time.	Do more paraphrasing.
Clarifying with questions	The listener asked two questions, but they were very defensive.	Questions should be probing for information, not defensive attempts to make the other person feel bad.
Confirming nods or other gestures	None	The listener could be more reassuring with nods and gestures.
Timing	The listener cut the speaker off three times.	Allow the speaker time to say what she needs to say.

Name _____ Class _____ Date _____

Listening Skills to Apply

Areas to Develop

List three areas you will develop over the next month to improve your ability to listen with understanding and empathy. Then complete the action plan to help you stay on task.

1.

2.

3.

Action Plan to Improve Listening Skills in One Month

In order to improve my skills, I will do the following things:

I can seek assistance from these sources:

I can monitor my improvement in these ways:

Expanding Capacities

Name _____ Class _____ Date _____

Listening Skills to Apply

Areas to Develop

List three areas you will develop over the next month to improve your ability to listen with understanding and empathy. Then complete the action plan to help you stay on task.

> Share the following sample answers with students to help them get started.

1. *I can improve my eye contact with people who are talking to me.*

2. *I can be better about letting people take the time to express their points of view. I have been known to interrupt.*

3. *I can stay calm when someone else is angry instead of getting angry and defensive myself.*

Action Plan to Improve Listening Skills in One Month

In order to improve my skills, I will do the following things:

- *Become more aware of how I am listening to someone.*
- *Actively practice using good learning techniques.*
- *Ask a trusted friend to role-play with me if I know I'll be in a difficult situation or to replay a situation I wish I had handled differently.*
- *Keep the Observation Chart around for reference.*

I can seek assistance from these sources:

> *My mom and my best friend*

I can monitor my improvement in these ways:

> *I can revisit this worksheet to remind me of my goals.*
> *I can create a listening rubric.*
> *I can self-assess my progress every Friday and every time I think I need a refresher.*

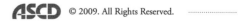

Expanding Capacities

Thinking Flexibly

PURPOSE OF THIS TOOL

In this tool, students explore how flexible thinking can be used to solve serious problems. They learn about the team of flexible thinkers who helped land Apollo 13 after it became damaged in space. Then they do their own research to report on a group or individual who achieved something remarkable with flexible thinking. Finally, they summarize the importance of this Habit of Mind by employing quotations, strategies, and illustrations in a poster. As students further apply the concept of thinking flexibly, they form a deeper understanding and begin to make it a true habit.

The resources in this tool will enable students to

- Discuss the importance of using flexible thinking to solve problems.
- Research and report on an individual or team of people who did something remarkable by thinking flexibly.
- Summarize the importance of the Thinking Flexibly Habit of Mind in a poster.

HOW TO USE THIS TOOL

The following list of resources includes the suggested sequence for using this tool:

- Seeing Anew discussion (Motivating Activity)
- "Great Thinking!" Research Project worksheet (Individual Research Project)
- Flexible Quotations worksheet (Reflection Activity)

The activities and tasks included in this tool should take two 60-minute class periods, one week or more apart, to complete. You will need the following materials:

- Poster board and markers
- *Apollo 13* movie (optional)
- A list of ideas of suitable subjects for an individual research project

TIPS AND VARIATIONS

1. Motivating Activity

- Write the following quotation on the board:

  No problem can be solved from the same consciousness that created it. We must learn to see the world anew.

  —Albert Einstein, scientist

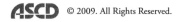

• Have students work in pairs to paraphrase what Einstein meant by this statement. Encourage students to think of an example from their own lives or from the wider world to illustrate the point.

• When everyone has finished, have a group conversation to share examples with the class.

2. Individual Research Project

• Recap for students the story of NASA's Apollo 13 flight:

In 1970, a ground team at the National Aeronautics and Space Administration (NASA) headquarters in Houston, Texas, had a serious problem. They had to bring the space rocket Apollo 13 back to Earth after the rocket had been severely damaged in space. The lives of three astronauts were on the line, and time was short. All the ground team had to work with was the equipment on board the Apollo 13 and the expertise of the astronauts. Team members had a very intense brainstorming session, thinking as flexibly as possible about all of the possible uses, combinations, and purposes of the equipment available to the astronauts. What was the end result? They succeeded. Apollo 13 made it safely back to Earth.

Show the movie *Apollo 13* or clips from it, if time and resources permit, or encourage students to watch it on their own to learn more about this great example of people who really knew how to think flexibly.

• Introduce the research project by telling students to each pick a famous person or group of people who have done something remarkable by thinking flexibly. Give students the "Great Thinking!" Research Project worksheet to get them started.

• Give students a week to do their research and submit a report. The day students turn in their reports, have them discuss their findings and the importance of thinking flexibly.

3. Reflection Activity

• Ask: Do you think it is challenging to think flexibly? What type of tools or strategies might help a person to think flexibly? Explain.

• Have students design a poster to explain this Habit of Mind, illustrating its importance and showing practical tools, strategies, and other ideas for achieving it. Tell students the intended audience of the poster is a 14-year-old student who doesn't know anything about the Habits of Mind.

Expanding Capacities

• Give students the Flexible Quotations worksheet. Tell them to include at least two of the quotes in their poster.

Name _____ Class _____ Date _____

"Great Thinking!" Research Project

Answer the following questions to direct your research.

Research Project Details	
Whom am I going to research?	
Why did I choose this person or group?	
What is an example of this person's or group's flexible thinking?	
When did this happen?	
Where did this happen?	
What thinking strategies, techniques, or tools were used?	
What might have happened if flexible thinking had not been used in this situation?	

Expanding Capacities

Name _____ Class _____ Date _____

"Great Thinking!" Research Project

Share the following sample answers with students to help them get started.

Research Project Details	
Whom am I going to research?	*The NASA Apollo 13 ground crew.*
Why did I choose this person or group?	*I am fascinated by space travel and am curious about how Apollo 13 ground control saved the astronauts.*
What is an example of this person's or group's flexible thinking?	*They figured out how to bring the astronauts home after an explosion seriously damaged their craft.*
When did this happen?	*April 1970*
Where did this happen?	*The Apollo 13 was somewhere between here and the moon. The ground crew was in Houston, Texas.*
What thinking strategies, techniques, or tools were used?	*Positive thinking, aggressive brainstorming, leadership on the ground and on the spacecraft, teamwork, sharing ideas, being receptive to any idea, calling for their own personal best.*
What might have happened if flexible thinking had not been used in this situation?	*Three astronauts would have died and the space program probably would have been set back even further.*

Name _____ Class _____ Date _____

Flexible Quotations

Think about the following quotations and how they might apply to the Thinking Flexibly Habit of Mind.

• *Only fools and dead men don't change their minds. Fools won't and dead men can't.*

—John H. Patterson, soldier and author

• *If you never change your mind, why have one?*

—Edward de Bono, writer and inventor

• *A person can grow only as much as his horizon allows.*

—John Powell, musician and composer

• *It is change, continuing change, inevitable change, that is the dominant factor in society today. No sensible decision can be made any longer without taking into account not only the world as it is, but the world as it will be.*

—Isaac Asimov, science fiction author

• *There is nothing so confining as the prisons of our own perceptions.*

—William Shakespeare, playwright, in *King Lear*

Thinking About Thinking (Metacognition)

PURPOSE OF THIS TOOL

In this tool, students explore whether a person can learn how to think or thinking just comes naturally. They test one model using a life-or-death scenario and then consider how the method might be used in ordinary situations, too. Then students consolidate their thoughts by teaching other students about this Habit of Mind via a brochure. As students flex their metacognitive muscles, they form a deeper understanding of the concept of thinking about thinking and begin to make it a solid Habit of Mind.

The resources in this tool will enable students to

- Discuss the value of learning how to think.
- Explore how using the P-D-R method might increase a person's odds of surviving in an extreme situation.
- Consider how the P-D-R method might be used in other situations.
- Design and create a brochure to teach other students about this Habit of Mind.

HOW TO USE THIS TOOL

The following list of resources includes the suggested sequence for using this tool:

- I Cannot Teach discussion (Motivating Activity)
- The P-D-R Method worksheet (Core Activity)
- I Can Only Make Them Think discussion (Reflection Activity)
- Thinking About Quoting worksheet (Synthesis Activity)

The activities and tasks included in this tool should take 75–90 minutes to complete.

TIPS AND VARIATIONS

1. Motivating Activity

- Write the following quotation on the board:

  I cannot teach anybody anything. I can only make them think.

  —Socrates, ancient Greek philosopher

- Have students work in pairs to analyze the quote. Mention that Socrates seems to be saying that a person can learn to think. Ask: Do you agree with the statement? Do you believe that is true? Is thinking something we learn how to do, or does it just come naturally? Ask students to support their opinions with examples.

Expanding Capacities

2. Core Activity

- Tell students that many young idealists have ventured to the Alaskan wilderness looking for excitement and sure they can conquer the world. Some Alaskan natives say that most of these people have little understanding of extreme wilderness. They tempt fate and almost always lose.

- Relate the following story to students:

  A young man hiked 20 miles into the extremely cold and untamed wilderness. He was alone. He had a map and a fishing pole but no formal training in how to use them. He had a guide book on native flora and what to eat and what not to eat, but he had no real experience in plant identification or foraging. In fact, he had no formal survival training. He was looking for adventure and sure he could conquer the wilderness. He didn't. He died because when he realized he needed to get back to civilization, the river was too high to cross. Instead of using his map to find an alternate route, he wasted away and slowly died of starvation. In fact, he would have found a way over the river less than a mile upriver or a safe crossing sound one mile down river.

Explain that this is a true story that happened and continues to happen. It is a tragedy. And it is only one example of how people can make grave mistakes by failing to adequately think about and prepare for a situation.

- Divide the class into small groups. Tell them to use the P-D-R Method (Plan-Do-Review) worksheet to discuss how the young adventurer might have better prepared himself for a positive experience.
- Divide class time into three equal phases. Have students spend the first phase planning (P) what the adventurer will do and what preparations he should make.
- During the second phase, have students imagine that they are in the adventurer's shoes doing (D) the journey themselves and monitoring the adventurer's thinking as he progresses. Students should raise key questions during this stage. Examples: This isn't working, so what else should I try? What could I use from my supplies to make this part of the journey better?
- In the third stage, have students review (R) the completed journey and consider how it could be done even better in the future. Ask: What were the highlights? What were the worst moments?

3. Reflection Activity

• Redirect students' attention to the Socrates quotation. Discuss with students whether their thinking has changed at all after reviewing the wilderness example and applying the P-D-R method. Say that sometimes people really have their minds set on doing something. In the end, we can't do anything to change their minds, but we can try to get them to carefully think through their plans.

• Remind students that they used the P-D-R method to analyze an extreme situation. Ask: Could the model be used to solve simpler situations? (Yes.) What are some examples?

4. Synthesis Activity

• Have students create a 2–3 page brochure that explains metacognition to students their age who have no knowledge of the Habits of Mind. Tell them the goal should be to get students their age to think about thinking.

• Distribute the Thinking About Quoting worksheet. Encourage students to include in their brochures one or more of the quotes from the worksheet, a picture, a catch phrase, and an example of how to apply this Habit of Mind.

• Have each student come to the front of the class to display her brochure and explain what she has included in it and why.

Expanding Capacities

Name _____ Class _____ Date _____

The P-D-R Method

Use the **Plan-Do-Review** (P-D-R) model to think through a situation before attempting it.

> **Mission: Camp in the extreme wilderness** for one month and live to tell about it.

Plan:

Do:

Review:

Name _____ Class _____ Date _____

The P-D-R Method

Use the Plan-Do-Review (P-D-R) model to think through a situation before attempting it.

> Mission: Camp in the extreme wilderness for one month and live to tell about it.

> The following are sample answers. You may wish to simplify the mission, or have students come up with their own goal. Keep this worksheet handy for students to use whenever they need to think through a situation.

Plan:

Get adequate training. Travel to the area and meet with experts. Get to know the area. Create a clear plan about when, where, and how far away you will go, and for how long. Let someone know where you will be and establish a way to get help if you need it. Research possible problems and what to do about them. Determine how many supplies will be needed, what kind of supplies will be needed, and what to do if the supplies run out.

Do:

Take wilderness survival courses, including orienteering, foraging, and classes specific to the area you will be going to. Learn to fish from an expert. Learn to problem-solve in extreme situations. Take short trips with a guide. Practice.

Review:

Show your plan to an expert to review possible problems and what you can do about them. Make sure this adventure is really worth the risk. Ask the expert: Do you think I can survive this mission, or do I need to prepare further?

Name _____ Class _____ Date _____

Thinking About Quoting

Think about the following quotations. How might they apply to Thinking About Thinking?

- *When the mind is thinking it is talking to itself.*

　　　　　　　　　　　　　　　　　　　　—Plato, ancient Greek philosopher

- *If I look confused it's because I'm thinking.*

　　　　　　　　　　　　　　　　　　　　—Samuel Goldwyn, film producer

- *To read without reflecting is like eating without digesting.*

　　　　　　　　　　　　—Edmund Burke, 18th century Irish politician and writer

- *Once we know our weaknesses they cease to do us any harm.*

　　　　　　　　　　　　—Georg C. Lichtenberg, 18th century German scientist

This moment deserves your full attention, for it will not pass your way again.

　　　　　　　　　　　　　　　　　　　　—Dan Millman, gymnast

Expanding Capacities

Striving for Accuracy and Precision

PURPOSE OF THIS TOOL

In this tool, students learn the importance of not making mistakes on the job. They research a job that depends on accurate and precise workmanship, and they explore the real-world consequences of imprecision and inaccuracy in the workplace. As they apply the concept of striving for accuracy in this way, they form a deeper understanding and begin to make it a true Habit of Mind. The result should be that students become more motivated to take pride in their work and learning experiences.

The resources in this tool will enable students to

- Brainstorm a list of jobs that require accuracy and precision.
- Choose one job and research why precision and accuracy are important.
- Explore how being in a job that requires accuracy and precision might look, sound, and feel for them.
- Discuss the importance of accuracy and precision in the workplace.

HOW TO USE THIS TOOL

The following list of resources includes the suggested sequence for using this tool:

- Confucius quote (Motivating Message)
- Precision Professions Research Project worksheet (Individual Research Project)
- Accuracy and Precision Y-Chart worksheet (Reflection Activity)
- Revisiting Confucius discussion (Synthesis Activity)

The activities and tasks included in this tool should take two 60-minute class periods to complete. Students will need access to the Internet or library. Plan to allow students time to do research. You may want to do some advance planning to direct students to helpful career information.

TIPS AND VARIATIONS

1. Motivating Message

- Write the following quotation on the board. Don't discuss it unless students ask questions. Just let it serve as motivation throughout this tool.

A man who has committed a mistake and doesn't correct it is committing another mistake.

—Confucius, ancient Chinese philosopher

2. Individual Research Project

• Have students individually brainstorm a list of occupations that require a high level of accuracy and precision on a day-to-day basis. Students can choose basically any occupation, such as one from the field of sports, arts, business, or medicine. Then ask students to choose a job from the list that looks interesting to them.

• Give students the Precision Professions Research Project worksheet to help them get started.

• Allow students time to go to the library or do Internet research to learn about the occupation they chose.

• Have students summarize their findings in a short report or essay.

3. Reflection Activity

• Give students the Accuracy and Precision Y-Chart worksheet. Instruct them to complete it as if they were already employed in the occupation they researched. Ask: If you were in that profession, what would you look like? What would you sound like? How would you feel?

• Have students share their findings with three other people.

• Then have students share their ideas as a class. Students may be surprised at the range of occupations that rely on accuracy and precision.

4. Synthesis Activity

• Redirect students' attention to the Confucius quotation. Ask: Does this quotation have a greater impact now than it did when we began this lesson? (Yes, because now we have seen some of the implications of imprecision and inaccuracy.)

Name _____ Class _____ Date _____

Precision Professions Research Project

Answer the following questions to direct your research.

Research Project Details	
Which job am I going to research?	
In what way do people in this occupation need to be accurate and precise?	
How do people in this occupation train to be accurate and precise?	
Are there rules or laws that govern the level of accuracy and precision?	
What are the consequences for people in this occupation who are not accurate and precise?	
Describe a specific example of those consequences.	

Expanding Capacities

Name _____ Class _____ Date _____

Precision Professions Research Project

Answer the following questions to direct your research.

> Share the following sample answers with students to help them get started.

Research Project Details	
Which job am I going to research?	*Brain surgeon*
In what way do people in this occupation need to be accurate and precise?	*The brain is a very delicate part of the body. Surgeons must be both accurate and precise when manipulating this internal organ or serious damage could result.*
How do people in this occupation train to be accurate and precise?	*Neurosurgical candidates train for at least 16 years: 4 years premed, 4 years to MD, and 6 years residency. Many train 2 years more to get a master's degree and follow their residency with a 1–2 year subspecialty fellowship. Some people even add significant PhD research in neuroscience.*
Are there rules or laws that govern the level of accuracy and precision?	*They must be licensed and certified to practice neurosurgery, and they must follow a host of procedural laws and rules to protect the health of the patient.*
What are the consequences for people in this occupation who are not accurate and precise?	*The patient could die or lose significant bodily function. If the surgeon is off by even a small amount, the patient can lose feeling, lose the ability to speak or move limbs, become childlike, or die.*
Describe a specific example of those consequences.	*One family filed a lawsuit because a neurosurgeon operated on the wrong side of a 15-year-old's brain. "Operation performed at incorrect site" continues to rank in the top five complications for insured physicians in neurosurgery and many other specialties.*

Name _____ Class _____ Date _____

Accuracy and Precision Y-Chart

Use this chart to explore your thoughts about being in a profession where you must possess the Habit of Mind of Striving for Accuracy and Precision.

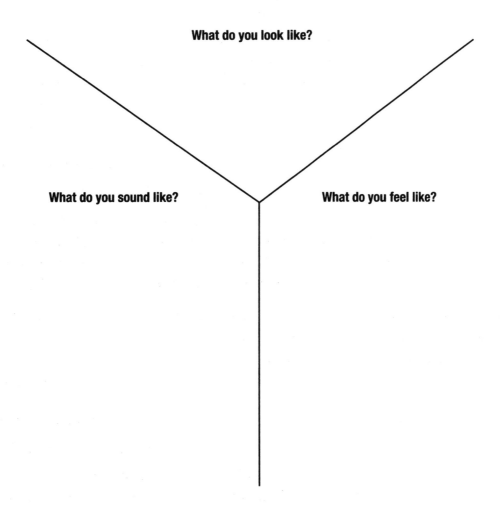

What do you look like?

What do you sound like?

What do you feel like?

Questioning and Posing Problems

PURPOSE OF THIS TOOL

In this tool, students focus intensely on the nature of questioning. They ask rapid-fire questions and then slow down to ponder age-old philosophical questions. They reflect on what questioning means to them and might say about others. As students further apply the concept of questioning and posing problems, they form a deeper understanding and begin to make it a true Habit of Mind.

The resources in this tool will enable students to

- Explore their thoughts about the way questioning looks, sounds, and feels.
- Play a game that involves a lot of questioning.
- Explore a philosophical question, mapping their process of unraveling meaning.
- Reflect on what a person's questions might reveal about him or her.

HOW TO USE THIS TOOL

The following list of resources includes the suggested sequence for using this tool:

- Questioning Y-Chart worksheet (Motivating Activity)
- Questions game (Core Activity)
- What Is Beauty? worksheet (Synthesis Activity)
- Questions or Answers? worksheet (Reflection Activity
- Questioning Y-Chart worksheet (Reflection Activity)

The activities and tasks included in this tool should take 60–90 minutes to complete.

TIPS AND VARIATIONS

1. Motivating Activity

- Give students the Questioning Y-Chart worksheet. Ask the following questions as students fill in each area of the worksheet:

  What does it look like when someone is in a questioning mood or search-ing for an answer to a problem? What does it look like at school versus in the world beyond school?

  What feelings do you have when you are in a questioning mood or trying to find answers to a problem? Do you always feel the same way? What range of feelings do you have?

Expanding Capacities

What does the process of questioning sound like to you? Is it noisy? pleasant? curious? strange?

• Have students share their findings as a class.

2. Core Activity

• Write the following rules on the board:

Rules for Questions Game
Ask your partner a question.
Respond to your partner's question with a related but different question.
Continue the process.
The person who answers the question (makes a statement) or asks an unrelated question loses.

• Have students find a partner. Read the rules on the board and explain as necessary. Tell students to begin the game by asking: What is your name? The partner could answer: What is your sister's name? or What is your middle name? and so on.

• Tell students that when the first round ends they should start again. Perhaps students could play "best two out of three" or continue playing for a specified amount of time.

• Discuss the activity with questions such as the following: What have you learned about asking questions? What types of questions were the most useful? What professionals might be required to ask many questions in the course of their day-to-day work?

3. Synthesis Activity

• Tell students that some questions just can't be answered easily, if at all. Philosophical questions, when discussed, often lead to more questions and still more questions. Some philosophical questions have occupied minds for thousands of years. Give students the worksheet What Is Beauty? Have them work in small groups to discuss at least one of the questions. (You may want to assign each group one question.) The point of this conversation is not to come up with answers to these age-old questions but to enjoy the process of exploring and questioning and challenging each other.

Expanding Capacities

• Encourage students to come up with a group answer to the questions. Remind them to be aware of new questions that arise and how they deal with them. Ask the groups to list their new questions and, if you wish, to map how they tried to answer them. Maps should show a clear explanation of thought processes and should include questions.

4. Reflection Activity

• Give students the Questions or Answers? worksheet. Have them work in small groups to discuss the quotation and answer the questions.

• Have students revisit their Questioning Y-Chart worksheet to see if they would like to add to or revise any of their previous thoughts about questioning.

Name _____ Class _____ Date _____

Questioning Y-Chart

Use this chart to explore your thoughts about the Habit of Mind of Questioning and Posing Problems.

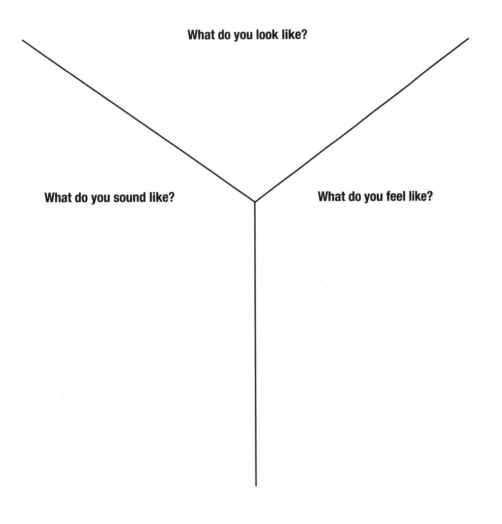

What do you look like?

What do you sound like?

What do you feel like?

Name _____ Class _____ Date _____

What Is Beauty?

Pick at least one of the following questions to discuss and define as a group. Be aware of any new questions that arise in the process. Map your thought process as you discuss the question.

What is knowledge?
What is beauty?
Do I have free will?
What is truth?
What is consciousness?
What is justice?

Map your thought processes here:

Name _____ Class _____ Date _____

Questions or Answers?

Read the following quotation, think about it for a moment, and then answer the questions that follow.

Judge a man by his questions rather than by his answers.

—Voltaire, 18th century French philosopher and writer

Questions

1. Rewrite the quotation in your own words:

2. To what extent do you agree with the quotation?

3. Name one or two people who ask good questions. Explain why you think so.

4. Do you judge a person by his or her questions? Explain.

Expanding Capacities

Name _____ Class _____ Date _____

Questions or Answers?

Read the following quotation, think about it for a moment, and then answer the questions that follow.

Judge a man by his questions rather than by his answers.

— Voltaire, 18th century French philosopher and writer

> The following are sample answers that you can use to help students get started.

Questions

1. Rewrite the quotation in your own words:

   A person's questions are more revealing than his or her answers.

2. To what extent do you agree with the quotation?

   I agree completely. I think people can memorize and smooth-talk with their answers, but a person who can ask really good questions is a thoughtful, curious, interested person, and I value those qualities.

3. Name one or two people who ask good questions. Explain why you think so.

   My piano teacher never asks an ordinary question, like "How are you?" He'll say something intriguing instead, like "Did you notice the first daffodil on your way in?" He keeps me thinking.

4. Do you judge a person by his or her questions? Explain.

   Yes, I think I do, because I think of people who ask good questions as intelligent, curious, and interested. They care more about what other people think and feel than about hearing themselves talk.

Expanding Capacities

Questions or Answers?

Applying Past Knowledge to New Situations

PURPOSE OF THIS TOOL

Students have several opportunities in this tool to see how past knowledge can be applied in current situations. They are encouraged to explore the value of the process by examining what it looks like, sounds like, and feels like. They also get a chance to demonstrate their understanding of this Habit of Mind through role playing. Students finish the lesson with a valuable tool in hand—the K-W-L chart. This handy method for assessing prior knowledge and then reflecting on it can be a regular classroom tool for students to consciously recall knowledge and actively build upon it. In this way students form a deeper understanding of the concept of applying past knowledge to new situations and make it a true Habit of Mind.

The resources in this tool will enable students to

- Discuss how a person links something learned in the past to new learning.
- See how characters in a classic tale applied past learning in new situations.
- Describe what someone looks like, sounds like, and may be feeling when he or she is applying something learned in the past to solve a current problem.
- Create a skit to demonstrate why people may be reluctant to give up learning.
- Use the K-W-L chart to recall past learning and document new knowledge.

HOW TO USE THIS TOOL

The following list of resources includes the suggested sequence for using this tool:

- Linking Learning (Introductory Discussion)
- Why, You Little …! worksheet (Motivating Activity)
- Past Knowledge Y-Chart worksheet (Core Activity)
- Hanging On skit (Synthesis Activity)
- K-W-L Chart worksheet (Ongoing Activity)

The activities and tasks included in this tool should take about 60 minutes to complete.

TIPS AND VARIATIONS

1. Introductory Discussion

- Tell students that we can often easily link something new we have learned to something we learned previously. Encourage students to provide examples. (Sample

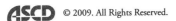 © 2009. All Rights Reserved.

Expanding Capacities

answers: Second-language students gradually write more sophisticated sentences that use vocabulary learned years earlier. In math, many of the concepts learned in high school are based on simpler concepts learned in elementary and junior high school.)

• Ask: Does this concept apply outside the classroom? Encourage students to provide examples. (Sample answers: Passing the driving test proves you have developed a level of competence necessary to safely drive on public roads. As you drive more and more, you learn to use your skills in new terrain, in new weather conditions, and with different cars.)

2. Motivating Activity

• Give students the Why, You Little …! worksheet. Call on someone to read the story aloud, or let students read it silently.

• Have students work in pairs to discuss how the tale relates to the Habit of Mind of Applying Past Knowledge to New Situations. After a few minutes, ask the pairs of students to join another pair to further compare ideas.

3. Core Activity

• Ask students to continue to work in pairs. Hand out the Past Knowledge Y-Chart worksheet.

• Read the following scenes:

Scene 1: You are in a mathematics class. The person facing you is stuck and has been stuck for a while. She suddenly remembers something she learned in a previous action tool that helps her move on. She is applying her past knowledge to a new situation.

Scene 2: You are playing soccer. It is a fast-moving game, and your entire team needs to be fast on their feet and thinking quickly at all times. You see one of your team members suddenly remember something about the goalie, apply that past knowledge, act fast, and score the winning goal.

• Tell students to use one of these scenes and complete the Y-Chart worksheet. To direct their thinking, ask: What words might you hear the person who remembered old knowledge say? What might they think to themselves? What might their facial expressions look like? What feelings might they go through as they move from being stuck to succeeding?

• Ask students to discuss situations in which they applied past knowledge to help in a new situation.

4. Synthesis Activity

- Write the following quotation on the board:

Once people learn something, they're reluctant to let it go.

—Robert Easton, actor

- Divide the class into groups of three or four. Ask the groups to write a short skit that explores the statement you wrote on the board. The skit should show how something learned in the past can be useful in the present. Encourage students to express why people may be reluctant to let knowledge and skills fade away.

5. Ongoing Activity

- Close this lesson by giving students the K-W-L Chart worksheet. Tell them that this worksheet is a useful tool for recalling past knowledge and documenting new learning. Explain that using the chart helps make the Applying Past Knowledge to New Situations Habit of Mind a conscious process until it becomes ingrained. Suggest that students use the chart anytime they are beginning a new topic or studying for a test.
- Keep copies of the chart handy in the classroom so students can use it regularly and get used to starting their learning by seeing what they already know and then building upon that knowledge.

Expanding Capacities

Name _____ Class _____ Date _____

Why, You Little . . . !

The following is a synopsis of the "Three Little Pigs" story. Discuss how the tale relates to the Habit of Mind of Applying Past Knowledge to New Situations.

Three Little Pigs

Three little pigs each decide to build a home. The first little pig makes a house of straw. A wolf comes along and blows his house down. The second little pig makes a house of sticks. The wolf blows that house down, too. The third little pig builds a house of bricks, and his two brothers come to his house to stay. The wolf tries to blow the house down but is not successful. He tries to trick the pig into coming out, but doesn't succeed. Finally, he climbs onto the roof and attempts to slide down the chimney to surprise the pig. The pig is waiting, though. He has boiled water in a pot in the fireplace. So when the wolf slides down the chimney, he lands in the boiling water. Then the pigs have the wolf for dinner!

How does this story relate to the Habit of Mind of Applying Past Knowledge to New Situations?

Name _____ Class _____ Date _____

Past Knowledge Y-Chart

Use this chart to explore your thoughts about Applying Past Knowledge to New Situations.

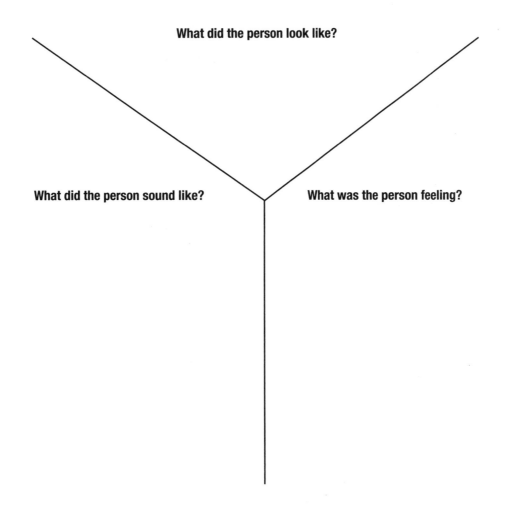

What did the person look like?

What did the person sound like?

What was the person feeling?

Name _____ Class _____ Date _____

K-W-L Chart

When you are about to start studying something new or are preparing for a test, complete this chart. Fill out the first two columns before you begin studying and fill out the last column after your studies.

What Do I **Know** Already?	What Do I **Want** to Learn?	What Have I **Learned**?

Name _____ Class _____ Date _____

K-W-L Chart

When you are about to start studying something new or are preparing for a test, complete this chart. Fill out the first two columns before you begin studying and fill out the last column after your studies.

What Do I <u>K</u>now Already?	What Do I <u>W</u>ant to Learn?	What Have I <u>L</u>earned?
This section is for prior knowledge. Have students list the knowledge or skills they have that are relevant to the topic.	This section is for listing learning goals. Have students list the questions they would like to answer about the topic or the things they need to know for the test.	This section is for students to reflect after they have completed their learning project. Have them list what they've gained after studying the topic. Tell students not to write everything they've learned, but instead to choose the three most interesting, surprising, or important things they learned. Then they can compare the information in this column with the information in the first column to see how much they have built upon their prior knowledge.

Thinking and Communicating with Clarity and Precision

PURPOSE OF THIS TOOL

In this tool, students learn firsthand why it is so important to think and communicate with clarity and precision. They define and describe how clear, thoughtful communication looks, sounds, and feels. Then they role-play an example of poor communication and discuss words and expressions that make communication difficult. Finally, they create a rubric to help improve their communication skills over time. As students further apply the concept of thinking and communicating with clarity and precision, they form a deeper understanding of it and make it a true Habit of Mind.

The resources in this tool will enable students to

- Define the concept of thinking and communicating with clarity and precision.
- Describe how this Habit of Mind looks and feels when it is put into practice.
- Participate in a role-play to demonstrate a specific type of communication.
- Discuss words and expressions that make communication difficult.
- Use a rubric to evaluate and improve their ability to think and communicate with clarity and precision.

HOW TO USE THIS TOOL

The following list of resources includes the suggested sequence for using this tool:

- On a Roll worksheet (Introductory Activity)
- Fuzzy Language resource page (Core Activity)
- Thinking and Communicating Rubric worksheet (Reflection Activity)

The activities and tasks included in this tool should take about 45 minutes to complete. You will need a watch or clock. Note that some advance preparation is needed.

TIPS AND VARIATIONS

1. Introductory Activity

- Ask students to discuss examples of this Habit of Mind in their lives, using questions such as the following: Where have you seen people think and communicate with clarity and precision? What movies or books feature characters that demonstrate this Habit of Mind? Who in your own life has shown the ability to think and communicate with clarity and precision?

- Give students the On a Roll worksheet and have them answer the questions. You may wish to have students work with a partner to complete this activity. When they have finished, tell them that thinking about what something sounds like, looks like, feels like, and means to you is a great tool for integrating it and that this lesson will help them better integrate this Habit of Mind.

2. Core Activity

- Advance Preparation: Copy the Fuzzy Language resource page and cut out the individual scenarios.
- Divide the class in half. Ask one half of the group to wait in the classroom while you take the other half out into the hallway for a moment.
- Give each member of the hallway group one of the scenarios on the Fuzzy Language resource page. Tell them they are being assigned a specific role to play. When they go back into the room, they will find a partner and role-play the scene described. However, they cannot use any specific language at all during the role-play. They can use only fuzzy, vague, and imprecise language. They should use a lot of nondescriptive words and phrases, such as "stuff," "you know," "um," "sorta," "like," "over there," "when the time is right," and so on. They should avoid using specific names, places, or times. They should not make any specific comparisons. In other words, they need to enact their scenario without revealing any concrete details about it.
- Have the hallway group return to the classroom and find a partner.
- Tell the unaware half of the class that their partner will role-play a scene. Their mission is to figure out the scenario; for example, if they figure out that their partner is attempting to borrow money, and the partner confirms it, they should raise their hand.
- Announce that students will have three minutes to guess their partner's scenario. After three minutes, tell students to stop and reveal their scenario to their partner (unless the partner has already guessed successfully).
- Lead a class discussion using questions such as the following: Did you come close to guessing the scenario? What happened? What words confused you? What was said and not said? Did the language used make the situation more complicated than it needed to be? If so, how? Do you ever use words that aren't very descriptive or meaningful?
- Conclude by acknowledging that this activity presented an extreme example, but note that in reality our vague and imprecise language often confuses other people.

Expanding Capacities

3. Reflection Activity

• Encourage students to better develop this Habit of Mind by thinking about how they can integrate it. Ask: Do you need to make a presentation? Are you part of a group project? Do you have written assignments to prepare? Do you need to solve any problems or work together with anyone else? How can this Habit of Mind help? Assure students that eventually this habit will become a natural state of mind that they can apply without having to stop and think about it. This process is called habituation.

• To help students assess their thinking and communicating abilities at any given time, give them the Thinking and Communicating Rubric worksheet. Encourage them to keep the rubric handy and to revisit it frequently.

Name _____ Class _____ Date _____

On a Roll

Sounds Like: When you are thinking and communicating with clarity and precision, your speech is …

1.

2.

3.

Looks Like: When you see a friend thinking and communicating with clarity and precision, he or she seems …

1.

2.

3.

Feels Like: When you are thinking and communicating with clarity and precision, you feel …

1.

2.

3.

Meaning to Me: Define the Thinking and Communicating with Clarity and Precision Habit of Mind using words or a picture.

Expanding Capacities

  ☐ 207

Name _____ Class _____ Date _____

On a Roll

Share the following sample answers with students to help them get started.

Sounds Like: When you are thinking and communicating with clarity and precision, your speech is …

1. *on target.*

2. *clear.*

3. *understood.*

Looks Like: When you see a friend thinking and communicating with clarity and precision, he or she seems …

1. *together.*

2. *knowledgeable.*

3. *trustworthy.*

Feels Like: When you are thinking and communicating with clarity and precision, you feel …

1. *powerful.*

2. *confident.*

3. *aware.*

Meaning to Me: Define the Thinking and Communicating with Clarity and Precision Habit of Mind using words or a picture.

Thinking and Communicating with Clarity and Precision means knowing what you are talking about and expressing yourself well so that other people understand exactly what you are saying.

Expanding Capacities

Fuzzy Language

Cut out the following statements and give them to half of your students for the Fuzzy Language game. Students should enact the following scenarios using nonspecific, imprecise language.

You are a coach talking to your team in the locker room. It is halftime, and your team is currently losing.	You are a teacher who is talking to a parent about the fact that every time her child attempts a science experiment, something blows up.
You are a professional boxer describing your technique for winning the national championship.	You are a coach talking to your team in the locker room. It is halftime, and your team is currently winning.
You are a dance instructor explaining a new move to a dancer over the phone.	You are telling your grandparent about what sort of puppy you would like her to get you for your birthday.
You want your parent to pick up you and your two friends at different locations and then drop you off at the skateboarding park at 3 p.m. and pick you up at 6 p.m.	You have commissioned a painting from an artist. You want the painting to be modern and colorful, but it should not include the colors red, orange, or yellow.
You are lost. You stop at a convenience store and ask the attendant for directions to a used car dealer at 5th & Arapahoe.	You are telling a friend to invite all of his friends to a party at the natural springs park on Blevins Road at 6 p.m. on Saturday.
You are a maintenance worker at a zoo. You are on the phone with the zoo manager explaining that someone opened all the cages and released the animals.	You are a deep-sea diver who just discovered the remains of a ship thought to be a 17th century pirate's schooner. You found gold, jewels, and weapons.
You are a professional musician who is describing your unique blend of rock and classic music to a record producer.	There is a large black bear trying to break in a window of your house and you are talking to a 9-1-1 operator.
You are a doctor who is telling a patient he contracted a fatal infectious disease during his last vacation to the rainforest. The patient has six months to live at best.	You are talking to the parent of a person you want to take out for dinner and a movie. Your date has requested that you make this call to get formal permission.

Expanding Capacities

Name _____ Class _____ Date _____

Thinking and Communicating Rubric

Use the following rubric to determine how well you are thinking and communicating. Add your own statements to the chart to further assess your abilities.

Do you ...	Always	Usually	Sometimes	Seldom	Never
communicate accurately in written form?					
communicate accurately when talking to other people?					
use precise terms in your speech?					
define unclear terms?					
use correct names?					
use universal labels and analogies?					
support statements with explanations, comparisons, quantification, and evidence?					
overgeneralize and exaggerate?					
leave out important information?					
distort information?					
use vague language such as "weird," "nice," "you know," "OK," "stuff," "junk," "things"?					
punctuate sentences with meaningless interjections such as "yeah," "like," "um," and "uh"?					
use vague or general nouns and pronouns such as "*They* told me to do it." "*Everybody* has one"?					
use unqualified comparisons such as "This book is *better*, I like it *more*"?					

Expanding Capacities

Gathering Data Through All Senses

PURPOSE OF THIS TOOL

In this tool, students explore different ways they can use the senses to gain information. They describe how the senses enhance a travel experience. They debate the relationship between knowledge and perception. As students further apply the concept of gathering data through the senses, they form a deeper understanding of it and begin to make it a true Habit of Mind. In the process, they become more open and alert to the environment around them.

The resources in this tool will enable students to

- Describe how they can use their senses in a thoughtful way.
- Demonstrate how the senses can guide and enhance a travel experience.
- Debate whether all knowledge has its origins in perceptions.
- Synthesize their thoughts by describing how people in different professions use the senses.
- Discuss how they use the senses at school.

HOW TO USE THIS TOOL

The following list of resources includes the suggested sequence for using this tool:

- Seeing, Hearing, Doing worksheet (Introductory Activity)
- Class Trip worksheet (Core Activity)
- Perceptions debate (Reflection Activity)
- Sensing on the Job worksheet (Synthesis Activity)

The activities and tasks included in this tool should take 60–75 minutes to complete.

TIPS AND VARIATIONS

1. Introductory Activity

- Give students the Seeing, Hearing, Doing worksheet.
- Have students work independently to come up with thoughtful examples of ways in which they can apply the senses in each scenario.

2. Core Activity

- Divide the class into groups of three or four.

- Give students the Class Trip worksheet. Have them work together to brainstorm ideas for a class trip. Give them ideas, such as a class ski trip or a historical journey to see ancient ruins. Once students have chosen the location, tell them to follow the worksheet to provide details about how the senses will heighten their experience.

3. Reflection Activity

- Write the following quotation on the board:

  All our knowledge has its origins in our perceptions.
  —Leonardo da Vinci, Italian artist, scientist, mathematician, inventor, futurist, and writer

- Call for a show of hands from people who support the statement. Record the number of supporters on the board.
- Have the class debate the statement. Divide them into groups of three. Tell half of the groups to support the statement and the other half to oppose it. Give students 10–15 minutes to prepare their arguments for or against da Vinci's statement.
- Ask all of the supporting groups to get together on one side of the room and all of the opposing groups to get together on the other side. Have these new teams map out a strategy for debating the issue. Students should work together to create notes and solidify an argument. Then have them pick at least two students to do the actual debating.
- Conduct the debate.
- At the conclusion of the debate, call for a show of hands from people who support the statement. Record the number on the board. Ask: Did anyone change his or her original opinion as a result of the debate? Discuss the results as a class.

4. Synthesis Activity

- Give students the Sensing on the Job worksheet. Ask them to describe how the listed professionals use the different senses on a daily basis.
- Ask: How do you use the senses in your role as a student? Have students work with a partner to describe at least two ways they use their senses at school to help them learn.

Expanding Capacities

Name _____ Class _____ Date _____

Seeing, Hearing, Doing

Review each of the scenarios below. Describe how you could use the three listed senses.

Scenario	Visual Sense	Auditory Sense	Kinesthetic and Tactile Senses
Following directions to a new destination			
Using a new piece of software for the first time			
Convincing the student council the school should be recycling			
Returning a defective item to the store			
Purchasing a new outfit			
Improving your skills in a sport			

Name _____ Class _____ Date _____

Seeing, Hearing, Doing

Review each of the scenarios below. Describe how you could use the three listed senses.

Share the following sample answers with students to help them get started.

Scenario	Visual Sense	Auditory Sense	Kinesthetic and Tactile Senses
Following directions to a new destination	*Look at a map or a compass.*	*Ask for spoken directions.*	*Walk to a major intersection so you can orient yourself.*
Using a new piece of software for the first time	*Watch a tutorial or read the instruction manual.*	*Have someone who is familiar with the program explain it to you.*	*Try using the program; learn as you move through.*
Convincing the student council the school should be recycling	*Write a letter.*	*Give a speech at the next council meeting.*	*Bring recycling bins and boxes to the meeting to demonstrate storage facilities.*
Returning a defective item to the store	*Show the agent the defective item.*	*Tell the agent what is wrong with the item.*	*Demonstrate that the item doesn't work as it should.*
Purchasing a new outfit	*Hold the item against yourself to see how it looks.*	*Ask your friends or a sales agent for their opinion about how the item looks.*	*Try on the item and see how it looks and feels.*
Improving your skills in a sport	*Read or watch videos about effective techniques for that sport.*	*Talk to your coach about how you could improve.*	*Try new strategies to see how your performance changes.*

Expanding Capacities

Name _____ Class _____ Date _____

Class Trip

Imagine that you are going on a class trip and that you get to help choose what sort of trip it will be and where you will go. Perhaps you imagine a skiing vacation or a historical journey through the Roman remains of Italy. In the spaces below, outline where your class will go and how each of your senses can be best used to help you gather data about this place.

1. For our class trip we will go to

2. Our sense of smell will be useful here because

3. Our sense of sight will be useful here because

4. Our sense of hearing will be useful here because

5. Our sense of taste will be useful here because

6. Our sense of touch will be useful here because

7. Our sense of movement will be useful here because

Name _____ Class _____ Date _____

Class Trip

Imagine that you are going on a class trip and that you get to help choose what sort of trip it will be and where you will go. Perhaps you imagine a skiing vacation or a historical journey through the Roman remains of Italy. In the spaces below, outline where your class will go and how each of your senses can be best used to help you gather data about this place.

> Share the following sample answers with students to help them get started.

1. For our class trip we will go to *Paris, France.*

2. Our sense of smell will be useful here because *we will tour the luscious gardens of Versailles, eat the most scintillating dishes, and tour a perfume-producing factory.*

3. Our sense of sight will be useful here because *we will go to the Louvre to examine some of the world's most precious pieces of art. We will also enjoy a view of the city from the top of the Eiffel Tower. We'll take in some of the city life by watching native Parisians and tourists from sidewalk cafes and from our balcony overlooking the Champs-Élysées. We'll need our sense of sight to peruse our guidebook for the best historical stops and restaurants. And I'm sure we'll spend a lot of time looking at our map!*

4. Our sense of hearing will be useful here because *French is such a beautiful language. We can appreciate it even if we can't understand it! For those of us who do speak a little French, we'll be listening carefully to figure out where to go and what to do. The rest of us will try our best to pick up and use a little French.*

5. Our sense of taste will be useful here because *Paris is famous for its delicious food, and we intend to make the most of it!*

6. Our sense of touch will be useful here because *Paris is also famous for its gorgeous clothing and fabrics. I can't wait to touch a fine French silk!*

7. Our sense of movement will be useful here because *we will do a lot of walking and dancing as we tour museums by day and later check out the Parisian nightlife.*

Expanding Capacities

Name _____ Class _____ Date _____

Sensing on the Job

Describe how the following professionals use each sense to regularly help them on the job.

Sense	Firefighters	Writers	Astronauts
Touch			
Sight			
Sound			
Taste			
Smell			
Kinesthesia			

Expanding Capacities

Name _____ Class _____ Date _____

Sensing on the Job

Describe how the following professionals use each sense to regularly help them on the job.

The following sample answers may help students get started.

Sense	Firefighters	Writers	Astronauts
Touch	They carry people; many are also paramedics who can treat wounds and other medical problems.	They use all the senses to share information; e.g., a scene might describe the way a mother touches her baby for the first time.	They conduct tests and touch instruments.
Sight	They scan a scene for potential danger, victims, and the source of danger, and to confirm the danger is over.	They read and reread their own work. They may use visual imagery. They review feedback from other readers.	They pay close attention to computer screens and instrument panels and make observations about their environment.
Sound	They listen for potential signs of distress, listen to heartbeats, and communicate with victims and other people.	They may read their work aloud to see how it sounds. They talk to others about it and may describe auditory experiences in the work.	They communicate with each other and home base; they are alert to warning sounds on the craft.
Taste	They enjoy cookies grateful rescued people bring them. They endure one another's cooking.	They incorporate scenes that describe the way things taste.	They eat dehydrated meals and may provide scientific feedback about the way things taste.
Smell	They are alert to smells that signal specific types of danger.	They incorporate scenes that describe various aromas.	They provide scientific feedback about the way things smell and are alert to dangerous smells.
Kinesthesia	They train to remain agile enough to perform rescue missions. They may be required to lift heavy objects, run, or climb.	They incorporate scenes that describe the way things move.	They move in zero gravity, which is completely different. They must physically train to prepare for the job.

Expanding Capacities

Creating, Imagining, and Innovating

PURPOSE OF THIS TOOL

In this lesson, students are encouraged to use a new creative-planning tool to transform an old object into something new. They evaluate the usefulness of the tool and brainstorm other ways it could be used. Finally, students explore the relationship between creativity and innovation. As students further define and apply the concepts of creating, imagining, and innovating, they form a deeper understanding of this habit and make it their own.

The resources in this tool will enable students to

- Learn an acronym for applying different strategies in a creative situation.
- Create a new object using the SCAMPER tool.
- Discuss the usefulness of this creative-thinking tool.
- Explore the relationship between creativity and innovation.

HOW TO USE THIS TOOL

The following list of resources includes the suggested sequence for using this tool:

- A New Tool (Introductory Discussion)
- SCAMPER worksheet (Core Activity)
- Creativity + Innovation worksheet (Reflection Activity)

The activities and tasks included in this tool should take about 60 minutes to complete. You will need a variety of basic art supplies.

TIPS AND VARIATIONS

1. Introductory Discussion

- Brainstorm with students a list of creative-thinking tools.
- Encourage discussion about the value of these tools.

2. Core Activity

- Write the letters S-C-A-M-P-E-R vertically on the board. Explain that this is an acronym that encompasses different methods for thinking creatively.
- Write the acronym's definition by adding the following words beside the appropriate letters. Explain how each term is a method for taking something that currently exists and making it entirely new.

Expanding Capacities

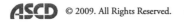

Substitute

Combine

Adapt

Modify

Put to other uses

Eliminate

Rearrange or reverse

Give students the SCAMPER worksheet.

• Divide the class into small groups. Let each group choose an object in the classroom that they can make over into something new. Challenge students to follow the SCAMPER process to create an original product from that existing object. Have them use the worksheet to record ideas as they brainstorm together.

• When everyone is finished, discuss the process with questions such as the following: Did you enjoy this process? Was it difficult? What helped you? What hindered you? Do you think you'll use it again? In what situations might it be a good tool?

3. Reflection Activity

• Write the following statement on the board:

Creativity is a necessary, but not sufficient, resource for innovation.

• Give students the Creativity + Innovation worksheet. Have them work in small groups to discuss the statement and answer the questions.

• Split the discussion groups into two smaller groups. Create new discussion groups by joining these smaller groups with other smaller groups, so students can compare and evaluate ideas with different students.

• Lead a class discussion to share ideas widely.

Name _____ Class _____ Date _____

SCAMPER

Let the guidelines in this creative-thinking strategy inspire you to create something new.

	Term	Key Ideas to Keep in Mind	New Ideas
S	Substitute	Who else? What else? When else? Where else? Change components, venue, setting, context.	
C	Combine	Join together, blend, synthesize; merge audiences, markets, purposes.	
A	Adapt	Alter, modernize, put into a new situation, employ a new purpose, add a constraint.	
M	Modify	Change size, color, fabric, material, direction, length, meaning; make smaller or larger.	
P	Put to other uses	Find unusual ways of using, other places to use, new ways to use, emergency uses.	
E	Eliminate	Take pieces away, remove, eradicate.	
R	Rearrange or reverse	Put together in a different order or sequence; change layout, design, or pattern; change direction or values; invert.	

Expanding Capacities

Name _____ Class _____ Date _____

Creativity + Innovation

Read the following statement. Then answer the questions that follow.

Creativity is a necessary, but not sufficient, resource for innovation.

Questions

1. To what extent do you agree with the statement? Explain.

2. Rewrite the statement to explain in your own words what you believe to be the relationship between creativity and innovation.

3. Sketch, diagram, or create a flowchart to show the relationship between creativity and innovation.

Name _____ Class _____ Date _____

Creativity + Innovation

Read the following statement. Then answer the questions that follow.

Creativity is a necessary, but not sufficient, resource for innovation.

Questions

> The following sample answers may help students get started.

1. To what extent do you agree with the statement? Explain.

I agree. In addition to creativity, a person needs mental agility and knowledge to create a new product. He or she also needs other resources such as money, materials, and a means for producing the product.

2. Rewrite the statement to explain in your own words what you believe to be the relationship between creativity and innovation.

I believe creativity is the starting point for innovation. Without creativity, innovation would never happen. It is also useful for solving problems and improving products as they are developed and new models come out.

3. Sketch, diagram, or create a flowchart to show the relationship between creativity and innovation.

Responding with Wonderment and Awe

PURPOSE OF THIS TOOL

In this tool, students describe positive experiences that have left a big impression. They use the terms *wonderment* and *awe* in several different ways to further explore the meaning of the concepts. In addition, they analyze the role of wonder in stimulating thinking, and they use their creative energies to design a logo for this Habit of Mind.

As students develop a deeper understanding of these concepts, they will find themselves responding with wonderment and awe more frequently and beginning to make this habit their own. In the process, they further cultivate their curious nature and enjoyment of the world around them.

The resources in this tool will enable students to

- Explore what the experience of something wonderful and awesome looks, sounds, and feels like.
- Describe a "fireworks" moment.
- Analyze a quotation from Socrates that links wonder to great beginnings.
- Design a new logo for this Habit of Mind.

HOW TO USE THIS TOOL

The following list of resources includes the suggested sequence for using this tool:

- Awesome Y-Chart worksheet (Motivating Activity)
- Fireworks worksheet (Core Activity)
- Wonderful Beginnings discussion (Reflection Activity)
- A New Logo (Extension Activity)

The activities and tasks included in this tool should take 45–60 minutes to complete. You will need color pencils or markers.

TIPS AND VARIATIONS

1. Motivating Activity

- Tell students that this Habit of Mind helps us realize and remember that things we witness can be truly awesome. Ask: What do you look like when you respond in awe? What actions or sounds might you witness? What feelings might you have? Does everyone feel the same way in such a situation?

• Give students the Awesome Y-Chart worksheet to "unpack," or explore, what this Habit of Mind means.

2. Core Activity

• Distribute and have students complete the Fireworks worksheet. Tell students the moment they describe doesn't have to be a huge event, such as watching a rocket explode into space. It can be something simple, such as watching fields of wheat move gently with the wind as far as the eye can see. Encourage students to explain a moment when they were overcome by a wonderful feeling, such as amazement, gratitude, joy, peace, or comfort. If students really have trouble with this exercise, suggest they close their eyes and imagine something realistic that they think would be awesome to see.

• If some students are willing to share their experiences with the class, have them do so.

• Have a class discussion on the final question about being open to such experiences.

3. Reflection Activity

• Write the following quotation on the board:

All thinking begins with wondering.

    —Socrates, ancient Greek philosopher

• Have students work in pairs to discuss the quote. Prompt students to answer questions such as the following: Do you agree? If you agree, do you agree 100 percent, 1 percent, or somewhere in between? Ask students to explain their answers.

• Ask the class: Can you think of any example from your studies at school or elsewhere that supports Socrates' statement?

• Ask whether anyone knows what the expression *the "wow" factor* means. Explain that people who are designing something, such as a TV show, a book, a tennis shoe, or an educational product, often use the term and that it refers to that aspect of something that really gets the attention of the intended audience. For example, it may be a surprising scene or dialogue in a movie or an innovative design or material in a product. Ask students to provide other examples.

4. Extension Activity

• Redirect students' attention to the Fireworks worksheet. Explain that the fireworks logo shown on the page is the official logo for this Habit of Mind. The fireworks represent the brilliance and beauty of an experience.

Expanding Capacities

• Have students create a new logo and catchphrase to publicize this Habit of Mind to students their age.

• Showcase students' designs in a class display. You may also choose to save their designs and use them in a display for students the next year.

Name _____ Class _____ Date _____

Awesome Y-Chart

Use this chart to explore your thoughts about the Habit of Mind of Responding with Wonderment and Awe.

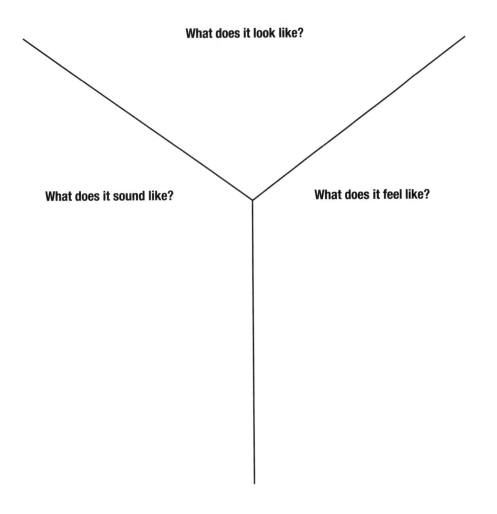

What does it look like?

What does it sound like?

What does it feel like?

Name _____ Class _____ Date _____

Fireworks

Think about a time when you were so inspired, impressed, awed, or amazed by something that fireworks went off in your head. Then answer the questions below.

1. Describe a moment when you were inspired, impressed, amazed, awed, or full of wonder about something. What happened?

2. How did you feel? Explain.

3. Had you ever felt that way before or have you since? Explain.

4. How might a person keep himself or herself open to being amazed?

Name _____ Class _____ Date _____

Fireworks

Think about a time when you were so inspired, impressed, awed, or amazed by something that fireworks went off in your head. Then answer the questions below.

1. Describe a moment when you were inspired, impressed, amazed, awed, or full of wonder about something. What happened?

When my baby brother was born, I got to go to the hospital and watch the live birth. I was grossed out at first and didn't want to be there—no one expected my mom's labor to be so short and I was the only person around to be with my mom. I'm so glad, because it was an unforgettable experience to see a brand new living thing come into the world, with tiny little hands and feet, all purple and scared. It's very difficult to explain how amazing it was.

2. How did you feel? Explain.

I felt like I really shouldn't be there at first. I didn't like seeing my mom in pain, and I didn't think I could handle what was about to happen. But I couldn't just leave her, and the nurse said I could hold her hand. Then she asked if I wanted to see the baby being born, and I did—oddly enough. Then I felt awed and so incredibly impressed with the process.

3. Have you ever felt that way before or since? Explain.

I've had some pretty terrific moments watching my brother grow up, but nothing comes close to watching him take his first breath.

4. How might a person keep himself or herself open to being amazed?

I think part of it is controlling your fear of the unknown and being open to seeing something for what it really is without attaching too many feelings or judgments to it.

Taking Responsible Risks

PURPOSE OF THIS TOOL

In this tool, students ponder several dilemmas. They methodically consider pros, cons, possible surprises, and most likely outcomes. Then they determine whether the risk is responsible or not and make a decision. As students gain more experience analyzing real-world situations, they become better equipped for taking responsible risks. They gain knowledge that allows them to make educated decisions about when and how to risk. In the process, they form a deeper understanding of this Habit of Mind and make it their own.

The resources in this tool will enable students to

- Analyze the pros, cons, and riskiness of a situation.
- Write or enact a dilemma.
- Help analyze several group dilemmas.
- Choose personal experiences or world events that involved taking a responsible risk and discuss the decision-making experience and results.

HOW TO USE THIS TOOL

The following list of resources includes the suggested sequence for using this tool:

- Jaspreet's Dilemma worksheet (Motivating Activity)
- Group Dilemmas (Core Activity)
- Risk Taking in the World (Synthesis Activity)

The activities and tasks included in this tool should take 60–90 minutes to complete.

TIPS AND VARIATIONS

1. Motivating Activity

- Read the following scenario to students:

  Jaspreet's best friend, Kim, is moving across the country. The two 15-year-old girls are devastated that they'll be so far apart, but they vow to remain lifelong friends. To help send Kim off in style, Jaspreet hosts a going-away party. She invites all of Kim's friends, many of whom she's never met because the two girls went to different schools.

At the party, Jaspreet meets Thomas, a guy Kim dated for a short time a few months ago. Thomas ended the relationship, but Jaspreet knows Kim wishes they were still dating. Thomas broke up with Kim because he said they didn't have much in common. Jaspreet didn't think he handled it very well and was crushed for her friend. When Jaspreet meets Thomas at the crowded party, she doesn't know who he is. They immediately realize how much they have in common and spend much of the evening getting to know each other. By the time Jaspreet realizes who Thomas is, she is irretrievably smitten. When Thomas asks Jaspreet if she would like to go out on a date, Jaspreet happily says yes. But when she tells Kim, Kim is furious.

What should Jaspreet do?

- Give students the worksheet Jaspreet's Dilemma. Ask them to work in small groups to use the worksheet and analyze Jaspreet's dilemma.
- Review the groups' decisions as a class.

2. Core Activity

- Divide the class into small groups again, or use the same groups as in the previous activity. Have the groups develop a scenario about someone their age who must decide whether it is responsible to take a risk. They can do this in one of the following ways:

  Write the situation as a short paragraph or story to be read to the class, such as the story about Jaspreet's dilemma.

  Prepare a short skit and act out the dilemma for the class.

  Write the dilemma in the form of an interview, with the dilemma gradually unfolding as the interview progresses, and act out the interview for the class.

- When the groups present their dilemmas to the class, have the class consider whether each risk is responsible. You may wish to record the pros and cons of each dilemma on the board and analyze as a class.

3. Synthesis Activity

- Relate this story to students:

  Several years ago, an ambitious 17-year-old sat ready to take the entrance exam for Cambridge University in England. He knew a lot was at stake—competition to get into this prestigious university is extremely fierce, and doing well on the entrance exam is absolutely vital. The entrance exam consisted of writing an essay on a given topic in 90 minutes. When the young man turned over the exam he saw the question: "What is risk?" The answer he wrote: "This is."

- Ask: What did the student mean by his answer? Discuss students' explanations.
- Ask students for a show of hands about whether the boy took a responsible risk. Have these students share and justify their points of view. Afterward, take another show of hands to see whether any students changed their opinion.

4. Extension Activity

- Challenge students to think of two or three examples of world events or to recall personal experiences in which someone took a responsible risk after considering an issue.
- Have students work in pairs to discuss the following questions about each risk they thought of: Was the risk academic, physical, social, or emotional? What consequences and considerations did the decision maker use to think through the consequences and ensure the risk was responsible? Why did you choose this example? What was the final outcome or decision?

Name _____ Class _____ Date _____

Jaspreet's Dilemma

Jaspreet said she would go on a date with Thomas. Analyze her situation below.

What good things could result from this decision?	What bad things could result from this decision?	What unlikely or unexpected things could result from this decision?

Explain the most likely outcome.

In light of these questions, is it responsible to take this risk?

Yes _____   No _____   Maybe _____

Name _____ Class _____ Date _____

Jaspreet's Dilemma

Jaspreet said she would go on a date with Thomas. Analyze her situation below.

> Keep copies of this form handy in the classroom. When students come to you with issues or if students want to be adventuresome in some way, suggest they use this form to analyze the situation. The following are sample answers.

What good things could result from this decision?	What bad things could result from this decision?	What unlikely or unexpected things could result from this decision?
Jaspreet and Thomas could be a very compatible couple and enjoy many happy times together.	Jaspreet could lose her long-term friendship with Kim over this issue. Thomas could dump Jaspreet and treat her badly, just as he did Kim.	This experience could help Kim let go of her past and be more fully open to experiences in her new home. If the relationship doesn't work out, Kim could help Jaspreet recover and their friendship could grow stronger. If Jaspreet's relationship with Thomas does work out, Kim could grow to understand and appreciate their bond and, in the process, learn something about why Thomas wasn't right for her and what she does need in a partner.

Explain the most likely outcome.

Jaspreet will go out with Thomas, and it will damage her relationship with Kim for a time. The relationship may not work, but Kim and Jaspreet will rekindle their friendship or they will let go and develop new friendships.

In light of these questions, is it responsible to take this risk?

Yes _____   No _____   Maybe _____

Jaspreet must decide whether she is willing to risk Kim's friendship.

Finding Humor

PURPOSE OF THIS TOOL

In this tool, students think a lot about where they find humor. They discuss personal examples of finding humor and are encouraged to begin keeping track of funny situations they can share with the class. They are also challenged to use a rubric to develop their ability to find humor in all the right places.

As students make finding humor a way of life, they form a deeper understanding of this habit and make it their own. As they do, they learn to assume the responsibility that comes along with finding humor and distinguish between situations that require compassion and those that are truly funny.

The resources in this tool will enable students to

- Define what it means to find humor and explore what it looks like, sounds like, and feels like.
- Discuss humor they have found in books, movies, and the media.
- Discuss personal examples of finding humor.
- Evaluate their skill at finding humor.
- Regularly look for and keep notes on humorous situations.

HOW TO USE THIS TOOL

The following list of resources includes the suggested sequence for using this tool:

- Investigating Finding Humor worksheet (Motivating Activity)
- Finding Humor Everywhere discussion (Core Activity)
- Finding Humor Rubric worksheet (Extension Activity)
- Noting Humor (Ongoing Activity)

The activities and tasks included in this tool should take about 45 minutes to complete.

TIPS AND VARIATIONS

1. Motivating Activity

- Ask students: What does it look like when someone around you is finding humor? What does it sound like? What noises or voices will you hear? What will you say to yourself? What does it feel like to find humor? What does it feel like to break a difficult silence or realize that you have made a mistake in front of others? Tell students that thinking about what something sounds like, looks like, feels like, and means to them is a great tool for integrating it.

• Give students the Investigating Finding Humor worksheet and have them answer the questions. You may wish to have students work with a partner to complete this activity.

2. Core Activity

• Have students choose a partner. Ask them to recall an example from a TV show, a book, a poem, a movie, a play, or other medium that effectively demonstrates the Finding Humor Habit of Mind and share it with their partner.

• Ask some of the pairs to share some of their examples with the class.

• Have students recall an example in which they personally demonstrated the Finding Humor Habit of Mind and share it with their partner.

• Lead a whole-class discussion with questions such as the following: How might you develop this habit? Why should you bother? What could you gain? What could those around you gain if you further developed the habit of finding humor?

3. Extension Activity

• Give students the Finding Humor Rubric worksheet and ask them to use it to evaluate their development of this Habit of Mind over time.

4. Ongoing Activity

• Tell students to pay attention over the next few weeks to situations in which humor added to an occasion, defused a difficult situation, relieved anxiety, or helped them look at things from a different viewpoint. Say that the class will revisit this Habit of Mind later, and at that time students can share examples they noted.

• If you wish, encourage students to create a humor journal to keep track of the funny things they see and do.

Expanding Capacities

Name _____ Class _____ Date _____

Investigating Finding Humor

Sounds Like: When you find humor, you might say to a friend …   1.   2.   3.
Looks Like: When a friend is finding humor, he or she may be …   1.   2.   3.
Feels Like: When you find humor, you may think to yourself …   1.   2.   3.
Meaning to Me: Define the Habit of Mind of Finding Humor with words or a picture.

Name _____ Class _____ Date _____

Investigating Finding Humor

> The following are sample answers.

Sounds Like: When you find humor, you might say to a friend …

1. *Check this out!*

2. *You've got to hear this hilarious story!*

3. *Want to hear something funny?*

Looks Like: When a friend is finding humor, he or she may be …

1. *laughing.*

2. *smiling.*

3. *nodding his or her head in delight.*

Feels Like: When you find humor, you may think to yourself …

1. *Whew! I needed that!*

2. *So things aren't so bad, after all!*

3. *Boy, that guy is funny!*

Meaning to Me: Define the Habit of Mind of Finding Humor with words or a picture.

Finding humor means different things in different situations. If I find something funny in a tense situation and everyone laughs when I share it, that means progress. That means there is hope. If I find humor in a problem I've been working on, that means perhaps I can stop taking myself so seriously and actually solve it. If I find and share humor with friends or family, it means I'm helping other people relax and enjoy themselves and helping to form bonds between us. Finding humor often means finding fun.

Name _____ Class _____ Date _____

Finding Humor Rubric

Use the following rubric to reflect on your ability to find humor. Add your own statements to the chart to further assess your abilities.

Do you ...	Always	Usually	Sometimes	Seldom	Never
look for a humorous way of engaging in a situation?					
perceive a situation from an original and interesting vantage point?					
initiate humor?					
place value on having a sense of humor?					
appreciate and seek to understand the humor of others?					
get verbally playful when interacting with others?					
have a whimsical frame of mind?					
find incongruity funny?					
perceive absurdities, ironies, and satire as funny?					
laugh at yourself?					
avoid laughing at ineptitude, injurious behavior, vulgarity, violence, profanity, or human differences?					
distinguish between situations that require compassion and those that are truly funny?					

Thinking Interdependently

PURPOSE OF THIS TOOL

In this tool, students explore how the idea of thinking interdependently looks, feels, and sounds to them. Then they show their opinions as a class during a human graph activity. Finally, students work interdependently to create skits showing effective and ineffective interdependent behaviors.

As students continue to practice thinking interdependently, they form a deeper understanding of this habit and make it their own. In the process, they become more open to feedback and more motivated to help others via constructive critiques.

The resources in this tool will enable students to

- Explore how the Thinking Interdependently Habit of Mind looks, sounds, and feels.
- Participate in a human graph to reflect opinions about working interdependently.
- Work with a team to create a skit showing effective and ineffective interdependent behaviors.

HOW TO USE THIS TOOL

The following list of resources includes the suggested sequence for using this tool:

- Interdependence Y-Chart worksheet (Introductory Discussion)
- Human Graph (Core Activity)
- Interdependent skits (Synthesis Activity)

The activities and tasks included in this tool should take about 60 minutes to complete.

TIPS AND VARIATIONS

1. Introductory Discussion

- Ask: What does it mean to work together or be part of a team? Does it mean thinking the same as everyone else? What is the difference between thinking the same as everyone else and thinking interdependently? (Interdependence is dependence upon each other. Thinking interdependently is thinking together, as a group, in such a way that the whole is greater than the sum of its parts. It does not mean that every part or person is the same or thinks the same; in fact, differences are necessary to create a productive team environment.)

Expanding Capacities

• Give students the Interdependence Y-Chart worksheet. Have them consider questions such as the following: What does it look like when people think together? What setting do you imagine them in? Do they need to see each other, or could they think interdependently over the phone or via the Internet? What facial expressions and body language might you expect to notice? What does a group of people thinking together sound like? What might you hear people say? What might it feel like to be part of such a group? What feelings might the individuals experience?

2. Core Activity

• Explain that a human graph is much like a written graph except that the classroom floor is the page and each student is a point on an axis. Assign the left side of the classroom to represent "Strongly Agree" and the right side of the room to represent "Strongly Disagree." (You may want to label these with signs.)

• Tell students that as you ask a series of questions they should respond by standing on one side of the room or the other according to their viewpoint. If their point of view is somewhere in the middle, they should stand in between the two end points.

• Read the following statements, pausing for students to move each time. Periodically call on one or more students to share the rationale for their position.

> I enjoy working on my own.
> I think well when others do not disturb me.
> I think doing a good job of thinking interdependently takes practice.
> I get a lot out of listening to the ideas and suggestions of other people.
> I have nothing to gain from listening to the ideas of others.
> I don't like sharing my ideas, because I worry that others will criticize me.
> I like working with others, but I get upset if they take my ideas and make them their own.
> I get more done when I work alone.
> I get a lot out of sharing my thinking with others.

• Have students pair up and talk about the experience. Give them the following questions to guide their discussion: How did I compare with other people in the class in relation to thinking interdependently? What aspects of this Habit of Mind do I already do well? What aspects could I improve?

3. Synthesis Activity

• Have students form small groups and write a five-minute skit that shows good and bad examples of thinking interdependently. Require the following: One character must demonstrate the ability to share his thinking and listen to the feedback of teammates; another character should have trouble sharing and listening to the group; the skit should not end well for the latter character.

• Have students enact their skits for the class. Have a class discussion after each. On the board, list the effective and ineffective behaviors depicted.

Expanding Capacities

Name _____ Class _____ Date _____

Interdependence Y-Chart

Use this chart to explore your thoughts about the Thinking Interdependently Habit of Mind.

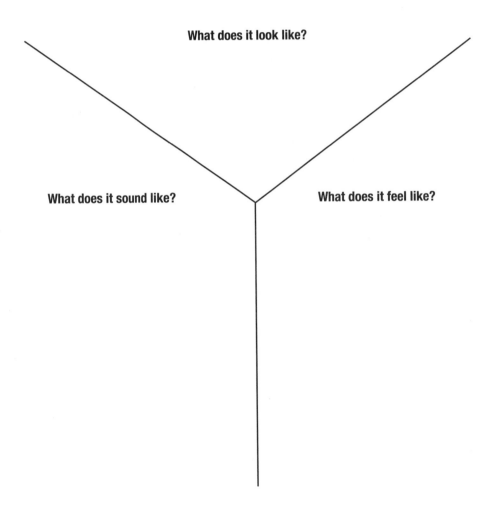

What does it look like?

What does it sound like?

What does it feel like?

Learning Continuously

PURPOSE OF THIS TOOL

In this tool, students explore attitudes toward learning continuously. They examine the consequences of open and closed attitudes about learning new things. They review their own extracurricular experiences and set goals to remain open to progress via new learning. Finally, students contemplate future careers and begin to think of ways they can remain open to new, related learning.

The resources in this tool will enable students to

- Describe what this Habit of Mind looks like, sounds like, and feels like.
- Take part in a role-play about people facing new learning experiences.
- Analyze different attitudes and levels of openness to learning and explore the different consequences of these attitudes.
- Review past extracurricular activities and skills and knowledge learned, and set new goals for learning.
- Contemplate future careers and skills they would like to develop.

HOW TO USE THIS TOOL

The following list of resources includes the suggested sequence for using this tool:

- Keep Learning Y-Chart worksheet (Introductory Discussion)
- New Skills role-play (Core Activity)
- Extracurricular Circles (Reflection Activity)
- Changing Careers discussion (Extension Activity)

The activities and tasks included in this tool should take about 60 minutes to complete. You will need one 11 x 17 piece of paper per student or large sheets of paper students can share.

TIPS AND VARIATIONS

1. Introductory Discussion

- Give students the Keep Learning Y-Chart worksheet. Work through the chart as a class by asking questions such as the following: What might a person who is open to learning look like? What might you see in her eyes or posture? What might this person have to say to you or to others? What other sounds might the person be interested in? What actions might she take? What sorts of things might she feel?

2. Core Activity

• Divide the class into groups of four. Have each group role-play a situation in which two people respond differently to the need to learn something new—for example, they both need to operate a machine at work or need to learn a new language to communicate with new neighbors or customers. Encourage students to come up with their own scenario.

• Explain that in each role-play, one student will portray a person who is open and willing to learn the new skill. Another student will portray a person who is reluctant. The other students can set the scene as supporting characters. Students should clearly portray the motivation of the characters facing the new task. The role-play should also clearly depict the consequences of each person's attitude in the short term and in the long term.

3. Reflection Activity

• Have students focus on skills they have gained outside the classroom by taking a look at their extracurricular activities and hobbies.

• Give students a large piece of paper. Tell them to list their favorite extracurricular activities in the center of the page and then draw a circle around the group of activities.

• Instruct them to draw a larger circle (with room to write) around the first circle. In this second circle, have students list the skills and knowledge they developed while participating in those activities.

• Have students draw a third outer circle, leaving plenty of room. Tell them to brainstorm ideas for how they might extend their abilities and knowledge. For example, they could practice more at a chosen sport and then try out for the school team, or learn to read music and take music lessons.

• Explain that the three circles show what students have learned and how they might learn more in the future. Note that the very act of brainstorming ideas for improvement suggests openness to continued learning. Example:

Inner circle: soccer; playing saxophone; swimming

Next circle: ball control skills, tackling techniques, passing skills, strategic thinking skills; tune and pitch skills, rhythm, reading music; front crawl, backstroke

Outer circle: Try other ball games, join soccer team in college; audition for college music scholarship, try other musical instruments—maybe trombone; try out for water polo team now or in college

Expanding Capacities

4. Extension Activity

- Tell students that experts predict that people of their generation will change careers four times during their working lives. That often means acquiring a whole new set of skills. Ask: What strengths do you have that will enable you to be open to continuous learning in future jobs? What skills might you want to develop?
- Encourage students to brainstorm ideas and list three target goals and an action plan for developing skills they have identified.

Expanding Capacities

Name _____ Class _____ Date _____

Keep Learning Y-Chart

Use this chart to explore your thoughts about the Habit of Mind of Learning Continuously.

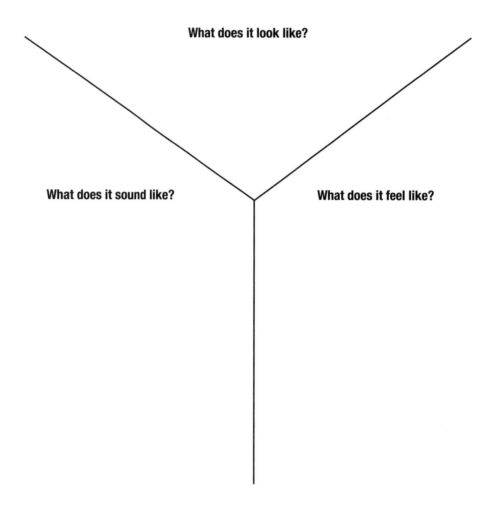

What does it look like?

What does it sound like?

What does it feel like?

Increasing Alertness

Example is not the main thing in influencing others. It is the only thing.

—Albert Schweitzer

This section takes the Expanding Capacities section one step further. By this time, students can identify the habits and their value and use them in specific situations. It is time for them to see the importance of developing the habits in and for themselves. Therefore, this section starts a shift away from teacher-led growth to student-led growth. It serves as a bridge between having an external understanding of the habits and forming a true internal, personal understanding. By the end of this section, the locus of control will begin to move from the teacher to the students. As a result, students will be empowered to use the habits to strengthen their skills as learners at school and in the world beyond.

This transfer of responsibility represents a key step in achieving student buy-in. Recognizing the Habits of Mind is not sufficient to generate personal activation. Students must see significant personal advantage in order to truly adopt and cultivate these habits. This section helps students become more alert to applications of the habits outside the classroom.

With the tools in this section, students will investigate people and situations that matter to them: famous people, world leaders, local people they respect, and significant global and local issues. As students identify applications of the Habits of Mind in the world around them via case studies, interviews, and research projects, they better understand that the habits can truly be beneficial to them in learning and in life.

In integrating the resources of this section into daily classroom practice, it is important to use as many personal, school, and local examples as possible. Continue to look for opportunities to integrate the Habits of Mind into your curriculum. Doing so will further increase the relevance of the habits to students.

CONTENTS

TITLE OF TOOL

Increasing Alertness

Looking Around Us

PURPOSE OF THIS TOOL

This tool focuses on specific examples of people using the Habits of Mind. First, students research a world leader as a group; then they conduct individual research on a famous person they admire. Finally, with a partner, they interview someone in the local area. With each activity, students explore how influential people adopt and apply various Habits of Mind to make contributions to society. As students look closely at people they admire and observe, they discover that these people use Habits of Mind to great benefit; this discovery ignites a greater desire in students to use the habits themselves.

The resources in this tool will enable students to

- Identify Habits of Mind as they are used by various people and in specific situations.
- Do a case study of a world leader to analyze how he or she uses or used Habits of Mind.
- Do a case study of a famous person to analyze how he or she uses or used Habits of Mind.
- Do a case study of a local leader to analyze how he or she uses or used Habits of Mind.
- Compare global, celebrity, and local examples in the application of Habits of Mind.

HOW TO USE THIS TOOL

This tool will support student understanding of how Habits of Mind apply to the world beyond the classroom, especially to their own direct experiences as well as observations of their environment. The following list of resources includes the suggested sequence for using this tool:

- Observing Others (Introductory Discussion)
- Case Study of a World Leader worksheet (Core Activity 1: Group Research)
- Key Research Questions worksheet (Core Activities 1 and 2)
- Habits of Mind Research worksheet (Core Activities 1 and 2)
- Case Study of a Famous Person worksheet (Core Activity 2: Independent Research)
- Case Study of a Local Leader worksheet (Core Activity 3: Partner Interviews)
- Looking for Habits of Mind (Reflection Activity)
- Obstacles on the Path worksheet (Extension Activity)

Increasing Alertness

The activities and tasks included in this tool should take several weeks, including research time, to complete. You will need access to a library or Internet resources. In addition, you will find Key Research Questions and Habits of Mind Research worksheets to aid students in all three research projects.

TIPS AND VARIATIONS

1. Introductory Discussion

- Ask: Can you identify other people's use of Habits of Mind? Can you name a few situations that were positively affected by somebody's use of a Habit of Mind? Have you seen other people benefit when one person used the habits?

2. Core Activity 1: Group Research Project

- Say to students: We can increase our alertness to the Habits of Mind by looking at case studies of people who have clearly used them. Analyzing case studies will help us identify the habits in others and pick up cues about when to use them.
- Introduce the first research project—a case study of a few famous people whose lives illustrate the potential of the habits. Divide the class into six groups. Assign each group one of the following great world leaders to analyze: Nelson Mandela of Africa, Martin Luther King of the United States, George Washington of the United States, Rosa Parks of the United States, Mother Teresa of India, Shirin Ebadi of Iran.
- Give students the Case Study of a World Leader worksheet. Point out that the worksheet employs the 5 Ws and 1 H model: Who, What, When, Where, Why, and How. Reinforce that the model is a great tool to use anytime students want to get core information about something. Tell students to use this worksheet to document basic facts about their great leader.
- As students delve into their research, they will undoubtedly have questions they want and need to pursue for more information. Give them the Key Research Questions worksheet so they can keep track of their questions.
- Encourage students to find specific examples of how their research subject used the Habits of Mind. To help with this process, give students the Habits of Mind Research worksheet (note that it is two pages in length).
- When students have finished their reports, have them present their findings to the class.

3. Core Activity 2: Independent Research Project

• Have students work independently to complete a similar research project. This time, ask them to pick a famous person from any walk of life—a political figure, a movie star, a journalist, a stage or TV actor, a model or designer, a sports hero, an astronaut, or any other public figure who fascinates them.

• Give students the Case Study of a Famous Person worksheet and tell them to now do individually exactly what they did in their group research project. Say that this time you would like them to zero in on things about the person that they especially admire or appreciate—perhaps the person's accomplishments or attitude. Tell them to find out how the person became successful and which Habits of Mind he or she regularly used or uses.

• Give students the Key Research Questions and Habits of Mind Research worksheets to use while conducting their research.

• When students have finished their reports, have them form a group with one or two other students to discuss what they learned about their famous people and how the people used or use the Habits of Mind.

4. Core Activity 3: Partner Interviews

• Have students choose a partner. Tell them they are going to use the same model again, this time to investigate a local person they respect. Give them the Case Study of a Local Leader worksheet as a guide.

• Tell students to pick a person in the local area they really respect—for example, a neighbor, local politician, local comedian, teacher, business leader, or professional in a career they aspire to. If students don't immediately have an idea of whom to research, suggest they ask a librarian about getting lists of people in the community who have received awards such as "volunteer of the year" or "teacher of the year."

• Have students contact their chosen individual by phone or e-mail to set up a 30-minute interview. Students could make arrangements to meet the person at school, a local coffee house, a restaurant, or a public area such as a park. Students can use their worksheet to guide the interview, come up with a few questions specific to their own interests about the person, and spend some time simply getting to know the individual on a personal level.

Note: Students are often nervous about doing an interview. Reassure them that the experience is usually far more rewarding than they anticipate.

- When students have finished their reports, have the partners form a group with another duo and share their findings.

5. Reflection Activity

- Lead a class discussion about the experience of looking for Habits of Mind in other people. Ask questions such as the following: Do you see any similarities between great national leaders, the famous person you admire, and the local person you respect? Do any of these people use similar Habits of Mind? Did you learn anything from them?
- Encourage students to elaborate as they respond to the questions and to one another's comments.

6. Extension Activity

- Give students the Obstacles on the Path worksheet and ask them to pick one or more of the people they researched and describe how the person or persons overcame obstacles.
- Encourage volunteers to share their responses aloud. Use these responses as a springboard to class discussion.

Increasing Alertness

Name _____ Class _____ Date _____

Case Study of a World Leader

Ask a variety of questions, and then record your answers.

Questions	Answers
Who?	
Where?	
When?	
Why?	
What?	
How? (Which Habits of Mind?)	

Name _____ Class _____ Date _____

Case Study of a World Leader

Ask a variety of questions, and then record your answers.

Share the following sample answers with students to help them get started.

Questions	Answers
Who?	*Mother Teresa*
Where?	*India*
When?	*Born 1910, died 1997*
Why?	*Winner of the Nobel Peace Prize in 1979, great humanitarian*
What?	*She ministered to the poor, sick, orphaned, and dying for over 40 years. She established and led missionaries throughout India and then in other countries. A documentary and book about her called* Something Beautiful for God, *by Malcolm Muggeridge, helped her garner international fame by the 1970s. She is known as a great humanitarian and advocate for the poor and helpless. Her Missionaries of Charity had expanded to 610 missions in 123 countries at the time of her death.*
How? (Which Habits of Mind?)	*Listening with Understanding and Empathy, Persisting, Responding with Wonderment and Awe, Questioning and Posing Problems*

Name _____ Class _____ Date _____

Key Research Questions

As you do your research, brainstorm questions that will help you learn more. The following are a few examples:

- Why was _____ famous?
- Why did many people respect him or her?
- What did _____ achieve in his or her lifetime?
- What lessons does _____ teach us?

Your Research Topic:

Questions:

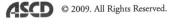
Increasing Alertness

Name _____ Class _____ Date _____

Habits of Mind Research

As you do your research, record notes on the Habits of Mind as you see them exemplified and put into practice.

Research Topic: _____

Habits of Mind: Part 1

Habit of Mind	Example	What did using this Habit of Mind achieve?
Persisting		
Managing Impulsivity		
Listening with Understanding and Empathy		
Thinking Flexibly		
Thinking About Thinking (Metacognition)		
Striving for Accuracy and Precision		
Questioning and Posing Problems		
Applying Past Knowledge to New Situations		

Increasing Alertness

Name _____ Class _____ Date _____

Habits of Mind Research, *continued*

Research Topic: _____

Habits of Mind: Part 2

Habit of Mind	Example	What did using this Habit of Mind achieve?
Thinking and Communicating with Clarity and Precision		
Gathering Data Through All Senses		
Creating, Imagining, and Innovating		
Responding with Wonderment and Awe		
Taking Responsible Risks		
Finding Humor		
Thinking Interdependently		
Learning Continuously		

Increasing Alertness

Name _____ Class _____ Date _____

Habits of Mind Research

As you do your research, record notes on the Habits of Mind as you see them exemplified and put into practice.

> Share the following sample answers with students to help them get started.

Research Topic: *Mother Teresa*

Habits of Mind: Part 1

Habit of Mind	Example	What did using this Habit of Mind achieve?
Persisting	*Many people thought she was crazy helping the outcast, miserable, and poor people, because there were too many and their lives were of questionable value.*	*Her ability to persist despite a lot of doubt and prejudice allowed people to see that everyone has value and everyone deserves food, shelter, and a safe environment.*
Managing Impulsivity		
Listening with Understanding and Empathy	*She ministered to the poor and won the Nobel Peace Prize for her efforts.*	*Her ability to see everyone as important and empathize with everyone's struggle helped her bring great relief and inspired thousands of other humanitarians.*

Habits of Mind: Part 1 (*continued*)

Habit of Mind	Example	What did using this Habit of Mind achieve?
Thinking Flexibly	*She identified problems and found new ways of solving them.*	*She found a way through the many obstacles to achieve her goal.*
Thinking About Thinking (Metacognition)		
Striving for Accuracy and Precision		
Questioning and Posing Problems		
Applying Past Knowledge to New Situations		

Increasing Alertness

Name _____ Class _____ Date _____

Case Study of a Famous Person

Ask a variety of questions, and then record your answers.

Questions	Answers
Who?	
Where?	
When?	
Why?	
What?	
How? (Which Habits of Mind?)	

Name _____ Class _____ Date _____

Case Study of a Famous Person

This is an example only. Students will have chosen their own topic.

Ask a variety of questions, and then record your answers.

Questions	Answers
Who?	*Mohammed Ali, previously known as Cassius Clay*
Where?	*Louisville, Kentucky, USA*
When?	*Born in 1942; won Olympic gold medal in 1960; throughout the 1960s and 1970s earned the title of WBA heavyweight boxing champion many times.*
Why?	*He was an amazing boxer with a unique "dancing" style and a fierce belief in his capabilities.*
What?	*Muhammad Ali won 56 matches and lost only 5; he was the three-time world heavyweight champion; he beat almost every top heavyweight in his era; he is an inductee into the International Boxing Hall of Fame and has beaten seven other Hall of Fame inductees; he is one of only three boxers to be named Sportsman of the Year by* Sports Illustrated; *he was awarded the Arthur Ashe Courage Award; he continues to contribute to society despite suffering from Parkinson's disease.*
How? (Which Habits of Mind?)	*Persisting; Thinking and Communicating with Clarity and Precision; Creating, Imagining, Innovating; Striving for Accuracy and Precision*

Increasing Alertness

Name _____ Class _____ Date _____

Case Study of a Local Leader

Ask a variety of questions, and then record your answers.

Questions	Answers
Who?	
Where?	
When?	
Why?	
What?	
How? (Which Habits of Mind?)	

Name _____ Class _____ Date _____

Case Study of a Local Leader

> This is an example only. Students will have chosen their own topic.

Ask a variety of questions, and then record your answers.

Questions	Answers
Who?	*Janie Smith*
Where?	*Austin, Texas, USA*
When?	*2009 Volunteer of the Year*
Why?	*She is determined to help people have adequate housing.*
What?	*Janie won the 2009 Volunteer of the Year award for her work with Habitat for Humanity. She helped build more than 35 houses last year. As a retired architect, Janie donated the plans for each home and logged countless hours hammering, sawing, lifting, painting, and gardening to make the homes special. Her efforts helped the Habitat program build twice as many homes this year as last. These homes now provide a safe place for 140 people to live. Janie is 75 years old.*
How? (Which Habits of Mind?)	*Persisting; Applying Past Knowledge to New Situations; Thinking and Communicating with Clarity and Precision; Creating, Imagining, and Innovating; Taking Responsible Risks; Thinking Interdependently; Learning Continuously; Listening to Others with Understanding and Empathy; Striving for Accuracy and Precision*

Increasing Alertness

Name _____ Class _____ Date _____

Obstacles on the Path

Complete the following tree map to show successes, failures, and obstacles the subject of your research experienced on his or her path to success.

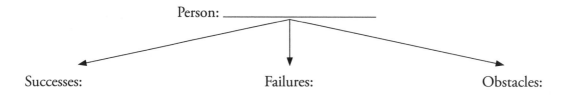

Person: _____

Successes: Failures: Obstacles:

Which Habits of Mind helped this person overcome obstacles?	How did the Habits of Mind help this person?	What evidence supports your claim?

Professional Applications

PURPOSE OF THIS TOOL

This tool helps students focus on how Habits of Mind are applied in the workplace. In groups, students analyze a number of professions to determine which habits are most relevant and why. They also examine possible consequences if those habits are not used regularly. Then students work independently to explore and compare professions of personal interest. They analyze the Habits of Mind most relevant to those careers and see how they match up with the students' own personal strengths. Then students target areas for improvement and create an action plan to develop useful Habits of Mind.

As they go through these exercises and think about their futures, students will increasingly recognize, without prompting, when to apply the habits. Students will also become more astute at observing people around them who are using Habits of Mind.

The resources in this tool will enable students to

- Explore how Habits of Mind are used in the workplace.
- Target a couple of professions of personal interest and analyze the most relevant Habits of Mind.
- Compare Habits of Mind needed for professions of interest to their own personal aptitudes.
- Create an action plan to improve a Habit of Mind.

HOW TO USE THIS TOOL

This tool will support student understanding of how Habits of Mind can contribute to their career success. The following is the suggested sequence for exploring this habit:

- Profession Cards (Advance Preparation)
- Profession Analysis worksheet (Motivating Activity)
- Summary of 16 Habits of Mind (Motivating Activity)
- Two Professions worksheet (Core Activity)
- Career Action Plan worksheet (Core Activity)
- Thinking Forward discussion (Reflection Activity)

Note: The Summary of 16 Habits of Mind worksheet is available in Appendix B.

The activities and tasks included in this tool should take about 60 minutes plus extra-curricular time for interested students to complete their career exploration. Some advance preparation is needed.

Increasing Alertness

Note: To use this tool with students in primary grades, see the suggestions provided for adapting it for younger students.

TIPS AND VARIATIONS

1. Advance Preparation

- Copy and cut out the items on the Profession Cards worksheet. If possible, use card stock.

2. Motivating Activity

- Divide the class into groups of two or three. Randomly distribute three or four Profession Cards so that each student has one. Give each group one copy of the Profession Analysis worksheet and the Summary of 16 Habits of Mind worksheet (Appendix B).
- Tell the groups to discuss each profession and fill in the analysis sheet. Encourage students to clearly describe all relevant Habits of Mind. Have additional copies of this form available in case students need it, or you may want to recreate the form on larger paper to allow students more room for description.
- Ask the groups to add two or three more professions to the Profession Analysis worksheet and analyze them.

3. Core Activity

- Once students have finished analyzing professions, instruct them to leave their completed worksheets at their group stations and then get up and move through all other group stations to see the range of careers their classmates have explored. Encourage them to pay special attention to professions that look interesting to them.
- Have students return to their own desks. Give them the Two Professions worksheet and ask them to compare and contrast two professions. Students can use professions their group or another group analyzed, or they can come up with two new professions that interest them. Allow students to do Internet or library research on these professions.
- Point out to students that the Two Professions worksheet can serves as a good starting place to explore careers of interest. To extend the activity, suggest that students visit a career counselor or interview persons in the professions. As students explore, encourage them to look for Habits of Mind relevant to each profession.
- Have students consider how well they themselves apply the Habits of Mind that are most relevant to their preferred careers. Give students the Career Action Plan

Increasing Alertness

worksheet as a guide. Help students analyze and reflect on the best Habits of Mind for their career aspirations, and help them create a good plan for monitoring and improving those habits.

4. Reflection Activity

- Have students work in small groups to discuss the following questions:

  Suppose you are in charge of training new police recruits. Which three Habits of Mind would you train them in, and why?

  Which Habits of Mind are most relevant to a career of interest to you?

  Think about up-and-coming jobs of the future, or jobs that have increasing demand every year. Which Habits of Mind are likely to be most useful for these jobs?

- Ask the groups to share some of their discussion highlights with the whole class.

ADAPTATIONS FOR YOUNGER CHILDREN

1. Advance Preparation

- If your students are in primary grades, you may wish to create several sets of the 16 Habits of Mind on labels so they can attach them to appropriate cards. You could make the cards with names and pictures so students can make clear associations.

2. Core Activity

- Have students work in small groups. Give them two or three Profession Cards and ask them to decide which Habit of Mind label is best for each profession. If students are older elementary students, simply have them write the Habits of Mind on appropriate cards.
- Hold a class discussion to review two or three careers.
- Ask volunteers to suggest a profession the class can analyze together.

3. Reflection Activity

- Have students work in small groups to discuss which careers are the most interesting to them.
- Ask the groups to share highlights of their discussion with the whole class.

Increasing Alertness

Profession Cards

Copy and cut out the following cards to distribute to students. If possible, use card stock. Several blank cards are included for you to add professions you think will interest your students. If necessary, create more class-specific cards.

Doctor	Nurse	Firefighter	Scientist
Museum Director	Teacher	Writer	Actor
King or Queen	Banker	Librarian	Carpenter
Dentist	Chef	Bridge Builder	Soldier
Referee	Minister	Nanny	Musician
Comedian	Inventor	Painter	Mechanic

Increasing Alertness

Name _____ Class _____ Date _____

Profession Analysis

The profession I am analyzing is: _____

Habits of Mind a person in this profession regularly uses	How this Habit of Mind relates to this job	Consequences if the Habit of Mind is not used

Increasing Alertness

Name _____ Class _____ Date _____

Two Professions

Use this worksheet to compare two professions that interest you.

The two professions I am comparing are

The similarities between Habits of Mind used in these professions are

The differences between Habits of Mind used in these professions are

Other similarities between these professions are

Other differences between these professions are

To better compare these professions, I would like to know more about

Increasing Alertness

Name _____ Class _____ Date _____

Career Action Plan

List Habits of Mind most relevant to careers of interest to you. Then complete this action plan to help you develop those habits.

Habits of Mind I Can Develop to Prepare for These Careers

1.

2.

3.

My Action Plan to Improve These Habits of Mind in One Month

I will do these specific things:

I can seek assistance from these sources:

I can monitor my improvement in these ways:

Increasing Alertness

Important Issues

PURPOSE OF THIS TOOL

Through this tool, students learn about a pressing global issue. They explore how Habits of Mind relate to the issue and how people are using Habits of Mind to address the issue today. Students explore the scope of global issues and particularly the relevance of the Thinking Interdependently Habit of Mind in resolving issues that cross international borders.

Students then brainstorm issues of concern in their local area. They work in groups to pick one issue and research it. They also explore relevant Habits of Mind and consequences related to not using the habits to resolve the issue. Finally, students are encouraged to interview someone working on the issue to see firsthand which Habits of Mind are being applied.

The resources in this tool will enable students to

- Explore a global issue.
- Determine how Habits of Mind relate to a global issue.
- Brainstorm local issues.
- Research a local issue.
- Determine how Habits of Mind relate to a local issue.
- Interview someone who is working on a local issue.

HOW TO USE THIS TOOL

This tool extends students' exploration of authentic, real-world applications of Habits of Mind in the world of international relations and global interdependence, as well as in their local area. The following set of resources is especially useful in helping students to expand their research and investigation competencies while considering a relevant global or local issue of concern to them.

- Issue Analysis worksheet (Introductory Activity)
- Summary of 16 Habits of Mind (Introductory Activity)
- Case Study of a Local Issue worksheet (Core Activity)
- Issue Analysis worksheet (Core Activity)
- Key Research Questions worksheet (Core Activity)
- Case Study of a Local Leader worksheet (Synthesis Activity)
- Obstacles on the Path worksheet (Synthesis Activity)

Increasing Alertness

Note: The Summary of 16 Habits of Mind, Case Study, and Obstacles on the Path worksheets can be found in Appendix B.

The activities and tasks included in this tool should take 1–2 weeks to complete, including research time.

TIPS AND VARIATIONS

1. Introductory Activity

- Tell students that the Secretary-General of the United Nations, Ban Ki-moon, has called climate change the "defining issue of our era" and has said that "how we address it will define us, our era, and ultimately the global legacy we leave for future generations."
- Explain that you would like to explore this issue as a class. Then show students all or part of a film or TV program that chronicles the issue of climate change. Suggestions:

  An Inconvenient Truth, Al Gore's 2007 documentary

  Global Warming: Too Hot Not to Handle, HBO 2008 documentary

  The 11th Hour, Leonardo di Caprio's 2007 documentary

  Global Warming: The Signs and the Science, PBS Home Video

  Earth to America! short features at www.stopglobalwarming.com

- After the film, give students the Issue Analysis worksheet and the Summary of 16 Habits of Mind worksheet (Appendix B). Ask them to pick five Habits of Mind that are related in some way to this issue and then complete the chart.
- Have a class discussion about the issue. Ask: What Habits of Mind might have prevented this situation? Why didn't nations do something about the global climate issue sooner? What Habits of Mind, had they been applied, might have helped prevent the current problem? What habits can be used now to help solve the problem? Predict what might happen if Habits of Mind were never used.
- Read another quote from the Secretary-General of the United Nations, Ban Ki-moon:

  We must … leave this conference with a sense of purpose and mission, knowing that we are allied in our determination to make a difference. Only by acting together, in partnership, can we overcome this crisis, today and for tomorrow. Hundreds of millions of the world's people expect no less. (Presentation at the High-Level Conference on World Food Security: The Challenges of Climate Change and Bioenergy, Rome, June 2008)

Increasing Alertness

- Ask: Which Habit of Mind does this quote exemplify? (Thinking Interdependently.) Point out that this statement was not made in relation to climate change but at a conference on world food security. Having enough food to feed the world's people is another global issue.

- Ask: What are some other global issues? Have students brainstorm in small groups. (Examples: endangered species, international peace, human rights, energy development, space travel, sustainable development, and disaster relief.)

2. Core Activity

- Write the following quotation on the board:

  Think globally, act locally.
  —David Brower

- Ask students what they think this statement might mean. (Having a global perspective is important. Everyone should realize that his or her actions affect the health of our global environment.) Because that scale is so large that it's difficult to fathom, ask: How can you—one little person—possibly save or prevent global crises? (By acting locally.) Point out that that if everyone improves his or her own relationship with the environment, the positive effects would spread across the globe.

- Have students work in small groups to discuss major social or environmental issues in your local area. Ask them to brainstorm a list of current, pressing issues. (Examples: protection of local water resources or species, suburban sprawl, farm support, pollution, waste management, energy resources, health care, homelessness, child protection and safety, and human rights.)

- Ask students to choose one of these issues to research. Allow them to work either individually or in small groups for this project. Give them the following worksheets to direct their research: Case Study of a Local Issue, Key Research Questions, and Issue Analysis.

- Have students create a presentation on their chosen topic to educate the class. Remind them to emphasize the relevance of Habits of Mind throughout their presentations.

3. Synthesis Activity

- Encourage students to interview someone who works or volunteers for a local organization working on the issue they studied. Afterward, have students use the Case

Increasing Alertness

Study of a Local Leader and Obstacles on the Path worksheets to analyze and summarize the experience.

- Have students share their findings with the class.

Name _____ Class _____ Date _____

Issue Analysis

The issue I am analyzing is _____

Related Habits of Mind	Relevance of Habits of Mind	Consequences of Not Using Habits of Mind

Name _____ Class _____ Date _____

Issue Analysis

The issue I am analyzing is _____ *Global Climate Change* _____

Related Habits of Mind	Relevance of Habits of Mind	Consequences of Not Using Habits of Mind
Gathering Data Through All Senses	The more scientific data we can get on this issue, the better off we will be. We need to monitor physical changes to the climate and document changes over time.	For years, people have ignored the reality of global climate problems. As more data are gathered and made public, it becomes more difficult to ignore the evidence.
Thinking Interdependently	Solving the global climate issue requires that the governments of many nations work together, think together, and brainstorm together.	This is a global problem; without support from nations all over the globe, it is going to be difficult to resolve.
Questioning and Posing Problems	We need to do a better job of questioning whether the things we do today are harming our environment now or may in the future.	If we continue to serve our interests without consideration of the future, we could seriously harm our environment and handicap future generations.
Learning Continuously	We need to continuously monitor and study. By looking at the situation in new and more detailed ways and continuously gathering data, we will be better equipped to solve the problem.	This is a dynamic issue. The environment is constantly changing and so are human technologies. We need to continue to learn about our effects on the climate and new ways to reduce harm.
Thinking and Communicating with Clarity and Precision	Solving this issue is highly dependent upon scientists, politicians, and others thinking carefully about the issue and then communicating evidence and future predictions with clarity and precision.	One of the reasons this is a global problem is that we did not have enough people communicating well about it. We need constant, clear, and convincing communication and thoughtful reflection.

Increasing Alertness

Name _____ Class _____ Date _____

Case Study of a Local Issue

Share the following sample answers with students to help them get started.

Ask a variety of questions and then record your answers.

Questions	Answers
What?	
Where?	
When?	
Why?	
Who?	
How?	

Name _____ Class _____ Date _____

Case Study of a Local Issue

Ask a variety of questions and then record your answers.

Questions	Answers
What?	Here students should describe the local issue.
Where?	What part or how much of the local area suffers from this issue?
When?	How long has this been an issue?
Why?	How did this issue come to be a problem?
Who?	What organizations or individuals are working to resolve this issue? Who contributes to the issue?
How?	How can this issue be resolved? What Habits of Mind could help?

Increasing Alertness

Name _____ Class _____ Date _____

Key Research Questions

As you do your research, brainstorm questions you would like to get answered in order to learn more. The following are a few examples:

- Why is this a problem?
- What are the short- and long-term consequences of this problem?
- What can be done to resolve this problem?
- Who is working on this issue?
- How widespread is the problem?

Your research topic:

Questions:

Increasing Alertness

Evaluating Progress

PURPOSE OF THIS TOOL

This tool provides an opportunity to evaluate how students are progressing in relation to their understanding of the Habits of Mind. In addition, students will conduct self-evaluations, then use their results to create an action plan for continued and future development of the Habits of Mind.

The resources in this tool will enable students to

- Self-evaluate their competence in using the Habits of Mind.
- Review a teacher evaluation of their competence in using the Habits of Mind and compare it to their own evaluation.
- Create an action plan to improve one area of competence.

HOW TO USE THIS TOOL

Striving for Accuracy and Precision and Metacognition are extremely important Habits of Mind for students to internalize and apply on a regular basis both in the classroom and in the world beyond it. This tool contains the following resources, each of which will help students evaluate their own progress toward understanding and applying the 16 Habits of Mind:

- Teacher Evaluation of Student checklist (Teacher Activity)
- Student Self-Evaluation checklist (Core Activity)
- Action Plan for Habits of Mind Development worksheet (Synthesis Activity)

The activities and tasks included in this tool should take 60–90 minutes to complete.

TIPS AND VARIATIONS

1. Teacher Activity

- By this stage, students should be alert to the use of Habits of Mind on a global level, in your local area, and in their personal lives.
- Take a moment to evaluate how competent each student is in using the Habits of Mind. Use the Teacher Evaluation of Student Checklist to assist you in this process. Include additional items in the blank spaces as necessary.

Increasing Alertness

□ 285

2. Core Activity

• Point out to students that by this stage they have become more alert to the use and potential of the Habits of Mind. Then ask: How can you know when you've mastered these skills? How will you know when you're ready to move on to the next stage in your learning journey?

• Say to students that you have a wonderful tool to help them keep track of their personal progress. Hand out the Student Self-Evaluation Checklist. Ask students to complete the checklist to gauge their understanding of the Habits of Mind right now. Tell them to be honest about their abilities. Encourage everyone to find a partner who can check their answers and give them honest feedback.

3. Synthesis Activity

• Give students your evaluation of their competence. Have them compare their own evaluation to yours. Encourage students to confer with you if they have any questions.

• Give students the Action Plan for Habits of Mind Development worksheet. Ask them to pick one area from their evaluations that requires improvement and develop a plan for improvement using this worksheet. You may wish to help students evaluate the best competency to target. Then work with them to create a good plan for monitoring and improving that competency.

Increasing Alertness

Name _____ Class _____ Date _____

Teacher Evaluation of Student Checklist

This student is able to	Seldom	Sometimes	Usually	Consistently
Recognize increasingly diverse, complex, and novel situations in which to apply the Habits of Mind.				
Spontaneously draw forth appropriate Habits of Mind when confronted with ambiguous and perplexing situations.				
Recognize a wide range of situations in which to apply the Habits of Mind.				
Recognize, without assistance, novel and complex situations in which to apply the Habits of Mind.				
Articulate the criteria upon which the decisions reflected in this review were made.				

Increasing Alertness

Name _____ Class _____ Date _____

Student Self-Evaluation Checklist

Complete this checklist to evaluate your progress in applying the Habits of Mind. In the blank rows, you can add areas you would like to be aware of and improve. Be honest with yourself!

I am able to	Seldom	Sometimes	Usually	Consistently
Recognize different and complex situations in which to use the Habits of Mind.				
Suggest which Habits of Mind are useful or relevant when looking at new situations.				
Recognize a wide range of situations in which to apply the Habits of Mind.				
Recognize, without assistance, new and complex situations in which to apply the Habits of Mind.				
Explain why I would use certain Habits of Mind in a situation.				

Increasing Alertness

Name _____ Class _____ Date _____

Action Plan for Habits of Mind Development

Pick one Habit of Mind competency that you would like to improve. Then create an action plan for improvement using the following form.

The competency I would like to improve is: _____

Action Plan to Improve This Competency in One Month

In order to improve, I will do these specific things:

I can seek assistance from these sources:

I can monitor my improvement in these ways:

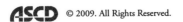
Increasing Alertness

Extending Values

Individually, we are one drop. Together, we are an ocean.

—Ryunosuke Satoro

This section explores the concept of extending values by suggesting strategies for creating a "school as a home for the mind" (Costa, 2007). This theme is central to Costa and Kallick's belief that the full potential of the Habits of Mind cannot be realized unless the program is employed schoolwide and in all aspects of school culture. Having teachers promote Habits of Mind in their own classrooms is a great start, but when they are applied on a larger scale, students are more likely to realize the full potential of the habits. The following activation model illustrates how a schoolwide, all-embracing adoption of the habits extends them beyond the classroom. The model outlines the different levels and responsibilities involved in creating a school that is truly a home for the mind. Its premise is that sustainable change happens from the center, or the leaders of an organization, and moves outward.

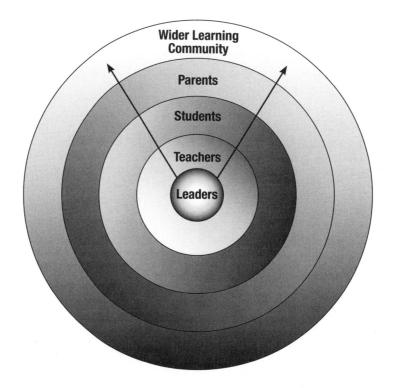

When a schoolwide, all-embracing adoption of the habits is complete, students, teachers, and school leaders see the habits as being of great value in everything that takes place across the school. As new developments, projects, and challenges arise in the school, the habits are automatically valued as part of the solution.

HOW TO USE THE ACTIVATION MODEL

The model shows an ideal method for implementing a Habits of Mind program so that it achieves the greatest impact. Leaders introduce the model to teachers. Then a schoolwide program teaches the habits to students. Parents learn from their children and from visits to the school. Leaders, teachers, students, and parents take the message to the community by modeling it.

This section includes a number of methods for setting up a schoolwide program. In addition, it provides teaching strategies, examples, and ideas from actual schools and students—some from elementary school experiences, others from secondary schools. Most, however, apply to both. Additional samples and ideas can be found in the Building Commitment section.

TIPS AND VARIATIONS FOR USING THE ACTIVATION MODEL

This section consists of a variety of individual tools to support your implementation of the activation model. The tools are grouped into two overall categories: ideas to promote high levels of schoolwide implementation and specific teaching strategies that can become a regular part of classroom practice, including ideas for teacher observation and walk-through processes. Through both types of tools, students are led to eventually take charge of their own mastery of the Habits of Mind.

Extending Values

CONTENTS

TITLE OF TOOL

Extending Values

Ideas for Schoolwide Implementation

The Habits of Mind offer the greatest potential when they are seen, heard, and felt across every aspect of school life. Achieving this goal requires strategic leadership. Suggestions for implementation approaches are described in this tool.

1. Outlining a Skills Vision for the School

Work with other school leaders to create a plan for widespread integration. Gather other school leaders together and begin by analyzing where you are and what you are hoping to achieve, using questions such as the following:

> Step 1: What skills and dispositions do lifelong learners in the 21st century need?
>
> Step 2: What skills and dispositions do you want your learners to have before graduating from your school?
>
> Step 3: To what extent do you achieve this already? Where are the gaps?
>
> Step 4: How could you fill in the gaps?

Then discuss whether and how a Habits of Mind program might help fill the gaps.

2. Having Schoolwide Thematic Assemblies

A great way of heralding the Habits of Mind across a school is to have a school assembly centered on one habit at a time. You could take a current event, a news story, a fairy tale, a parable, or an issue within the school and use it to outline the appropriate habit.

Example: Several years ago a principal introduced the Habit of Mind of Persisting in a whole-school assembly. The audience consisted of girls ages 11–18. The principal told the girls a story of a young French woman who had recently climbed to the top of Mt. Blanc. The principal described the incredible obstacles the girl faced during her climb. Despite these difficulties, the girl persevered and pushed forward, determined to reach her goal—and she was successful. The principal concluded the story by asking the girls to consider the "mountains" they themselves had climbed in the past and might climb in the future and by assuring them that if they persisted in their efforts they would reach their personal summits.

3. Using Other Methods to Deliver Consistent Messages

Look for opportunities to deliver consistent schoolwide messages both to students and staff. For example, discuss a Habit of Mind at every pep rally, or at regular times (e.g.,

Extending Values

once a week or once a month) via the school announcement system. Ask teachers to display Habits of Mind materials at school open house events for parents; highlighting different habits in different classrooms would allow parents to learn about several Habits of Mind. School newsletters, other school publications, the school Web site, and award certificates are also useful ways to reinforce the message of the habits.

Example: The principal of a private school introduces or reinforces the Habits of Mind during chapel time. She links the topic of Managing Impulsivity to a suitable illustrative story and discusses the importance of this habit in today's world. On appropriate occasions, this creative school principal also links songs and actions to illustrate her point.

4. Sharing a Common Language

One important method for applying the Habits of Mind in a meaningful way is to have all teachers use similar words to describe concepts, make assignments, and communicate with students. Teachers and administrators use many Habits of Mind on a daily basis. Encourage them to make that process transparent for students by using language that identifies the habits. Leaders can model the use of this language for other teachers, who can then model it for students.

Examples: The following methods are particularly useful for teachers to use in the classroom.

- Create word splashes to "unpack" each habit. Word splashes generate multiple ways of defining a concept so that it has meaning for students. For example, "Think before you act" is another way to say Managing Impulsivity.
- Use thinking words to create a new type of literacy—literacy in the communication of *thinking*. Using specific, cognitive terminology—or mindful language—during instruction will increase the likelihood that students will use mindful language in their communications.

Rather than ...	Use mindful language by saying ...
"Let's look at these two pictures."	"Let's compare these two pictures."
"What do you think will happen when ..."	"What do you predict will happen when ..."

- Reinforce terminology by recognizing, identifying, and labeling student uses of the Habits of Mind.

  "You really *persisted* on that problem."

  "That is an intriguing *problem* you are *posing*."

- Use mindful discipline. Discourage and reinforce behaviors at once.

Rather than ...	Use mindful discipline by saying ...
"Sarah, get away from Kathryn."	"Sarah could you find someplace better to do your best work?"
"Stop running."	"Why do we have a rule about always walking in the hall?"

- Provide data, not solutions. Allow students to become more autonomous by providing them with data to aid their decision making rather than making their decisions for them.

When a student ...	Use mindful language by saying ...
Repeatedly taps his pencils on the desk ...	"I want you to know that your pencil tapping is disturbing me."
Interrupts other students ...	"I like it when you take turns to speak."

- Promote autonomous learning. Avoid treating students like robots, feeding them information and getting a specific action in return. Instead, lead them to analyze a task, decide what is needed, and then act autonomously.

Extending Values

Rather than ...	Use mindful language by saying ...
"Remember to write your name in the top left corner."	"What must you remember to do for me to know whom the test belongs to?"
"The bell is about to ring. Pack up your desk, put up your chairs, and line up at the door."	"The bell is about to ring. What do we need to do before we leave?"

• Apply metacognitive strategies. The Thinking About Thinking Habit of Mind begets more thinking. Discussing the thinking process can cause that process to become more overt.

When a student says ...	Use mindful language by saying ...
"I don't know how to solve this problem."	"What can you do to get started?"
"I'm finished."	"How do you know you are correct?"

• Avoid negative presuppositions. Many times, teacher comments to students carry implicit meaning involving negative presuppositions. Over time, such remarks can damage students' self-esteem and their self-concept as thinkers and lead to negative behaviors.

Rather than ...	Use mindful language by saying ...
"Why did you forget your assignment?"	"As you plan for your assignment, what materials do you need and what is your time line?"
"When will you grow up?"	"As we grow older, we learn how to solve these problems from experiences such as these."

5. Displaying Posters Around the School

Displaying Habits of Mind posters around the school is a great way to increase student consciousness of the habits and extend their value. You may want to use purchased posters, or you may prefer to have teachers or students design their own posters to further increase their sense of ownership of the habits.

Examples:

Design a poster that includes pictures of students or teachers demonstrating a particular habit via an activity.

Have students design their own posters, including their own icon or logo to represent the habit.

After a field trip, design a poster that includes photographs of different activities that highlight a particular habit. Students could create posters like these in groups or as a class.

6. Coaching Teachers to Be Coaches

Support and nurture teachers who are enthusiastic in their adoption of the Habits of Mind and who consistently model the habits. Invest in professional development for these passionate teachers. Showcase their achievements and encourage them to share their experiences. They will then serve as valuable models for schoolwide implementation and become the core of a network of inspired teachers. When other teachers see that these early adopters of the program are valued, they understand that school leadership is serious about implementing the habits and developing the school as a home for the mind.

Example: When reviewing teaching practice, the curriculum, or the success of a school event with colleagues, employ the language of the habits in your discussions.

The strategies and examples provided here are just a few of many ways to teach and instill Habits of Mind schoolwide. Keep in regular communication with other leaders to share ideas.

You may also choose to use activities described in other sections of this ASCD Action Tool as springboards for developing additional strategies for schoolwide implementation. The next tool in this section offers even more strategies for consideration.

Extending Values

Specific Teaching Strategies

Here you will find numerous specific teaching strategies and examples to inspire the schoolwide integration of the Habits of Mind.

1. Solving Problems with Specific Habits of Mind

The following is a powerful example of what can happen when teachers get together to discuss a learning issue and use the Habits of Mind to problem-solve.

> Teachers in a high school mathematics department were hoping that Habits of Mind could help their students think and behave more like mathematicians. At a department meeting, they discussed exactly what aspects of student behavior they wanted to improve. They asked: If students were to behave more like mathematicians and less like students doing math, how would their behavior change?
>
> The teachers quickly and unanimously realized that the students' behavior would be less risk-adverse. They noted that their students were inclined to ask for help the moment they got stuck, rather than to look for strategies to solve a problem themselves; they were too dependent on teachers to find ways they could complete their work.
>
> To encourage the students to act like mathematicians and find ways around being stuck, the teachers focused on the Taking Responsible Risks Habit of Mind. In every math class, they asked students to write the capital letters RR in the margins of their tests or Habits of Mind assignments to indicate a place when they got stuck. They would then take a responsible risk (RR) and do their best to answer the question.
>
> The teachers praised and rewarded students for taking a responsible risk even if their work was not accurate. The independent strategizing behavior was more important than the final answer, which students would learn later. In this way, students began thinking and behaving like mathematicians.

Another idea, useful at the elementary level, is to use a "Success-o-Meter" as a rubric. The example shown on page 289 is designed to help students who are working on a writing assignment. It helps them analyze their work, think about their thinking, and see exactly what they need to do to improve. A Success-o-Meter or other symbol of progress toward a goal (e.g., a large mountain to be climbed) can be used in other content areas as well.

Extending Values

2. Adjusting Wait Time

Focusing on wait time (or think time) is a powerful strategy for managing impulsivity. According to a study by Mary Budd Rowe in the *Journal of Teacher Education* (1986, January/February), after asking a question, the average teacher waits one second before either calling on a student, asking another question, or answering the question herself. As a result, students do not have time to think. It is unrealistic to expect anyone to provide an informed answer in one second. Instead, Rowe recommends that teachers wait at least 7–10 seconds before calling on a student. That way, students have adequate time to think.

The following are three waiting strategies:

Wait Time I: Pause at least 7–10 seconds after asking a question.

Wait Time II: After a student replies or asks a related question, pause at least 3 seconds for a basic question and at least 5 seconds for a higher-order question.

Wait Time III: After a student asks a question, pause and model thoughtfulness.

As students benefit from seeing wait time modeled, they will learn to be better listeners and to better manage their impulsive urges.

3. Using the Think-Pair-Share Model

The Think-Pair-Share model provides an excellent strategy for helping students develop thinking skills. With this model, students start with a problem or task. They begin by thinking alone for a specified period of time. Then they form pairs to discuss the question or task. Finally, students share their thoughts and ideas with the whole class.

4. Employing Paired Verbal Fluency

This strategy encourages active listening. Students work as partners, facing each other; they are designated as Partner A and Partner B. At the signal "Go," Partner A brainstorms for one minute; Partner B must sit and quietly listen. At the end of one minute, Partner B brainstorms for one minute without repeating any of Partner A's ideas. Then Partner A brainstorms again, this time for 45 seconds and not repeating anything that has been said so far. Partner B does the same. In the final round, each partner has a turn for 30 seconds, again with neither partner repeating anything that has been said so far. Students must be good listeners to master this activity.

5. Creating a Human Graph or Continuum Graph

This activity is a powerful tool for reflecting on experiences and opinions and for learning from others. One excellent application for beginning a course of study on a Habit of

Extending Values

Mind is as follows: Choose a Habit of Mind. Have students line up along one wall. Ask if they have ever experienced this habit. Direct those who have experienced the habit to one end of the line and those who haven't to the other end. Have those who aren't sure or who don't want to commit position themselves anywhere along the continuum. Ask those students who are at the "expert" end of the graph to become group leaders, then divide the rest of the class into groups and allocate one "expert" to each group. Have each group leader describe his or her experience of the habit to the group. Then encourage other group members to think about whether they might have experienced the habit without realizing it. After hearing from a peer, students usually realize that they have indeed experienced the habit for themselves in some way.

6. Sharing Stories

Many teachers are accustomed to reading stories to or with their classes. Many rich and exciting varieties of stories from numerous cultures exemplify the Habits of Mind in different contexts. A powerful way of motivating students to value the habits is to highlight one or more habits relevant to the story. For example, introduce a tale as a story about the Habit of Mind of Persisting and, later, encourage students to identify additional relevant habits. Or read the story to the class and then ask students to identify the habits they believe are involved. To extend this exercise, ask students to analyze which habits might have prevented a problem from arising or might have helped solve a difficult issue. In this way, students can see the habits valued in a variety of ways and in many different contexts.

7. Considering Frame of Reference

The frequent infusion of the Habits of Mind into all aspects of learning, rather than isolating them into specific lessons, sends a clear message to students that the habits are valuable. If the habits are used as a frame of reference across the curriculum, students learn to analyze new situations in terms of the habits and become more adept at personally cultivating the habits.

8. Using Bookmarks

A teacher in Christchurch, New Zealand, uses Habits of Mind bookmarks to encourage students to set goals and focus on developing each habit. At the beginning of the term, the teacher has each student choose a habit he would like to develop, then gives students bookmarks that display information about their chosen habit. Students can write personal goals on the reverse of the bookmark and laminate it. They keep the bookmark in

Extending Values

their reading book to refer to every day. This is a simple but highly effective way of helping children maintain focus on Habits of Mind.

9. Modeling the Habits

An excellent example of modeling occurred when one teacher was instructing students on writing. As the teacher was writing a story on the board, she openly discussed and challenged her own thinking. She wrote: "'Oh no!' said John" on the board and then she said, "Oh! I already used *said John* in the last sentence. This time I want to use *exclaimed* instead because John is shocked and upset, so *exclaimed* is a more accurate word and it prevents my saying the same thing over again." With just these few words, the teacher modeled her thinking process and enabled students to become more aware of their own thinking processes when writing. When teachers show that they value the habits, students will respond to teachers' cues and find their own value in the habits.

10. Using Thinking Verbs

If your goal is to encourage students to think, explicitly use thinking words such as those below. Students will then become better adept at understanding and using them.

Examples of Thinking Verbs

analyze	observe
apply	organize
classify	paraphrase
compare	predict
connect	respond
contrast	support
describe	represent
discuss	visualize
elaborate	reason
explore	verify
diagram	solve
identify	summarize
interpret	simplify
judge	determine

Extending Values

These key thinking words are of universal application across subject areas. Investing time to teach these terms to students can have a significant impact on skillful thinking across a school.

11. Using Checklists, Rubrics, Action Plans, and Other Evaluation Tools

Evaluation is an important part of the Habits of Mind program. A Success-o-Meter and a Group Work Evaluation are provided as examples. Other assessment tools are incorporated throughout this action tool. Appendix B includes both specific and generic evaluation tools.

You can also encourage students to take charge of their own mastery of the Habits of Mind. For example, they can design their own rubrics, table tops, desk liners, and games. They can employ self-management tools such as variations of the Before-During-After model to chronicle what they knew before, learned during, and knew after studying a topic.

Journal writing is another highly effective method of promoting evaluation. As students record their thoughts in an ongoing manner, they practice the metacognitive process and can track their growth over time, gaining skills in self-assessment and self-regulation. Introduce students to journal writing with simple idea starters, or ask them to describe the thinking, steps, and sequences related to a task (before, during, and after), with an emphasis on a particular Habit of Mind.

12. Managing Student Behavior

In addition to their value as a framework for learning and teaching, the Habits of Mind can be valuable in classroom management and issues of student behavior. For example, students who have been involved in behavior problems or incidents with other students can be asked to sit down and write a "think paper" in which they reflect upon their thinking and behaviors in response to prompts such as those provided on page 291.

Extending Values

Success-o-Meter

> This is an example of a type of rubric students can use to evaluate one another's writing skills.

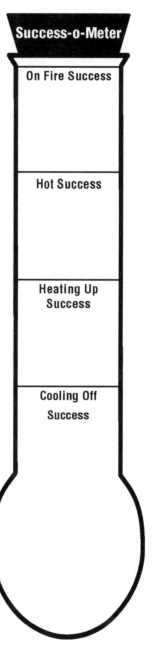

Success-o-Meter

On Fire Success

Hot Success

Heating Up Success

Cooling Off Success

Excellent description.
Mixture of short, medium, and long sentences with interesting words to start each sentence.

Good description.
Some long, medium, and short sentences.
Start sentences with different words. Great punctuation.

No description.
Simple, short sentences. Some punctuation.

No description.
Only one long sentence. No punctuation—
needs capital letter at beginning and period at end.

Extending Values

Name _____ Class _____ Date _____

Group Work Evaluation

1. When I knew an idea I shared it with my group. ☺ ☹

2. I encouraged others in my group. ☺ ☹

3. I used people's names. ☺ ☹

4. When I did not understand, I asked my partner. ☺ ☹

5. When my partner did not understand, I helped. ☺ ☹

Goal Setting:

What could you do to improve your group work?

Extending Values

Suggested Prompts for a Student "Think Paper"

What was the incident in which you were involved?

What caused this incident?

Which Habits of Mind should you have used to avoid this situation?

What are the consequences of this situation for you, the other person, and others in the school?

Which Habits of Mind are you going to put into play to repair the situation with the others involved?

Which Habits of Mind would you like to see the other people use to help you repair the situation?

Which Habits of Mind would help prevent another situation like this from happening again?

How will you incorporate these Habits of Mind into your behavior from now on?

Extending Values

Building Commitment

Excellence is not a singular act but a habit. You are what you repeatedly do.

—Shaquille O'Neal

This section relates to the final goal of the Habits of Mind program: making the habits automatic. The tools provided here take learners from thinking consciously about using a habit to internalizing the habit to such a degree that it is a regular part of how the learners think, learn, and live. In other words, the habits become a part of a learner's being such that they naturally and unconsciously direct the person's behavior.

This process, which is called habituation, is the ultimate goal for any mindful, independent learner. However, we cannot become complacent as we habituate the Habits of Mind. We must find ways of continuously growing and improving. The model on the next page demonstrates how the Habits of Mind provide a continuous disposition for lifelong learning.

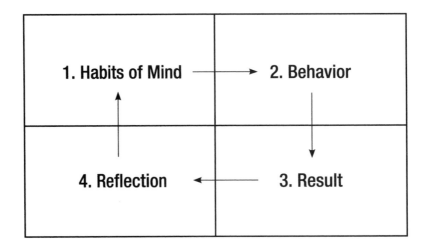

As the diagram shows, the Habits of Mind unconsciously give form to learners' thinking and shape their behaviors. Their behaviors then lead to results, or outcomes, which may be positive or negative. Learners then take time to reflect on the results and the processes.

By the time learners have reached the habituation stage, this self-reflection is an automatic process if they intend to change results or outcomes. Two key components of the reflection stage are to evaluate how the habits were used and to consider how to refine their use to achieve the desired change.

CONTENTS

TITLE OF TOOL

Building Commitment

School Leaders Building Commitment

Watch your thoughts for they become words,
watch your words for they become actions,
watch your actions for they become habits,
watch your habits for they become character,
watch your character for it becomes your destiny.
　　　　　　　　　　　—Ralph Waldo Emerson

PURPOSE OF THIS TOOL

This tool provides a series of recommendations and strategies for helping school leaders—especially administrators and teacher leaders—to promote the growth and sustain the use of Habits of Mind within the school as a learning organization. It provides an overview of suggestions proven effective in schools that have been successful in making the 16 Habits of Mind a clear and continuous part of the school's climate, culture, policies, and practices.

HOW TO USE THIS TOOL

School leaders may elect to incorporate the materials in this tool into school improvement planning sessions as well as faculty meetings devoted to Habits of Mind. Specifically, study groups responsible for introducing and sustaining the use of Habits of Mind as part of ongoing school improvement planning and professional development will find these recommendations both practical and immediately applicable. Leaders may elect to have members of a Habits of Mind study group discuss and debate which of the recommendations presented here have the most immediate relevance.

TIPS AND VARIATIONS

This tool addresses six topics related to integrating Habits of Mind into key aspects of organizational change and strategic planning processes. School leaders may choose whichever topics are most appropriate for their particular circumstances.

1. Revisiting Strategic Plans

When the Habits of Mind are an integral part of a school's strategic plan, building commitment is inherent in school goals. The Boyes-Watts Model of Activation can help you create strategic purpose. Use of the model to increase alertness is described in the previous

Building Commitment

section (Extending Values) of this action tool. By revisiting your strategic plan every year to review and reflect on goals and current practices, you can change your use of the Habits of Mind as necessary to build commitment and improve your program. It is all too easy for any initiative to be sidelined as new initiatives are implemented. By committing to annual strategic planning, your program will improve with time.

The following are three sets of sample questions for reviewing the effectiveness of current Habits of Mind implementation. Make sure school leaders, teachers, and students are all involved in the review process. This way, you have a shared understanding and a common sense of purpose and direction.

- Strategic Planning Questions for School Leaders

    Are you displaying the leadership qualities required to sustain the Habits of Mind?

    Are you using mindful language in your conversations?

    Are you investing in the ongoing development of your school as a home for the mind?

- Strategic Planning Questions for Teachers

    Are you using mindful language?

    Do you model your own thinking for students?

    Do you allow wait time for students to answer questions?

    Do you allow opportunities for the development of the Habits of Mind in your teaching?

- Strategic Planning Questions for Students

    Are you improving your use of the Habits of Mind?

    Have you set targets to further develop the habits?

    Are you transferring Habits of Mind from one situation to another?

    Are you using the habits in your life outside the classroom?

2. Supporting Ongoing Professional Development

Support and nurture the enthusiasm of teachers who are using Habits of Mind and modeling the habits. When teachers get regular opportunities to grow their personal skills, they understand that school leadership is serious about an ongoing, continued implementation of the habits to keep the school as a "home for the mind." With regular professional development, teachers can continue to build and maintain their commitment to teaching and modeling Habits of Mind.

Building Commitment

3. Inducting New Staff and Students

Introduce new students and teachers to the Habits of Mind and their role at your school as soon as possible. Induction may take the form of an information booklet, a training DVD, staff meetings, parent evenings, or assemblies. The sooner those new to the school are familiar with the habits, the sooner they can grow their understanding and build commitment.

4. Maintaining a Universal, Mindful Language

The importance of maintaining a shared language cannot be overemphasized. When school leaders, teachers, students, and parents all understand and use a shared vocabulary of learning, they can build on common ground. The previous section of this action tool (Extending Values) discusses the importance of mindful language and the need for school leaders, teachers, and parents to consciously use mindful language every day to support student learning. To build commitment, the Habits of Mind must become the fabric of learning that weaves through the school community and beyond. In other words, the habits must become "the way we do it around here."

5. Creating School Newsletters

Newsletters are a great tool for facilitating communication between school and home. With this tool, you can explain the function and role of the Habits of Mind. You can also include articles that focus on a particular habit relevant at that time or explain how the habits are preparing students to be lifelong learners. Remember that the habits are of service to the parents since they are the students' teachers and guides at home; parents who adopt the habits find them to be a powerful tool in parenting. So newsletters not only let parents know what is happening at the school but also give them a useful tool to help them help their children learn and build commitment.

6. Routinely Allowing Time for Thinking

If students have time to think and reflect, they can apply the Habits of Mind to new situations and in their own ways. So if you want students to think, give them the time they need. The following are three strategies for providing sufficient time for thinking:

- Pause at least 7–10 seconds after asking a question.
- After a student replies or asks a related question, pause at least 3 seconds for a basic question and at least 5 seconds for a higher-order question.
- After a student asks you a question, pause and model thoughtfulness.

Building Commitment

Teachers Building Commitment

The only limit to your impact is your imagination and commitment.

—Anthony Robbins

PURPOSE OF THIS TOOL

Teachers who are embarking on teaching the Habits of Mind or who have been involved in the program for some time may ask questions such as these: How do you know if you are building commitment? What is internalizing the Habits of Mind like? To answer these questions, a good starting place and invaluable ongoing resource is self-reflection. In teacher training sessions, you can give teachers a tool for self-reflection and then discuss how teachers might target specific areas to improve. Teachers can then periodically use the tool to check their personal progress. The resources in this tool will support instructional leaders and other educators in this process.

HOW TO USE THIS TOOL

One Teacher Self-Reflection tool is provided on page 302. On this form, teachers can score their current level of mastery of each Habit of Mind on a scale of 1–10. (For additional reflection tools, see Appendix B.) In addition to using data from the implementation of this tool, leaders may wish to share examples of how they can work with staff members to create Habits of Mind signals within the school environment.

TIPS AND VARIATIONS

1. Encourage teachers to reflect frequently on their own use of the Habits of Mind. The Teacher Self-Reflection provided on page 302 is an example of one instrument you might use.

2. Display the Habits of Mind throughout the school to demonstrate the program's value and your commitment to it. Ideas for displays can come from teachers, students, and administrators. You can create songs, posters, plaques, acronyms, or a school motto to broadcast the habits and create cues for learning, remembering, and integrating the habits. See the examples on the following pages to help you get started.

Building Commitment

3. Provide awards to students and teachers for demonstrating use of various habits or for creating artwork or some other instrument for publicizing the habits and helping students learn and use them.

4. Review the previous section (Extending Values) for specific teaching strategies and samples.

Teacher Self-Reflection Tool

Habit of Mind	I am a teacher who ...
Persisting	Perseveres with challenging students and ensures all students have a depth of understanding and skills as a learner. *Rate yourself: 1 2 3 4 5 6 7 8 9 10*
Managing Impulsivity	Uses wait time and the techniques of pausing, paraphrasing, and probing; I demonstrate thoughtfulness. *Rate yourself: 1 2 3 4 5 6 7 8 9 10*
Listening with Understanding and Empathy	*Actively listens to others; I make genuine attempts to understand where others are coming from and to perceive their points of view.* *Rate yourself: 1 2 3 4 5 6 7 8 9 10*
Thinking Flexibly	Is open to the points of view of others; changes plans and strategies when needed to better meet groups' needs; grasps the teachable moment to foster interest and achievement. *Rate yourself: 1 2 3 4 5 6 7 8 9 10*
Thinking About Thinking (Metacognition)	Is aware of my own thinking processes; I invest time in reflection; I model my thinking processes to those around me. *Rate yourself: 1 2 3 4 5 6 7 8 9 10*
Striving for Accuracy and Precision	Sets high standards in the things I do and in relations with others. I check for accuracy in written documents and communications. *Rate yourself: 1 2 3 4 5 6 7 8 9 10*
Questioning and Posing Problems	Is skilled in composing and asking complex questions. *Rate yourself: 1 2 3 4 5 6 7 8 9 10*
Applying Past Knowledge to New Situations	Uses past experiences, resources, and knowledge to ensure good practice. I offer wide knowledge to support student learning. *Rate yourself: 1 2 3 4 5 6 7 8 9 10*
Thinking and Communicating with Clarity and Precision	Strives to be accurate in all communications. I use thinking verbs when giving instructions. *Rate yourself: 1 2 3 4 5 6 7 8 9 10*
Gathering Data Through All Senses	Stays alert to people and situations by gathering data through my senses. *Rate yourself: 1 2 3 4 5 6 7 8 9 10*

Building Commitment

Habit of Mind	I am a teacher who ...
Creating, Imagining, and Innovating	Is creative and innovative in finding new ways and alternatives. *Rate yourself:* 1 2 3 4 5 6 7 8 9 10
Responding with Wonderment and Awe	Is enthusiastic about my teaching, my students' learning, and new discoveries. *Rate yourself:* 1 2 3 4 5 6 7 8 9 10
Taking Responsible Risks	Moves outside my comfort zone and becomes adventurous after thoughtful consideration. *Rate yourself:* 1 2 3 4 5 6 7 8 9 10
Finding Humor	Can laugh with others and at myself; I do not take myself too seriously. *Rate yourself:* 1 2 3 4 5 6 7 8 9 10
Thinking Interdependently	Works collaboratively with others; I can learn from those around me. *Rate yourself:* 1 2 3 4 5 6 7 8 9 10
Learning Continuously	Has the humility and pride to admit when I don't know something; I resist complacency. *Rate yourself:* 1 2 3 4 5 6 7 8 9 10

Building Commitment

Examples and Ideas for Building Commitment

FOCUSING ON ONE HABIT OF MIND PER WEEK

- Refer to the habit of the week whenever possible during content instruction and class activities. Examples:

  Introduce words related to the habit during vocabulary lessons.
  Discuss characters' use (or lack of use) of the habit during literature lessons.
  Assign homework that will assure students practice or focus on the habit at
      home in some way.

- Have students create posters, artworks, poems, songs, or other products that demonstrate the habit. Allow students to display their work in the classroom or hallway for other students to see and enjoy.
- Create a class mural depicting aspects or examples of the habit of the week.
- Award a small prize or certificate at the end of the week to students who most frequently exhibited the habit in class or to students who showed the most improvement in the habit during the week.

CREATING SLOGANS

- Write a catchy phrase that can become a tag line on school stationery, the school's Web site, the masthead of the school newspaper, or elsewhere. Examples:

  Berkshire Elementary: A Habits of Mind Learning Community
  Amherst Academy: Specializing in Habits of Mind for Lifelong Learning
  Brentford School: Where learning is Habit (of Mind)-forming
  Canterbury School: Habits of Mind, tales of success

- Use a familiar advertising slogan for an organization, an industry, or a product—but give it a twist. Examples:

  For Thinking Flexibly: Better living through better thinking.
  For Striving for Accuracy: Because it absolutely, positively should be right!
  For Creating, Imagining, and Innovating: Let your imagination do the walking.

- Incorporate the school mascot in a slogan. Examples:

  For Thinking and Communicating with Clarity and Precision: Taylor School
      Tigers "paws" to think.

Building Commitment

For Learning Continuously: Braddock High School—Where Bruin power is brain power; Braddock High School—Where Bruins use their brains; Braddock High School—Our Bruins have powerful brains.

For Taking Responsible Risks: Whittier Wildcats take responsible risks.

For Learning Continuously: Lakewood Lions take "pride" in learning.

For Thinking Flexibly: At Edgar Allan Poe School, we're "raven"ous about learning with Habits of Mind.

USING ACRONYMS

- Use the school name to create an acronym. Examples:

  Burke Middle School: **B**uilding **U**nderstanding, **R**esponsibility, and **K**nowledge to achieve **E**xcellence

  Holmes Elementary School: Our **H**abit **O**f **L**earning **M**akes **E**xcellent **S**tudents

  Dunleigh Academy: **D**eep **UN**derstanding and **L**earning, **E**xciting **I**nnovation, **G**reat **H**abits

DESIGNING POSTERS AND OTHER MESSAGES

- Place posters throughout the school to inspire students to make the habits their own.
- Sponsor a contest in which classes compete to design a unique way to foster the habits schoolwide. Reward the winning class with a pizza party or other suitable celebration. This could be a monthly event with different requirements each month—for example, one month all entries must be rap song lyrics, another month posters, another cheers ("Two-four-six-eight; come see how we innovate!"), and so on.
- If the school has a Web site, feature the Habits of Mind on the home page, perhaps with a link to information about the habits, reports of how students are learning them, photographs of student creations that illustrate them, and so on.
- Coordinate a schoolwide art show of student and teacher artifacts that illustrate or demonstrate various Habits of Mind. Suggest that the PTA hold one of its meetings at the time the art show is set up, so parents can tour it. Invite a panel of judges to view all works and award ribbons of excellence to deserving pieces.
- Put a Habit of Mind of the Month bulletin board in a prominent place in the school—for example, the lobby or cafeteria.

Building Commitment

- Institute a Habits of Mind column for the school newspaper or newsletter. Teachers or students could be the writers, describing how their class has learned about and used each featured habit.
- Plan a schoolwide or grade-level assembly in which parents or community volunteers are invited to participate in a panel. Have student representatives ask questions about how the panelists use different Habits of Mind in their work or at home. Afterward, have students write a summary of the event in a form of their choosing (a descriptive paragraph, a review for the newspaper, an editorial commentary, and so on).
- Think about other creative ways to show commitment to the Habits of Mind philosophy. For example, one school symbolized growing the habits by planting a tree on school property for each habit and placing a marker for each habit at the tree's base.

Students Building Commitment

Effort only fully releases its reward after a person refuses to quit.

—Napoleon Hill

PURPOSE OF THIS TOOL

Like the rest of us, students build commitment progressively. Periodically take a moment to stop and reflect on their progress with questions such as these: How have the Habits of Mind influenced student decision making about learning? What were some effects of a particular habit on a student or students? As students reflect on their work, which habits do they feel have served them most?

HOW TO USE THIS TOOL

The strategies in this tool will help you and your students keep track of student progress and build upon what they are learning. The central impetus of the models, strategies, and suggestions included here is to create classrooms as learning communities in which Habits of Mind are discussed, revisited, and used as catalysts for promoting high levels of student metacognition, self-regulation, and self-assessment. Additional strategies can be found in the previous section (Extending Values).

TIPS AND VARIATIONS

Share the ideas and strategies included with this tool as samples and models for staff members to identify and implement ways to help students build momentum, ownership, and sustained use of the Habits of Mind.

1. Building Portfolios

Portfolios are a wonderful resource. They allow students to keep track of their work, and they allow both you and the student to see growth over time. The following is one method you can use for building a portfolio. It can be summed up in four steps as follows:

- Collect: Deposit class work and other materials in a central area such as a folder or binder.
- Select: Pick work samples that show learning and growth.
- Reflect: Think about the learning the items show, and identify evidence of growth.

Building Commitment

- Connect: Build links across classes, disciplines, and semesters. Strengthen connections between school, community, and work.

A typical Habits of Mind portfolio includes work samples, journal writings, self-assessments and other reflection tools, information and ideas, and action plans. Stress that students do some reflection and attach a description of why each piece is included in a portfolio. The following are a few sample starters:

- I chose this piece of work because ...
- My parents liked this piece of work because ...
- I will remember this piece of work in 20 years because ...
- The Habit of Mind called ... was useful with this piece of work because ...
- This piece of work would have been better if I had focused on the Habit of Mind called ... because ...
- The Habit of Mind I have improved the most is ... because ...
- The Habit of Mind that will add the most to my work in the future is ... because ...

2. Earning Rewards

Certificates, stickers, ribbons, calendars, and other items make great rewards. Students can take these items home to develop a link between the Habits of Mind taught at school and principles taught at home. For example, early in the year, a teacher could introduce parents to a habit the class will study, then periodically send home a certificate with blank spaces for students and parents to complete together. Many students are eager to complete the certificates, so they look for opportunities to practice the habit. Parents also learn about the Habits of Mind and are able to support their children's learning at home.

3. Reading Relevant Literature

Why not have a display of books, both fiction and nonfiction, to help build awareness and commitment to a particular Habit of Mind? Give your library staff sufficient notice and ask them to select books that illustrate a particular habit. Then put together a display of books and posters to help attract students to learn more about the habit. Suggest that students who read the books write a review for the school newspaper or write a letter to a story character congratulating him or her on use of a habit.

4. Using Learning Ladders

Using learning ladders helps students become competent and proficient with the Habits of Mind. The ladders allow students to reflect on how they use a habit on a regular basis. The bottom rung of a learning ladder lists beginning skills. The next rungs show developing, proficient, and expert skills, respectively. Students can define each step for clarity. Then they can regularly return to the ladder to reflect on their current level of development. The ladder might be in a student's notebook, on a wall, on a table, or inside a desk. You could post one ladder if you are focusing on a specific habit, or display several ladders to focus on habits that are key to your students' learning at a particular time. If you have enough time and space, have students create a ladder for each of the 16 habits. Another possibility is to have them create digital resources to represent the ladders.

5. Creating Wall Charts or Posters

Students can make colorful and creative reminders of the Habits of Mind to post in the classroom and around the school. You might like to have students compete to create sets or summaries of the habits. Suggest that students use the Summary of 16 Habits of Mind (Appendix B) as a resource. Help students compile their products into a personalized book that they can keep.

6. Designing New Logos

As you have seen throughout this ASCD Action Tool, each Habit of Mind has a thoughtful and interesting logo; these can be excellent tools for teaching. You can help students integrate a personal understanding of the habits by asking them to design their own logos. By collecting and keeping these student artworks over the years, you can build a unique set. You could take the idea one step further and have students create objects, sculptures, toys, or other items to represent the habits. For example, they might produce posters, toys, or stories with titles such as *Mount Persistence*, *The Wiggly Worm of Thinking Flexibly*, the *Dart Board of Accuracy*, the *Lightbulb of Creating*, or the *Happy Face of Finding Humor*. Students are often the best resources for finding creative new ways to signify and symbolize the habits; their products often create lasting impressions and help students internalize.

7. Extending Beyond the Classroom

Students who are involved in extracurricular activities both in school and outside of school can practice, appreciate, and extend the Habits of Mind in a variety of ways.

Building Commitment

Examples:

- Athletes in both individual and team sports take responsible risks, apply past knowledge to new situations, gather data through all senses, and think interdependently. These students can share their use of and reflections on such habits with classmates, coaches, sponsors, and fans.
- After-school special-interest clubs and organizations can focus on various habits as part of their activities and assessment of their events (chess team members use metacognition, science club members learn continuously, student office assistants strive for accuracy, and so on).
- Cheerleaders can publicize Habits of Mind by composing cheers about them. They can then choreograph motions to accompany the cheers and perform them at assemblies, rallies, and even athletic events.
- The student council could organize a Habits of Mind parade as part of a schoolwide event such as the annual carnival, family fun fair, field day, spirit week, or homecoming activities. Various teams or classes could make a festive float or other parade entry about a chosen habit. Students might enjoy competing for various awards (best design, most unusual, etc.) for their creations.

8. Extending Beyond the School

Students can look for opportunities to extend the Habits of Mind beyond the school grounds. For example, students can

- Participate in the school's hosting of a training session for parents to teach them to model the habits and use mindful language.
- Encourage their parents and families to use the habits at home.
- Encourage their friends and classmates to use the habits in making decisions that affect their personal life, such as what kinds of friends to choose, how to handle conflicts with siblings, how to spend their money wisely, and so on.
- Request that the PTA sponsor a special event to highlight the habits, such as a Habits of Mind fair, or that the PTA work the habits into a regular event such as Back-to-School Night.
- Assume responsibility for the Habits of Mind portion of the school's Web site, designing it and keeping it fresh with ideas and information submitted by all classes.
- Volunteer to be Habits of Mind columnists for the school newsletter or newspaper.
- Create a video of skits depicting each Habit of Mind and then show the video to younger classes and to parents.

9. Regularly Reflecting and Assessing

Ongoing assessment is an important part of integration. Tools and activities throughout this ASCD Action Tool incorporate ways for students to analyze specific growth at a point in time. A sample self-assessment tool for students is available on the next page. Additional resources are available in Appendix B.

Building Commitment

Student Self-Assessment: Assess Your Persisting Skills

Rate your skills by circling a number from 1 to 10, with 1 representing the lowest level and 10 the highest level of development.

I can ...	Rating
stay on task.	1 2 3 4 5 6 7 8 9 10
use a broad range of strategies to solve a problem.	1 2 3 4 5 6 7 8 9 10
keep going until the solution is found.	1 2 3 4 5 6 7 8 9 10
keep going until the assignment is finished.	1 2 3 4 5 6 7 8 9 10
keep attempting new ways to solve a problem.	1 2 3 4 5 6 7 8 9 10
put up with frustration and confusion to achieve my goals.	1 2 3 4 5 6 7 8 9 10
refuse to quit even when it gets tough.	1 2 3 4 5 6 7 8 9 10
persevere even when answers or solutions are not immediately apparent.	1 2 3 4 5 6 7 8 9 10
enjoy the satisfaction of succeeding in a challenging new task.	1 2 3 4 5 6 7 8 9 10
keep trying even if something gets difficult.	1 2 3 4 5 6 7 8 9 10

Internalization

All of a sudden these new concepts stopped churning within you, and a new reality is born: You and the concepts are one. They have literally become you. You have become them.

—Tom Hopkins

PURPOSE OF THIS TOOL

This tool provides a brief but powerful summary of ideas and conclusions about how students can be supported toward the act of internalization—that is, making their use of Habits of Mind an automatic and spontaneous part of their lifelong learning process. Perhaps most significant, the ideas presented here reinforce the idea that internalization is always a work in progress, never an end point.

HOW TO USE THIS TOOL

Share ideas presented on the previous pages of this section with staff members, parents, and community members as part of outreach and development efforts to reinforce the significance and power of the 16 Habits of Mind. Consider with participants the following essential question: How do we make Habits of Mind a significant, sustainable, and powerful part of our organizational culture and commitment to lifelong learning for every student?

TIPS AND VARIATIONS

An ideal format for reviewing and discussing the ideas presented throughout this Building Commitment section is a cooperative learning jigsaw activity. Participants can select a partner or a small group to process one or more of the ideas presented in this tool. The ideas are also good starting points for follow-up study groups and inquiry teams.

1. Adopting a New Way of Being

Building commitment refers not just to learning within school but to life outside of and after school. A teacher in New Zealand commented that "the Habits of Mind have made me a better father." This recognition that the habits are not just for students in the classroom but are also for all teachers to live by is significant. To fully benefit from the Habits of Mind, we need to understand they are a way of being. They are not something teachers turn on when they arrive at school in the morning and turn off when they leave.

Building Commitment

The habits offer service to professional practice and enhance teachers' participation in the wider world.

2. Reinforcing That No Internalization Is Final

So what is meant by *internalization*? Costa and Kallick suggest that the Habits of Mind can never be fully mastered. As continuous learners, we must continually practice, modify, and refine them. When we are truly habituated to a Habit of Mind, we demonstrate that habit automatically, spontaneously, and without prompting. When confronted with complex decisions, ambiguous tasks, challenging problems, or perplexing dilemmas, we ask ourselves questions such as these: What is the most flexible thing I can do right now? What questions do I need to ask myself and others? Who else do I need to think about? How can I refine the problem to make it clearer? What intrigues me about this problem? Realizing that we are all works in progress, we can be metacognitive about how the habits serve us and how they can serve others. Suppose, for example, that you are in a group in which problem solving is not going well and one group member says, "This is too hard. Let's quit." The person with commitment might advocate for the Habit of Mind of Persisting by saying, "C'mon. Problems are hard to solve but if we stay with it, I bet we can do it! Imagine how great we will all feel if we actually come up with a solution rather than living with this frustration." At this point, the habit has become internalized as a way of life.

3. Determining How We Can Truly Internalize the Habits of Mind

You cannot hope to build a better world without first improving the individuals. To that end, each of us must work for our own improvement and, at the same time, share a general responsibility for all humanity.

—Marie Curie

Begin by clarifying goals and purposes. For example, ask yourself: What do you want to achieve? Then make a plan of action, take action, experiment, gather evidence and become aware, monitor growth, and reflect on the successes of your strategies. Ask yourself: What did I achieve? Is this the best way of doing it? Then use the answers to those questions to modify your plans as needed to get better results. Next, revisit your goals and purposes to ensure you are on track. At this point, start over again. Thus, as the figure on the next page shows, the spiral continues ever onward.

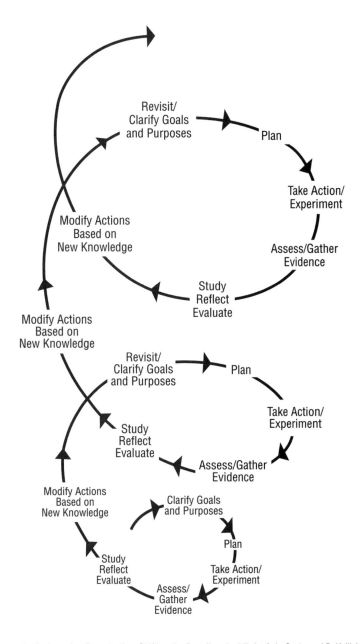

Source: From *Assessment in the Learning Organization: Shifting the Paradigm* (p. 27), by A. L. Costa and B. Kallick, 1995, Alexandria, VA: ASCD. Copyright 1995 by ASCD.

Building Commitment

Appendix A

WHAT ARE HABITS OF MIND?

This appendix provides a brief background of the Habits of Mind for those who are new to the program. Habits of Mind are behaviors associated with effective learning. When faced with new challenges or problems to solve, these behaviors can be used to effectively manage a learning situation. The Habits of Mind are long-range, enduring skills that allow us to cope with a rapidly changing world. The behaviors promote powerful thinking skills for intelligently navigating moral, ethical, and spiritual challenges.

GUIDING PRINCIPLES

Habits of Mind serve as guiding principles for learning in the classroom and outside the school walls throughout students' life experiences. The habits are powerful tools for

- Establishing and maintaining positive relationships.
- Developing effective communication techniques.
- Applying flexible-thinking strategies in complex situations.
- Learning powerful character traits such as self-reflection and resilience.

RELEVANCE TO ALL

Habits of Mind are as useful for adults as they are for students. When teachers internalize these dispositions themselves, they can better model desirable behavior in their students. In addition, Habits of Mind are relevant to students of all ages and in all subject areas. In fact, Habits of Mind can extend beyond a single classroom to create a whole-school learning culture.

Noted educators Arthur L. Costa and Bena Kallick identify and describe 16 types of intelligent behavior in several of their publications. Their recent book, *Learning and Leading with Habits of Mind: 16 Essential Characteristics for Success* (ASCD, 2008), defines and summarizes the habits on pages 15–38.

Describing 16 Habits of Mind

By Arthur L. Costa and Bena Kallick

By definition, a problem is any stimulus, question, task, phenomenon, or discrepancy, the explanation for which is not immediately known. Thus, we are interested in focusing on student performance under those challenging conditions that demand strategic reasoning, insightfulness, perseverance, creativity, and craftsmanship to resolve a complex problem. We are interested not only in how many answers students know but also in how they behave when they *don't* know. We are interested in observing how students produce knowledge rather than how they merely reproduce it. The critical attribute of intelligent human beings is not only having information but also knowing how to act on it.

A Habit of Mind is a disposition toward behaving intelligently when confronted with problems that do not have immediately known answers. When humans experience dichotomies, are confused by dilemmas, or come face to face with uncertainties, our most effective actions require drawing forth certain patterns of intellectual behavior. When we draw upon these intellectual resources, the results that are produced are more powerful, of higher quality, and of greater significance than if we fail to employ those patterns of intellectual behaviors.

Employing Habits of Mind requires a composite of many skills, attitudes, cues, past experiences, and proclivities. It means that we value one pattern of thinking over another; therefore, it implies choice making about which pattern should be employed at which time. It includes sensitivity to the contextual cues in a situation that signal an appropriate time and circumstance in which the employment of a pattern would be useful. It requires a level of skillfulness to employ and carry through the behaviors effectively over time. It suggests that as a result of each experience in which the behaviors were employed, the effects of their use are reflected upon, evaluated, modified, and carried forth to future applications.

Habits of Mind attend to

- Value: Choosing to employ a pattern of intellectual behaviors rather than other, less productive patterns.
- Inclination: Feeling the tendency toward employing a pattern of intellectual behaviors.
- Sensitivity: Perceiving opportunities for and appropriateness of employing the pattern of behaviors.

- Capability: Possessing the basic skills and capacities to carry through with the behaviors.
- Commitment: Constantly striving to reflect on and improve performance of the behaviors.

DESCRIBING HABITS OF MIND

> *When we no longer know what to do we have come to our real work and when we no longer know which way to go we have begun our real journey. The mind that is not baffled is not employed. The impeded stream is the one that sings.*
>
> —Wendell Berry

What behaviors are indicative of the efficient, effective problem solver? Just what do human beings do when they behave intelligently? Research in effective thinking and intelligent behavior by Feuerstein (1980), Glatthorn and Baron (1985), Sternberg (1985), Perkins (1985), and Ennis (1985) indicates that there are some identifiable characteristics of effective thinkers. These are not necessarily scientists, artists, mathematicians, or the wealthy who demonstrate these behaviors. These characteristics have been identified in successful mechanics, teachers, entrepreneurs, salespeople, and parents—people in all walks of life.

Following are descriptions and an elaboration of 16 attributes of what human beings do when they behave intelligently. We choose to refer to them as Habits of Mind. They are the characteristics of what intelligent people do when they are confronted with problems that do not have immediately apparent resolutions.

These behaviors are seldom performed in isolation. Rather, clusters of such behaviors are drawn forth and employed in various situations. When listening intently, for example, one employs flexibility, metacognition, precise language, and perhaps questioning.

These are not the only 16 ways in which humans display their intelligence. It should be understood that this list is not meant to be complete. It should serve to initiate the collection of additional attributes. Although 16 Habits of Mind are described here, you, your colleagues, and your students will want to continue the search for additional Habits of Mind by adding to and elaborating on this list and the descriptions.

1. Persisting

> *Persistence is the twin sister of excellence.*
> *One is a matter of quality; the other, a matter of time.*
> —Marabel Morgan
> *The Electric Woman*

Efficacious people stick to a task until it is completed. They don't give up easily. They are able to analyze a problem and to develop a system, structure, or strategy to attack it. They employ a range and have a repertoire of alternative strategies for problem solving. They collect evidence to indicate their problem-solving strategy is working, and if one strategy doesn't work, they know how to back up and try another. They recognize when a theory or idea must be rejected and another employed. They have systematic methods of analyzing a problem, which include knowing how to begin, knowing what steps must be performed, and knowing what data need to be generated or collected. Because they are able to sustain a problem-solving process over time, they are comfortable with ambiguous situations.

Students often give up in despair when the answer to a problem is not immediately known. They sometimes crumple their papers and throw them away saying, "I can't do this," or "It's too hard," or they write down any answer to get the task overwith as quickly as possible. Some have attention deficits; they have difficulty staying focused for any length of time, they are easily distracted, they lack the ability to analyze a problem or to develop a system, structure, or strategy of problem attack. They may give up because they have a limited repertoire of problem-solving strategies. If their strategy doesn't work, they give up because they have no alternatives.

2. Managing Impulsivity

> *[A] goal-directed, self-imposed delay of gratification is perhaps the essence of emotional self-regulation: the ability to deny impulse in the service of a goal, whether it be building a business, solving an algebraic equation, or pursuing the Stanley cup.*
>
> Daniel Goleman
> *Emotional Intelligence* (1995, p. 83)

Effective problem solvers have a sense of deliberativeness: they think before they act. They intentionally form a vision of a product, plan of action, goal, or destination before they begin. They strive to clarify and understand directions, develop a strategy for approaching a problem, and withhold immediate value judgments about an idea before fully understanding it. Reflective individuals consider alternatives and consequences of several possible directions prior to taking action. They decrease their need for trial and error by gathering information, taking time to reflect on an answer before giving it, making sure they understand directions, and listening to alternative points of view.

Often, students blurt out the first answer that comes to mind. Sometimes they shout out an answer, start to work without fully understanding the directions, lack an organized plan or strategy for approaching a problem, or make immediate value judgments about an idea—criticizing or praising it—before fully understanding it. They may take the first suggestion given or operate on the first idea that comes to mind rather than considering alternatives and consequences of several possible directions.

3. Listening to Others with Understanding and Empathy

> *Listening is the beginning of understanding...*
> *Wisdom is the reward for a lifetime of listening.*
> *Let the wise listen and add to their learning and let the discerning get guidance.*
>
> Proverbs 1:5

Highly effective people spend an inordinate amount of time and energy listening (Covey, 1989). Some psychologists believe that the ability to listen to another person and to empathize with and understand their point of view is one of the highest forms of intelligent behavior. Being able to paraphrase another person's ideas, detecting indicators (cues) of feelings or emotional states in oral and body language (empathy), accurately expressing another person's concepts and emotions and problems—all are indications of listening behavior (Piaget called it "overcoming ego-centrism"). Effective listeners are able to see through the diverse perspectives of others. They gently attend to another person, demonstrating their understanding of and empathy for an idea or feeling by paraphrasing it accurately, building upon it, clarifying it, or giving an example of it.

Senge and his colleagues (1994) suggest that to listen fully means to pay close attention to what is being said beneath the words. You listen not only to the "music" but also to the essence of the person speaking. You listen not only for what someone knows but also for what he or she is trying to represent. Ears operate at the speed of sound, which is far slower than the speed of light the eyes take in. Generative listening is the art of developing deeper silences in yourself, so you can slow your mind's hearing to your ears' natural speed, and hear beneath the words to their meaning.

We spend 55 percent of our lives listening, yet it is one of the least-taught skills in schools. We often say we are listening, but in actuality we are rehearsing in our head what we are going to say next when our partner is finished. Some students ridicule, laugh at, or put down other students' ideas. They interrupt or are unable to build upon, consider the merits of, or operate on another person's ideas. We want our students to learn to devote their mental energies to another person and invest themselves in their partner's ideas.

We want students to learn to hold in abeyance their own values, judgments, opinions, and prejudices in order to listen to and entertain another person's thoughts. This is a very complex skill, requiring the ability to monitor one's own thoughts while at the same time attending to the partner's words. This does not mean that we can't disagree with someone. A good listener tries to understand what the other person is saying. In the end he may disagree sharply, but because he disagrees, he wants to know exactly what it is he is disagreeing with.

4. Thinking Flexibly

> *If you never change your mind, why have one?*
> —Edward deBono

An amazing discovery about the human brain is its plasticity—its ability to "rewire," change, and even repair itself to become smarter. Flexible people are the ones with the most control. They have the capacity to change their mind as they receive additional data. They engage in multiple and simultaneous outcomes and activities, draw upon a repertoire of problem-solving strategies, and can practice style flexibility, knowing when it is appropriate to be broad and global in their thinking and when a situation requires detailed precision. They create and seek novel approaches and have a well-developed sense of humor. They envision a range of consequences.

Flexible people can approach a problem from a new angle using a novel approach—deBono (1970) refers to this as lateral thinking. They consider alternative points of view or deal with several sources of information simultaneously. Their minds are open to change based on additional information and data or reasoning that contradicts their beliefs. Flexible people know that they have and can develop options and alternatives to consider. They understand means-ends relationships; are able to work within rules, criteria, and regulations; and can predict the consequences of flouting the rules. They not only understand immediate reactions but are also able to perceive the bigger purposes that such constraints serve. Thus, flexibility of mind is essential for working with social diversity, enabling an individual to recognize the wholeness and distinctness of other people's ways of experiencing and making meaning.

Flexible thinkers are able to shift, at will, through multiple perceptual positions. One perceptual orientation is what Jean Piaget called egocentrism—perceiving from our own point of view. By contrast, allocentrism is the position in which we perceive through another person's orientation. We operate from this second position when we empathize with others' feelings, predict how others are thinking, and anticipate potential misunderstandings.

Another perceptual position is macrocentric. It is similar to looking down from a balcony at ourselves and our interactions with others. This bird's-eye view is useful for discerning themes and patterns from assortments of information. It is intuitive, holistic, and conceptual. Since we often need to solve problems with incomplete information, we need the capacity to perceive general patterns and jump across gaps of incomplete knowledge.

Yet another perceptual orientation is microcentric—examining the individual and sometimes minute parts that make up the whole. This "worm's-eye view," without which science, technology, and any complex enterprise could not function, involves logical analytical computation searching for causality in methodical steps. It requires attention to detail, precision, and orderly progressions.

Flexible thinkers display confidence in their intuition. They tolerate confusion and ambiguity up to a point, and are willing to let go of a problem, trusting their subconscious to continue creative and productive work on it. Flexibility is the cradle of humor, creativity, and repertoire. While there are many possible perceptual positions—past, present, future, egocentric, allocentric, macrocentric, visual, auditory, kinesthetic—the flexible mind is activated by knowing when to shift perceptual positions.

Some students have difficulty in considering alternative points of view or dealing with more than one classification system simultaneously. Their way to solve a problem seems to be the only way. They perceive situations from a very ego-centered point of view: "My way or the highway!" Their mind is made up: "Don't confuse me with facts; that's it."

5. Thinking About Thinking (Metacognition)

> *When the mind is thinking it is talking to itself.*
>
> —Plato

Occurring in the neocortex, metacognition is our ability to know what we know and what we don't know. It is our ability to plan a strategy for producing what information is needed, to be conscious of our own steps and strategies during the act of problem solving, and to reflect on and evaluate the productiveness of our own thinking. While "inner language," thought to be a prerequisite, begins in most children around age 5, metacognition is a key attribute of formal thought flowering about age 11.

Probably the major components of metacognition are developing a plan of action, maintaining that plan in mind over a period of time, then reflecting back on and evaluating the plan upon its completion. Planning a strategy before embarking on a course of action assists us in keeping track of the steps in the sequence of planned behavior at the conscious awareness level for the duration of the activity. It facilitates making temporal and comparative judgments, assessing the readiness for more or different activities, and monitoring our interpretations, perceptions, decisions, and behaviors. An example of this would be what superior teachers do daily: developing a teaching strategy for a lesson, keeping that strategy in mind throughout the instruction, then reflecting back upon the strategy to evaluate its effectiveness in producing the desired student outcomes.

Intelligent people plan for, reflect on, and evaluate the quality of their own thinking skills and strategies. Metacognition means becoming increasingly aware of one's actions and the effect of those actions on others and on the environment; forming internal questions as one searches for information and meaning; developing mental maps or plans of action, mentally rehearsing them prior to performance, and monitoring those plans as they are employed—being conscious of the need for midcourse correction if the plan is

Resources and References

not meeting expectations; reflecting on the plan upon completion of the implementation for the purpose of self-evaluation; and editing mental pictures for improved performance.

Interestingly, not all humans achieve the level of formal operations (Chiabetta, 1976). As Alexander Luria, the Russian psychologist, found, not all adults metacogitate (Whimbey, 1976). The most likely reason is that we do not take the time to reflect on our experiences. Students often do not take the time to wonder why we are doing what we are doing. They seldom question themselves about their own learning strategies or evaluate the efficiency of their own performance. Some children virtually have no idea of what they should do when they confront a problem and are often unable to explain their strategies of decision making (Sternberg & Wagner, 1982). When teachers ask, "How did you solve that problem? What strategies did you have in mind?" or say, "Tell us what went on in your head to come up with that conclusion," students often respond by saying, "I don't know, I just did it."

We want our students to perform well on complex cognitive tasks. A simple example of this might be drawn from a reading task. It is a common experience while reading a passage to have our minds wander from the pages. We see the words but no meaning is being produced. Suddenly we realize that we are not concentrating and that we've lost contact with the meaning of the text. We recover by returning to the passage to find our place, matching it with the last thought we can remember, and, once having found it, reading on with connectedness. This inner awareness and the strategy of recovery are components of metacognition.

6. Striving for Accuracy and Precision

> *A man who has committed a mistake and doesn't correct it is committing another mistake.*
> —Confucius

Embodied in the stamina, grace, and elegance of a ballerina or a shoemaker is the desire for craftsmanship, mastery, flawlessness, and economy of energy to produce exceptional results. People who value accuracy, precision, and craftsmanship take time to check over their products. They review the rules by which they are to abide; they review the models and visions they are to follow; and they review the criteria they are to employ and confirm that their finished product matches the criteria exactly. To be craftsmanlike means knowing that one can continually perfect one's craft by working to attain the highest possible standards and pursuing ongoing learning in order to bring a laser-like focus of energies to task accomplishment. These people take pride in their work and have a desire for accuracy as they take time to check over their work. Craftsmanship includes exactness, precision, accuracy, correctness, faithfulness, and fidelity. For some people, craftsmanship requires continuous reworking. Mario Cuomo, a great speechwriter and politician, once said that his speeches were never done—it was only a deadline that made him stop working on them.

Some students may turn in sloppy, incomplete, or uncorrected work. They are more anxious to get rid of the assignment than to check it over for accuracy and precision. They are willing to suffice with minimum effort rather than to invest their maximum. They may be more interested in expedience rather than excellence.

7. Questioning and Posing Problems

The formulation of a problem is often more essential than its solution, which may be merely a matter of mathematical or experimental skill. To raise new questions, new possibilities, to regard old problems from a new angle, requires creative imagination and marks real advances ....

—Albert Einstein

One of the distinguishing characteristics between humans and other forms of life is our inclination and ability to find problems to solve. Effective problem solvers know how to ask questions to fill in the gaps between what they know and what they don't know. Effective questioners are inclined to ask a range of questions. Examples:

- They request data to support others' conclusions and assumptions with such questions as

  What evidence do you have about ...?
  How do you know that's true?
  How reliable is this data source?

- They pose questions about alternative points of view:

  From whose viewpoint are we seeing, reading, or hearing?
  From what angle, what perspective, are we viewing this situation?

- They pose questions about causal connections and relationships:

  How are these people (or events or situations) related to each other?
  What produced this connection?

- They pose hypothetical problems characterized by "if" questions:

  What do you think would happen if ...?
  If that is true, then what might happen if ...?

Inquirers recognize discrepancies and phenomena in their environment and probe into their causes. Examples: Why do cats purr? How high can birds fly? Why does the hair on my head grow so fast, while the hair on my arms and legs grows so slowly? What would happen if we put the saltwater fish in a fresh water aquarium? What are some alternative solutions to international conflicts other than wars?

Some students may be unaware of the functions, classes, syntax, or intentions in questions. They may not realize that questions vary in complexity, structure, and purpose. They may pose simple questions intending to derive maximal results. When confronted with a discrepancy, they may lack an overall strategy of search and solution finding.

8. Applying Past Knowledge to New Situations

> *I've never made a mistake. I've only learned from experience.*
>
> —Thomas A. Edison

Intelligent human beings learn from experience. When confronted with a new and perplexing problem, they will often draw forth experience from their past. They can often be heard to say, "This reminds me of ..." or "This is just like the time when I ..." They explain what they are doing now in terms of analogies with or references to previous experiences. They call upon their store of knowledge and experience as sources of data to support, theories to explain, or processes to solve each new challenge. Furthermore, they are able to abstract meaning from one experience, carry it forth, and apply it in a new and novel situation.

Too often, students begin each new task as if it were being approached for the very first time. Teachers are often dismayed when they invite students to recall how they solved a similar problem previously and students don't remember. It's as if they never heard of it before, even though they had the same type of problem just recently. It's as if each experience is encapsulated and has no relationship to what has come before or what comes afterward. Their thinking is what psychologists refer to as an episodic grasp of reality (Feuerstein, 1980). That is, each event in life is a separate and discrete event with no connections to what may have come before or with no relation to what follows. Furthermore, their learning is so encapsulated that they seem unable to draw forth learning from one event and apply it in another context.

9. Thinking and Communicating with Clarity and Precision

I do not so easily think in words ... after being hard at work having arrived at results that are perfectly clear .... I have to translate my thoughts in a language that does not run evenly with them.

—Francis Galton
Geneticist

Language refinement plays a critical role in enhancing a person's cognitive maps and ability to think critically, which is the knowledge base for efficacious action. Enriching the complexity and specificity of language simultaneously produces effective thinking.

Language and thinking are closely entwined. Like either side of a coin, they are inseparable. When you hear fuzzy language, it is a reflection of fuzzy thinking. Intelligent people strive to communicate accurately in both written and oral form, taking care to use precise language, defining terms, using correct names and universal labels and analogies. They strive to avoid overgeneralizations, deletions, and distortions. Instead, they support their statements with explanations, comparisons, quantification, and evidence.

We sometimes hear students and other adults using vague and imprecise language. They describe objects or events with words like "weird," "nice," or "OK." They refer to specific objects using such nondescriptive words as "stuff," "junk," and "things." They punctuate sentences with meaningless interjections such as "ya know," "er," and "uh." They use vague or general nouns and pronouns: "They told me to do it." "Everybody has one." "Teachers don't understand me." They use nonspecific verbs: "Let's do it" and unqualified comparatives: "This soda is better; I like it more."

10. Gathering Data Through All Senses

> *Observe perpetually.*
> —Henry James

The brain is the ultimate reductionist. It reduces the world to its elementary parts—photons of light, molecules of smell, sound waves, vibrations of touch—which send electrochemical signals to individual brain cells that store information about lines, movements, colors, smells, and other sensory inputs.

Intelligent people know that all information gets into the brain through the sensory pathways: gustatory, olfactory, tactile, kinesthetic, auditory, visual. Most linguistic, cultural, and physical learning is derived from the environment by observing or taking in through the senses. To know a wine, it must be drunk; to know a role, it must be acted; to know a game, it must be played; to know a dance, it must be danced; to know a goal, it must be envisioned. Those whose sensory pathways are open, alert, and acute absorb more information from the environment than those whose pathways are withered, immune, and oblivious to sensory stimuli.

Furthermore, we are learning more about the impact of arts and music on improved mental functioning. Forming mental images is important in mathematics and engineering; listening to classical music seems to improve spatial reasoning.

Social scientists solve problems through scenarios and role playing; scientists build models; engineers use cad-cam; mechanics learn through hands-on experimentation; artists experiment with colors and textures; musicians experiment by producing combinations of instrumental and vocal music.

Some students, however, go through school and life oblivious to the textures, rhythms, patterns, sounds, and colors around them. Sometimes children are afraid to touch, get their hands dirty, or feel some object that might be "slimy" or "icky." They operate within a narrow range of sensory problem-solving strategies, wanting only to "describe it but not illustrate or act it," or "listen but not participate."

11. Creating, Imagining, and Innovating

> *The future is not some place we are going to but one we are creating. The paths are not to be found, but made, and the activity of making them changes both the maker and the destination.*
>
> —John Schaar,
> Political Scientist and Author
> *Loyalty in America*

All human beings have the capacity to generate novel, original, clever, or ingenious products, solutions, and techniques—if that capacity is developed. Creative human beings try to conceive problem solutions differently, examining alternative possibilities from many angles. They tend to project themselves into different roles using analogies, starting with a vision and working backward, imagining they are the objects being considered. Creative people take risks and frequently push the boundaries of their perceived limits (Perkins, 1985). They are intrinsically rather than extrinsically motivated, working on the task because of the aesthetic challenge rather than the material rewards. Creative people are open to criticism. They hold up their products for others to judge and seek feedback in an ever-increasing effort to refine their technique. They are uneasy with the status quo. They constantly strive for greater fluency, elaboration, novelty, parsimony, simplicity, craftsmanship, perfection, beauty, harmony, and balance.

Students, however, are often heard saying, "I can't draw," or "I was never very good at art," or "I can't sing a note," or "I'm not creative." Some people believe creative humans are just born that way in their genes and chromosomes.

12. Responding with Wonderment and Awe

> *The most beautiful experience in the world is the experience of the mysterious.*
> —Albert Einstein

Describing the 200 best and brightest of the All-USA College Academic Team identified by *USA Today*, Tracey Wong Briggs (1999) states, "They are creative thinkers who have a passion for what they do." Efficacious people have not only an "I can" attitude but also an "I enjoy" feeling. They seek problems to solve for themselves and to submit to others. They delight in making up problems to solve on their own and request enigmas from others. They enjoy figuring things out by themselves and continue to learn throughout their lifetime.

Some children and adults avoid problems and are turned off to learning. They make such comments as, "I was never good at these brain teasers," or "Go ask your father; he's the brain in this family," or "It's boring," or "When am I ever going to use this stuff?" or "Who cares?" or "Lighten up, teacher, thinking is hard work," or "I don't do thinking!" Many people never enrolled in another math class or other "hard" academic subjects after they didn't have to in high school or college. Many people perceive thinking as hard work and, therefore, recoil from situations that demand "too much."

We want our students, however, to be curious, to commune with the world around them, reflect on the changing formations of a cloud, feel charmed by the opening of a bud, sense the logical simplicity of mathematical order. Students can find beauty in a sunset, intrigue in the geometric design of a spider web, and exhilaration at the iridescence of a hummingbird's wings. They see the congruity and intricacies in the derivation of a mathematical formula, recognize the orderliness and adroitness of a chemical change, and commune with the serenity of a distant constellation. We want them to feel compelled, enthusiastic, and passionate about learning, inquiring, and mastering.

13. Taking Responsible Risks

> *There has been a calculated risk in every stage of American development—the pioneers who were not afraid of the wilderness, businessmen who were not afraid of failure, dreamers who were not afraid of action.*
>
> —Brooks Atkinson

Flexible people seem to have an almost uncontrollable urge to go beyond established limits. They are uneasy about comfort; they live on the edge. They seem compelled to place themselves in situations where they do not know what the outcome will be. They accept confusion, uncertainty, and the higher risks of failure as part of the normal process and they learn to view setbacks as interesting, challenging, and growth producing. However, they are not behaving impulsively. Their risks are educated. They draw on past knowledge, are thoughtful about consequences, and have a well-trained sense of what is appropriate. They know that not all risks are worth taking.

Risk taking can be considered in two categories: those who see it as a venture and those who see it as adventure. The venture part of risk taking might be described by the venture capitalist. When a person is approached to take the risk of investing in a new business, she will look at the markets, see how well organized the ideas are, and study the economic projections. If she finally decides to take the risk, it is a well-considered one.

The adventure part of risk taking might be described by the experiences from project adventure. In this situation, there is a spontaneity, a willingness to take a chance in the moment. Once again, a person will take the chance only if he either knows that there is past history that suggests that what he is doing is not going to be life threatening or believes that there is enough support in the group to protect him from harm. Ultimately, the learning from such high-risk experiences is that people are far more able to take actions than they previously believed. It is only through repeated experiences that risk taking becomes educated. It often is a cross between intuition, drawing on past knowledge, and a sense of meeting new challenges.

Bobby Jindal, Executive Director of the National Bipartisan Commission on the Future of Medicare, states, "The only way to succeed is to be brave enough to risk failure" (Briggs, 1999, p. 2A).

Those who hold back from taking risks are confronted constantly with missed opportunities. Some students seem reluctant to take risks. Some students hold back on games, new learning, and new friendships because their fear of failure is far greater than their experience of venture or adventure. They are reinforced by the mental voice that says, "If you don't try it, you won't be wrong" or "If you try it and you are wrong, you will look stupid." The other voice, which might say, "If you don't try it, you will never know," is trapped in fear and mistrust. These students are more interested in knowing whether their answer is correct or not, rather than being challenged by the process of finding the answer. They are unable to sustain a process of problem solving and finding the answer over time and, therefore, avoid ambiguous situations. They have a need for certainty rather than an inclination for doubt.

We hope that students will learn how to take intellectual as well as physical risks. Students who are capable of being different, going against the grain of the common, thinking of new ideas, and testing them with peers as well as teachers are more likely to be successful in this age of innovation and uncertainty.

14. Finding Humor

> *Where do bees wait? At the buzz stop.*
> —Andrew, Student, Age 6

Another unique attribute of human beings is our sense of humor. Laughter transcends all human beings. Its positive effects on psychological functions include a drop in the pulse rate, the secretion of endorphins, and increased oxygen in the blood. It has been found to liberate creativity and provoke such higher-level thinking skills as anticipation, finding novel relationships, visual imagery, and making analogies. People who engage in the mystery of humor have the ability to perceive situations from an original and often interesting vantage point. They tend to initiate humor more often, to place greater value on having a sense of humor, to appreciate and understand others' humor, and to be verbally playful when interacting with others. Having a whimsical frame of mind, they thrive on finding incongruity and perceiving absurdities, ironies, and satire; they find discontinuities and are able to laugh at situations and themselves. Some students find humor in all the wrong places—human differences, ineptitude, injurious behavior, vulgarity, violence and profanity. They laugh at others yet are unable to laugh at themselves.

We want our student to acquire the characteristic of creative problem solvers, so that they can distinguish between situations of human frailty and fallibility, which are in need of compassion, and those that are truly funny (Dyer, 1997).

15. Thinking Interdependently

Take care of each other. Share your energies with the group. No one must feel alone, cut off, for that is when you do not make it.

—Willie Unsoeld
Mountain Climber

Human beings are social beings. We congregate in groups, find it therapeutic to be listened to, draw energy from one another, and seek reciprocity. In groups we contribute our time and energy to tasks that we would quickly tire of working alone. In fact, we have learned that one of the cruelest forms of punishment that can be inflicted on an individual is solitary confinement.

Cooperative humans realize that all of us together are more powerful, intellectually and physically, than any one individual. Probably the foremost disposition in postindustrial society is the heightened ability to think in concert with others; to find ourselves increasingly more interdependent and sensitive to the needs of others. Problem solving has become so complex that no one person can go it alone. No one has access to all the data needed to make critical decisions; no one person can consider as many alternatives as several people can.

Some students may not have learned to work in groups; they have underdeveloped social skills. They may feel isolated and prefer their solitude: "Leave me alone—I'll do it by myself." "They just don't like me." "I want to be alone." Some students seem unable to contribute to group work either by being a "job hog" or, conversely, letting others do all the work.

Working in groups requires the ability to justify ideas and to test the feasibility of solution strategies on others. It also requires the development of a willingness and openness to accept feedback from a critical friend. Through this interaction the group and the individual continue to grow. Listening, consensus seeking, giving up an idea to work with someone else's, empathy, compassion, group leadership, knowing how to support group efforts, altruism—all are behaviors indicative of cooperative human beings.

16. Learning Continuously

Insanity is continuing to do the same thing over and over and expecting different results.
—Albert Einstein

Intelligent people are in a continuous learning mode. Their confidence, in combination with their inquisitiveness, allows them to constantly search for new and better ways. People with this Habit of Mind are always striving for improvement, always growing, always learning, always modifying and improving themselves. They seize problems, situations, tensions, conflicts, and circumstances as valuable opportunities to learn.

A great mystery about humans is that we confront learning opportunities with fear rather than mystery and wonder. We seem to feel better when we know rather than when we learn. We defend our biases, beliefs, and storehouses of knowledge rather than inviting the unknown, the creative, and the inspirational. Being certain and closed gives us comfort, while being doubtful and open gives us fear. From an early age, employing a curriculum of fragmentation, competition, and reactiveness, students are trained to believe that deep learning means figuring out the truth rather than developing capabilities for effective and thoughtful action. They are taught to value certainty rather than doubt, to give answers rather than to inquire, to know which choice is correct rather than to explore alternatives.

Our wish for our students is that they become creative people who are eager to learn. We include in that wish the humility of knowing that they don't know, which is the highest form of thinking we humans will ever learn. Paradoxically, unless we start off with humility we will never get anywhere, so as the first step we have to have what will eventually be the crowning glory of all learning: the humility to know—and admit—that we don't know, and then we must not be afraid to find out.

SUMMARY

Drawn from research on human effectiveness, descriptions of remarkable performers, and analyses of the characteristics of efficacious people, we have presented descriptions of 16 Habits of Mind. This list is not meant to be complete but to serve as a starting point for further elaboration and description.

These Habits of Mind may serve as mental disciplines. When confronted with problematic situations, students, parents, and teachers might habitually employ one or more of these Habits of Mind by asking themselves questions such as

- What is the most intelligent thing I can do right now?
- How can I learn from this? How can I draw on my past successes with problems like this? What do I already know about the problem? What resources do I have available or need to generate?
- How can I approach this problem flexibly? How might I look at the situation in another way? How can I draw upon my repertoire of problem-solving strategies? How can I look at this problem from a fresh perspective?
- How can I illuminate this problem to make it clearer, more precise? Do I need to check out my data sources? How might I break this problem down into its component parts and develop a strategy for understanding and accomplishing each step?
- What do I know or not know? What questions do I need to ask? What strategies are in my mind now? What am I aware of in terms of my own beliefs, values, and goals with this problem? What feelings or emotions am I aware of that might be blocking or enhancing my progress?

Interdependent thinkers might turn to others for help. They might ask: How can this problem affect others? How can we solve it together? What can I learn from others that would help me become a better problem solver?

Taking a reflective stance in the midst of active problem solving is often difficult. For that reason, all Habits of Mind are situational and transitory. There is no such thing as perfect realization of any of them. They are utopian states toward which we constantly aspire. Csikszentmihalyi (1993, p. 23) states, "Although every human brain is able to generate self-reflective consciousness, not everyone seems to use it equally."

Few people, notes Kegan (1994), ever fully reach the stage of cognitive complexity, and rarely before middle age.

These Habits of Mind transcend all subject matters commonly taught in school. They are characteristic of peak performers whether they be in homes or schools; on athletic fields; or in organizations, the military, governments, churches, or corporations. They are what make marriages successful, learning continual, workplaces productive, and democracies enduring.

The goal of education, therefore, should be to support others and ourselves in liberating, developing, and habituating these Habits of Mind fully. Taken together, they are a force directing us toward increasingly authentic, congruent, ethical behavior. They are the touchstones of integrity. They are the tools of disciplined choice making. They are the primary vehicles in the lifelong journey toward integration. They are the "right stuff" that makes human beings efficacious.

> *We are what we repeatedly do. Excellence, then, is not an act but a habit.*
> —Aristotle

REFERENCES

Briggs, T. W. (1999, Feb. 25). Passion for what they do keeps alumni on first team. *USA Today*, pp. 1A–2A.

Chiabetta, E. L. A. (1976). Review of Piagetian studies relevant to science instruction at the secondary and college levels. *Science Education, 60,* 253–261.

Costa, A. (1991). The search for intelligent life. In A. L. Costa (Ed.), *Developing minds: A resource book for teaching thinking* (pp. 100–106). Alexandria, VA: Association for Supervision and Curriculum Development.

Csikszentmihalyi, M. (1993). *The evolving self: A psychology for the third millennium.* New York: Harper Collins.

Covey, S. (1989). *The seven habits of highly effective people.* New York: Simon & Schuster.

DeBono, E. (1991). The Cort thinking program. In A. L. Costa (Ed.), *Developing minds: Programs for teaching thinking* (pp. 27–32). Alexandria, VA: Association for Supervision and Curriculum Development.

Dyer, J. (1997). Humor as process. In A. Costa & R. Liebmann (Eds.), *Envisioning process as content: Toward a Renaissance curriculum* (pp. 211–229). Thousand Oaks, CA: Corwin Press.

Ennis, R. (1991). Goals for a critical thinking curriculum. In A. L. Costa (Ed.), *Developing minds: A resource book for teaching thinking* (Rev. ed., Vol. 1, pp. 68–71). Alexandria, VA: Association for Supervision and Curriculum Development.

Feuerstein, R., Rand, Y. M., Hoffman, M. B., & Miller, R. (1980). *Instrumental enrichment: An intervention program for cognitive modifiability.* Baltimore: University Park Press.

Resources and References

Glatthorn, A., & Baron, J. (1985). The good thinker. In A. L. Costa (Ed.), *Developing minds: A resource book for teaching thinking.* Alexandria, VA: Association for Supervision and Curriculum Development.

Goleman, D. (1995). *Emotional intelligence: Why it can matter more than IQ.* New York: Bantam Books.

Kegan, R. (1994). *In over our heads: The mental complexity of modern life.* Cambridge, MA: Harvard University Press.

Perkins, D. (1985). What creative thinking is. In A. L. Costa (Ed.), *Developing minds: A resource book for teaching thinking* (pp. 85–88). Alexandria, VA: Association for Supervision and Curriculum Development.

Perkins, D. (1995). *Outsmarting IQ: The emerging science of learnable intelligence.* New York: The Free Press.

Senge, P., Ross, R., Smith, B., Roberts, C., & Kleiner, A. (1994). *The fifth discipline fieldbook: Strategies and tools for building a learning organization.* New York: Doubleday/Currency.

Sternberg, R., & Wagner, R. (1982). *Understanding intelligence: What's in it for education?* Paper submitted to the National Commission on Excellence in Education.

Sternberg, R. (1984). *Beyond IQ: A triarchic theory of human intelligence.* New York: Cambridge University Press.

Sternberg, R. (1983). *How can we teach intelligence?* Philadelphia, PA: Research for Better Schools.

Whimbey, A., & Whimbey L. S. (1975). *Intelligence can be taught.* New York: Lawrence Erlbaum Associates.

This article is adapted from Costa, A. & Kallick, B. (2000), *Habits of Mind: A Developmental Series.* Alexandria, VA: Association for Supervision and Curriculum Development.

Book I: *Discovering and exploring habits of mind*

Book II: *Activating and engaging habits of mind*

Book III: *Assessing and reporting growth in habits of mind*

Book IV: *Integrating and sustaining habits of mind*

Appendix B

TEMPLATES, EVALUATIONS, AND RUBRICS

Throughout this action tool, you will find a variety of assessment and planning resources specific to relevant content. This appendix provides additional resources. Included are generic planning tools and resource templates, such as a summary of the 16 Habits of Mind and a template for creating your own lesson plans. You will also find self-evaluation and teacher-evaluation tools, action plans, and checklists. In addition, a rubric for every Habit of Mind is available.

CONTENTS

Summary of 16 Habits of Mind

1. Persisting: *Stick to it.* Persevering in a task through to completion; remaining focused.	**2. Managing Impulsivity:** *Take your time.* Thinking before acting; remaining calm, thoughtful, and deliberative.
3. Listening with Understanding and Empathy: *Understand others.* Devoting mental energy to another person's thoughts and ideas; holding in one's own thoughts in order to perceive another's point of view and emotions.	**4. Thinking Flexibly:** *Look at it another way.* Being able to change perspectives, generate alternatives, and consider options.
5. Thinking About Thinking (Metacognition): *Know your knowing.* Being aware of one's own thoughts, strategies, feelings, and actions and their effects on others.	**6. Striving for Accuracy and Precision:** *Check it again.* A desire for exactness, fidelity, and craftsmanship.
7. Questioning and Posing Problems: *How do you know?* Having a questioning attitude; knowing what data are needed and developing questioning strategies to produce data; finding problems to solve.	**8. Applying Past Knowledge to New Situations:** *Use what you learn.* Accessing prior knowledge; transferring knowledge beyond the situation in which it was learned.
9. Thinking and Communicating with Clarity and Precision: *Be clear.* Striving for accurate communication in both written and oral form; avoiding over generalizations, distortions, and deletions.	**10. Gathering Data Through All Senses:** *Use your natural pathways.* Gathering data through all the sensory pathways: gustatory, olfactory, tactile, kinesthetic, auditory, and visual.
11. Creating, Imagining, and Innovating: *Try a different way.* Generating new and novel ideas, fluency, and originality.	**12. Responding with Wonderment and Awe:** *Have fun figuring it out.* Finding the world awesome and mysterious and being intrigued with phenomena and beauty.
13. Taking Responsible Risks: *Venture out.* Being adventuresome; living on the edge of one's competence.	**14. Finding Humor:** *Laugh a little.* Finding the whimsical, incongruous, and unexpected; being able to laugh at oneself.
15. Thinking Interdependently: *Work together.* Being able to work with and learn from others in reciprocal situations.	**16. Learning Continuously:** *Learn from experiences.* Having humility and pride when admitting one doesn't know; resisting complacency.

Lesson Plan Template

Lesson Title:

Lesson Overview:

Objectives	Materials Needed
•	•
•	•
•	•
•	•
Estimated Time Required	**Notes**

Suggested Sequence of Activities

- Motivational Activity:

- Core Activity:

- Reflection Activity:

- Synthesis Activity:

- Extension Activity:

Name _____ Class _____ Date _____

Y-Chart

You can use this chart to explore your thoughts about many different topics.

Topic:

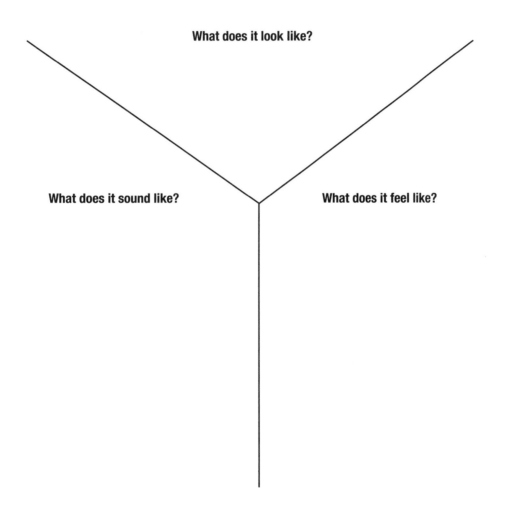

What does it look like?

What does it sound like?

What does it feel like?

Name _____ Class _____ Date _____

The C-A-F Model:
Consider All Factors

Use the C-A-F model when you need to make a decision. To consider all the relevant factors, brainstorm a list of questions to ask yourself. The following will get you started. You can add more. When you are finished brainstorming, answer the questions to help you make a decision.

Key Questions:

What factors are involved?

Who is affected by my decision?

Have I thought of everything?

Do I have everything I need?

Name _____ Class _____ Date _____

The P-D-R Method: Plan-Do-Review

Use the Plan-Do-Review method to think through a situation before attempting it.

> **Example:**
> Mission: Camp in the extreme wilderness for one month and live to tell about it.

Plan:

Do:

Review:

Name _____ Class _____ Date _____

K-W-L Chart

When you are about to start studying something new or are preparing for a test, complete this chart. Fill out the first two columns before you begin studying and fill out the last column after your studies.

What Do I Know Already?	What Do I Want to Learn?	What Have I Learned?

Name _____ Class _____ Date _____

Case Study _____

Ask a variety of questions, and then record your answers.

Questions	Answers
Who?	
Where?	
When?	
Why?	
What?	
How? (Which Habits of Mind?)	

Name _____ Class _____ Date _____

Key Research Questions

As you do your research, brainstorm questions you would like to get answered in order to learn more. The following are a few examples:

- Why was this person famous?
- Why did many people respect this person?
- What did this person achieve in his or her lifetime?
- What lessons does this person teach us?

Your Research Topic:

Questions:

Name _____ Class _____ Date _____

Obstacles on the Path

Complete the following tree map to show successes, failures, and obstacles that the subject of your research experienced on his or her path to success.

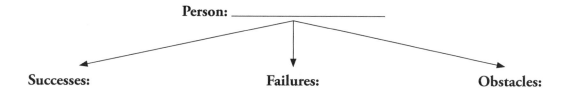

Person: _____

Successes: **Failures:**   **Obstacles:**

Which Habits of Mind helped this person overcome obstacles?	How did the Habits of Mind help this person?	What evidence supports your claim?

Name _____ Class _____ Date _____

Issue Analysis

The issue I am analyzing is: _____

Related Habits of Mind	Relevance of Habits of Mind	Consequences of Not Using Habits of Mind

Student Name _____ Class _____ Date _____

Teacher Evaluation of Student

This student is able to	Seldom	Sometimes	Usually	Consistently
Recognize increasingly diverse, complex, and novel situations in which to apply the Habits of Mind.				
Spontaneously use appropriate Habits of Mind when confronted with ambiguous and perplexing situations.				
Recognize a wide range of situations in which to apply the Habits of Mind.				
Recognize, without assistance, novel and complex situations in which to apply the Habits of Mind.				
Articulate the criteria upon which the decisions reflected in this review were made.				

Resources and References

Name _____ Class _____ Date _____

Student Self-Evaluation

Use this checklist to evaluate your progress in applying the Habits of Mind. Be honest with yourself! In the blank rows, include additional areas you would like to be aware of and improve.

I am able to	Seldom	Sometimes	Usually	Consistently
Recognize different and complex situations in which to use the Habits of Mind.				
Suggest which Habits of Mind are useful or relevant when looking at new situations.				
Recognize a wide range of situations in which to apply the Habits of Mind.				
Recognize, without assistance, new and complex situations in which to apply the Habits of Mind.				
Explain why I would use certain Habits of Mind in a situation.				

Teacher Self-Reflection Tool

Habit of Mind	I am a teacher who ...
Persisting	Perseveres with challenging students and ensures all students have a depth of understanding and skills as learners. *Rate yourself: 1 2 3 4 5 6 7 8 9 10*
Managing Impulsivity	Uses wait time and pausing, paraphrasing, and probing techniques; I demonstrate thoughtfulness. *Rate yourself: 1 2 3 4 5 6 7 8 9 10*
Listening with Understanding and Empathy	Actively listens to others. I make genuine attempts to understand where others are coming from and perceive their points of view. *Rate yourself: 1 2 3 4 5 6 7 8 9 10*
Thinking Flexibly	Is open to the points of view of others; changes plans and strategies when needed to better meet group needs; grasps the teachable moment to foster interest and achievement. *Rate yourself: 1 2 3 4 5 6 7 8 9 10*
Thinking About Thinking (Metacognition)	Is aware of my own thinking processes. I invest time in reflection; I model my thinking processes to those around me. *Rate yourself: 1 2 3 4 5 6 7 8 9 10*
Striving for Accuracy and Precision	Sets high standards in the things I do and in relations with others. I check for accuracy in written documents and communications. *Rate yourself: 1 2 3 4 5 6 7 8 9 10*
Questioning and Posing Problems	Is skilled in composing and asking complex questions. *Rate yourself: 1 2 3 4 5 6 7 8 9 10*
Applying Past Knowledge to New Situations	Uses past experiences, resources, and knowledge to ensure good practice. I offer wide knowledge to support student learning. *Rate yourself: 1 2 3 4 5 6 7 8 9 10*
Thinking and Communicating with Clarity and Precision	Strives to be accurate in all communications. I use thinking verbs when giving instructions. *Rate yourself: 1 2 3 4 5 6 7 8 9 10*
Gathering Data Through All Senses	Stays alert to people and situations by gathering data through my senses. *Rate yourself: 1 2 3 4 5 6 7 8 9 10*

Teacher Self-Reflection Tool

Habit of Mind	I am a teacher who ...
Creating, Imagining, and Innovating	Is creative and innovative in finding new ways and alternatives. *Rate yourself:* 1 2 3 4 5 6 7 8 9 10
Responding with Wonderment and Awe	Is enthusiastic about my teaching, my students' learning, and new discoveries. *Rate yourself:* 1 2 3 4 5 6 7 8 9 10
Taking Responsible Risks	Moves outside my comfort zone and becomes adventurous after thoughtful consideration. *Rate yourself:* 1 2 3 4 5 6 7 8 9 10
Finding Humor	Can laugh with others and at myself. I do not take myself too seriously. *Rate yourself:* 1 2 3 4 5 6 7 8 9 10
Thinking Interdependently	Works collaboratively with others. I can learn from those around me. *Rate yourself:* 1 2 3 4 5 6 7 8 9 10
Learning Continuously	Has the humility and pride to admit when I don't know something. I resist complacency. *Rate yourself:* 1 2 3 4 5 6 7 8 9 10

Student Self-Reflection Tool

Name _____ Class _____ Date _____

Habit of Mind	I am a student who …
Persisting	Perseveres with my studies to gain a depth of understanding and skills as a learner. *Rate yourself: 1 2 3 4 5 6 7 8 9 10*
Managing Impulsivity	Controls impulses; stops and thinks before acting; demonstrates thoughtfulness. *Rate yourself: 1 2 3 4 5 6 7 8 9 10*
Listening with Understanding and Empathy	Actively listens to others; makes genuine attempts to understand where others are coming from and perceive their points of view. *Rate yourself: 1 2 3 4 5 6 7 8 9 10*
Thinking Flexibly	Is open to the points of view of others. I can change plans and strategies when needed to better meet group needs. *Rate yourself: 1 2 3 4 5 6 7 8 9 10*
Thinking About Thinking (Metacognition)	Is aware of my thinking processes and invests time in reflection. I can explain my thinking to others. *Rate yourself: 1 2 3 4 5 6 7 8 9 10*
Striving for Accuracy and Precision	Sets high standards in the things I do and in relations with others. I check for accuracy in written documents and communications. *Rate yourself: 1 2 3 4 5 6 7 8 9 10*
Questioning and Posing Problems	Is skilled in composing and asking complex questions. *Rate yourself: 1 2 3 4 5 6 7 8 9 10*
Applying Past Knowledge to New Situations	Uses past experiences, resources, and knowledge to ensure good practice. *Rate yourself: 1 2 3 4 5 6 7 8 9 10*
Thinking and Communicating with Clarity and Precision	Strives to be accurate in written and oral communication. *Rate yourself: 1 2 3 4 5 6 7 8 9 10*

Habit of Mind	I am a student who …
Gathering Data Through All Senses	Stays alert to people and situations by gathering data through my senses. *Rate yourself: 1 2 3 4 5 6 7 8 9 10*
Creating, Imagining, and Innovating	Is creative and innovative in coming up with ideas and alternatives. *Rate yourself: 1 2 3 4 5 6 7 8 9 10*
Responding with Wonderment and Awe	Is enthusiastic about learning and new discoveries. *Rate yourself: 1 2 3 4 5 6 7 8 9 10*
Taking Responsible Risks	Can move outside my comfort zone and become adventurous after thoughtful consideration. *Rate yourself: 1 2 3 4 5 6 7 8 9 10*
Finding Humor	Can laugh with others and at myself. I do not take myself too seriously. *Rate yourself: 1 2 3 4 5 6 7 8 9 10*
Thinking Interdependently	Works collaboratively with others and can learn from those around me. *Rate yourself: 1 2 3 4 5 6 7 8 9 10*
Learning Continuously	Looks for opportunities to learn and improve; is open to growth and change. *Rate yourself: 1 2 3 4 5 6 7 8 9 10*

Resources and References

Name _____ Class _____ Date _____

Improving Habits

Select at least three Habits of Mind you need to improve. Explain why you think each is important. Then rank the habits in their order of importance.

Habits of Mind	How will this Habit of Mind help me?	Rank
Persisting		
Managing Impulsivity		
Listening with Understanding and Empathy		
Thinking Flexibly		
Thinking About Thinking (Metacognition)		
Striving for Accuracy and Precision		
Questioning and Posing Problems		
Applying Past Knowledge to New Situations		
Thinking and Communicating with Clarity and Precision		
Gathering Data Through All Senses		
Creating, Imagining, and Innovating		
Responding with Wonderment and Awe		
Taking Responsible Risks		
Finding Humor		
Thinking Interdependently		
Learning Continuously		

Name _____ Class _____ Date _____

Action Plan for Habits of Mind Development

Pick one Habit of Mind competency that you would like to improve. Then use this form to create an action plan for improvement.

The competency I would like to improve is _____

Action Plan to Improve This Competency in One Month

I will do these specific things:

I seek assistance from these sources:

I can monitor my improvement in these ways:

Name _____ Class _____ Date _____

Rubric for Persisting

Rating	Description
4 **EXPERT:** **Unconsciously Competent**	Does not give up no matter how difficult the solution is to find; has a repertoire of alternative strategies and will use them to find answers; evaluates the use of strategies, developing systematic methods for further use, including how to begin, steps to take, and relevant data to collect.
3 **PRACTITIONER:** **Consciously Competent**	Stays on task; develops a broad range of strategies and will use them when searching for an answer; does not give up until a solution is found or the assignment is finished.
2 **APPRENTICE:** **Consciously Incompetent**	Tries to complete tasks when answers are not readily available, but gives up easily if a task becomes difficult; fluctuates in staying focused for any length of time; uses few strategies to solve problems.
1 **NOVICE:** **Unconsciously Incompetent**	Does not complete any tasks; gives up easily; cannot think of or use strategies to solve problems.

Name _____ Class _____ Date _____

Rubric for Managing Impulsivity

Rating	Description
4 **EXPERT:** **Unconsciously Competent**	Carefully evaluates situations and seeks advice from other sources before taking appropriate action; is a thorough and careful researcher; effectively gathers important information; sets clear goals and describes each step taken to achieve goals; schedules and monitors progress.
3 **PRACTITIONER:** **Consciously Competent**	Thinks and searches for more information before taking action; evaluates a situation before taking appropriate action; has clear goals and can describe steps needed to achieve goals.
2 **APPRENTICE:** **Consciously Incompetent**	Searches for obvious information and then acts on impulse; will seek more information only if needed and easily available; is developing some steps to gather information to form decisions; is beginning to make goals and taking a few steps to achieve goals.
1 **NOVICE:** **Unconsciously Incompetent**	Acts before thinking; says the first answer that comes to his or her mind; rushes ahead with incomplete or inadequate information; shows little inclination to gather further data to form decisions; has random goals and is unclear about the steps needed to achieve goals.

Name _____ Class _____ Date _____

Rubric for Listening with Understanding and Empathy

Rating	Description
4 **EXPERT:** **Unconsciously Competent**	Is an attentive listener; demonstrates an understanding of other people's ideas via accurate paraphrasing, building upon statements, clarifying statements, or providing examples.
3 **PRACTITIONER:** **Consciously Competent**	Is an attentive listener; shows understanding and empathy for other people's ideas; is able to paraphrase and question to develop further understanding.
2 **APPRENTICE:** **Consciously Incompetent**	Is easily distracted and not a consistent listener; is able to repeat some parts of what has been said; has difficulty with other people, either because of a lack of comprehension or because of ridiculing, putting down, or mocking other people's ideas.
1 **NOVICE:** **Unconsciously Incompetent**	Is easily distracted from listening by outside and classroom noises; interrupts, daydreams; loses focus; can't paraphrase any part of spoken words.

Name _____ Class _____ Date _____

Rubric for Thinking Flexibly

Rating	Description
4 **EXPERT:** **Unconsciously** **Competent**	Looks at situations creatively and makes useful evaluations; values the opinions of other people and can incorporate or adjust thinking to accommodate new perspectives; consistently explores many alternatives when approaching tasks; illustrates diversity, originality, and effectiveness in ideas and solutions.
3 **PRACTITIONER:** **Consciously** **Competent**	Sees a variety of ways to view a situation and can make a supportive evaluation of each viewpoint; sees the points of view of other people; consistently generates alternative ways of approaching tasks and analyzes how those alternatives will affect tasks; shows some originality in approaching tasks.
2 **APPRENTICE:** **Consciously** **Incompetent**	Will occasionally view and describe different ways to see a situation; sees only his or her own perspective; sporadically generates alternative ways of approaching tasks with originality.
1 **NOVICE:** **Unconsciously** **Incompetent**	Looks at situations in only one way; doesn't generate alternative ideas and cannot see alternative ways of approaching tasks.

Name _____ Class _____ Date _____

Rubric for Thinking About Thinking (Metacognition)

Rating	Description
4 **EXPERT:** **Unconsciously** **Competent**	Describes steps of thinking in detail when solving problems or doing other mental tasks; explains in detail how and why metacognition helped improve work and learning; describes a plan before solving a problem; monitors steps and develops strategies while working; reflects on the efficiency of strategies and will improvise and develop further as needed.
3 **PRACTITIONER:** **Consciously** **Competent**	Describes thinking while problem solving, posing questions, making inferences, or reaching a conclusion; can explain how and why metacognition helped improve work or learning.
2 **APPRENTICE:** **Consciously** **Incompetent**	Includes sparse or incomplete information when describing thoughts on a topic; has difficulty coming to conclusions, formulating opinions, and recalling information in depth; is inconsistent when linking concepts, thinking sequentially, and solving problems.
1 **NOVICE:** **Unconsciously** **Incompetent**	Is confused about the relationship between thinking and problem solving; sees no link between thinking and learning; is unable to describe thinking when asked to reflect, recall, infer, provide an opinion, or suggest a solution; frequently answers, "I don't know."

Name _____ Class _____ Date _____

Rubric for Striving for Accuracy and Precision

Rating	Description
4 **EXPERT:** **Unconsciously** **Competent**	Always checks for accuracy and precision without being asked; always takes great care with a project, assignment, or assessment work; ensures all completed work is free of errors; sets a standard of excellence in all areas of his or her school life (academic, athletic, creative); strives to meet or exceed expectations in all areas.
3 **PRACTITIONER:** **Consciously** **Competent**	Checks work for accuracy; takes the time and care to check over work so that it is completely free of errors; sets high standards for accurate work and maintains those standards.
2 **APPRENTICE:** **Consciously** **Incompetent**	Is beginning to check work for errors and correct these errors when prompted; is showing some improvement in handing in work that shows some care has been taken to be more accurate and precise.
1 **NOVICE:** **Unconsciously** **Incompetent**	Does not and will not see errors in work; is doing incomplete, incorrect, and careless work; is settling for minimum effort rather than investing time and attention; will not take the time to revisit work to correct errors.

Name _____ Class _____ Date _____

Rubric for Questioning and Posing Problems

Rating	Description
4 **EXPERT:** **Unconsciously** **Competent**	Asks questions out of curiosity, intrigue, and interest; knows how to ask appropriate questions and has strategies in place to solve problems; uses questions to make causal connections and relationships; has a wide range and repertoire of question types.
3 **PRACTITIONER:** **Consciously** **Competent**	Asks appropriate questions and has strategies to solve problems; has a wide range of question types.
2 **APPRENTICE:** **Consciously** **Incompetent**	Is beginning to question and problem-solve; is developing strategies; is able to use a small range of question types.
1 **NOVICE:** **Unconsciously** **Incompetent**	Is oblivious to questions that arise in situations; cannot pose a simple problem or formulate a question; lacks strategies to search for or find a solution; is unaware of functions, types, or intentions in questions and questioning.

Name _____ Class _____ Date _____

Rubric for Applying Past Knowledge to New Situations

Rating	Description
4 **EXPERT:** **Unconsciously Competent**	Always builds a knowledge structure by revisiting previous information and drawing it forth; is able to use past knowledge and experiences as data to support, theories to explain, or processes to solve new challenges; transfers and applies information from past knowledge to new situations; modifies and develops new information from past knowledge, both inside and outside of school.
3 **PRACTITIONER:** **Consciously Competent**	Uses past knowledge as a framework to incorporate new information; uses prior knowledge to solve new challenges both in and out of school curriculum-based work.
2 **APPRENTICE:** **Consciously Incompetent**	Is recalling past information; will sometimes use prior knowledge to help solve simple challenges but becomes confused with more difficult situations; has difficulty transferring past knowledge across all areas of school life.
1 **NOVICE:** **Unconsciously Incompetent**	Is unsure of using past knowledge as a basis for learning new things; begins a new task as if it were being approached for the first time; cannot remember recent experiences; treats each event in life as separate, making no connections with what has come before and no relationship to what follows.

Name _____ Class _____ Date _____

Rubric for Thinking and Communicating with Clarity and Precision

Rating	Description
4 **EXPERT:** **Unconsciously Competent**	Always uses precise language; speaks and writes with precision in all subjects, elaborating on ideas and thoughts and using concise and descriptive language; is able to coherently state reasons for generalizations and provide data to support conclusions.
3 **PRACTITIONER:** **Consciously Competent**	Uses precise language in everyday speech; is able to clearly and effectively communicate thoughts using accurate language; is able to support statements with explanations, comparisons, and evidence.
2 **APPRENTICE:** **Consciously Incompetent**	Is beginning to use correct terms, labels, and names for ideas and objects; is broadening descriptive vocabulary such that similes and comparisons are used when prompted; is developing oral and written sentence structures.
1 **NOVICE:** **Unconsciously Incompetent**	Uses vague language to describe thoughts; speaks and writes in phrases rather than in complete sentences; punctuates communication with meaningless interjections such as "um," "er," and "uh" and names specific objects with nondescriptive words such as "stuff," "junk," and "things"; uses unqualified comparatives such as "I like lunch better."

Name _____ Class _____ Date _____

Rubric for Gathering Data Through All Senses

Rating	Description
4 **EXPERT:** **Unconsciously** **Competent**	Has strong powers of perception; efficiently and collectively engages and explores all the senses for observation and information gathering; has sensory pathways that are open, alert, and ready to absorb more information from the environment.
3 **PRACTITIONER:** **Consciously** **Competent**	Efficiently and collectively uses several senses to make observations and gather information.
2 **APPRENTICE:** **Consciously** **Incompetent**	Is beginning to use more than one sense to gather and present information; is beginning to notice and describe some textures, rhythms, and other sensory materials.
1 **NOVICE:** **Unconsciously** **Incompetent**	Has dull and sluggish senses; is oblivious to the textures, rhythms, patterns, sounds, and colors around him or her.

Name _____ Class _____ Date _____

Rubric for Creating, Imagining, and Innovating

Rating	Description
4 **EXPERT:** **Unconsciously Competent**	Thinks outside the box; has a variety of creative strategies to call upon; enjoys generating creative solutions; examines alternative possibilities from many angles; has an active imagination; strives to find new, inventive ways to work on a task; expands the possibility of creative insight by researching a topic in great detail; is eager to seek advice and use the ideas of others to find solutions; frequently reflects and uses metacognition; offers detailed feedback about whether ideas are acceptable; uses a variety of media to present ideas and projects.
3 **PRACTITIONER:** **Consciously Competent**	Generates new ideas to solve problems; develops and uses several strategies to complete tasks; is inventive; does detailed research; generates options and possibilities from attained knowledge; finishes the task no matter the length of time; shows well-developed reflection and metacognition skills.
2 **APPRENTICE:** **Consciously Incompetent**	Is beginning to volunteer one or two imaginative ideas; is increasingly developing strategies; needs encouragement to develop creative thinking; will stop persisting if answer is not gained after a short time; is developing metacognition with guidance.
1 **NOVICE:** **Unconsciously Incompetent**	Says things such as, "I was never good at art," "I can't draw," "I'm not creative," and "I can't." Has no strategies to call upon for new ideas; is afraid to be creative; will not seek alternative methods for solving new problems.

Name _____ Class _____ Date _____

Rubric for Responding with Wonderment and Awe

Rating	Description
4 **EXPERT:** **Unconsciously Competent**	Is actively aware of his or her surroundings and takes great care in protecting and conserving them; is very observant and derives pleasure from thinking and seeking answers to questions that stem from observations; has compassion and empathy for other life forms; is enraptured with awesome phenomena, intriguing situations, and jaw-dropping experiments.
3 **PRACTITIONER:** **Consciously Competent**	Is aware of his or her surroundings and understands the need to protect the environment; is developing an enthusiasm and passion about the physical world and will seek answers to inquiries with increasing independence; has respect and awe for other life forms.
2 **APPRENTICE:** **Consciously Incompetent**	Is making more detailed observations; has a developing curiosity and is asking questions about the immediate environment; is developing respect and empathy for other life forms.
1 **NOVICE:** **Unconsciously Incompetent**	Has no desire to learn about the world; does not search for knowledge; has limited observation skills and no eye for detail.

Name _____ Class _____ Date _____

Rubric for Taking Responsible Risks

Rating	Description
4 **EXPERT:** **Unconsciously** **Competent**	Always draws on past knowledge; applies considerable thought to consequences; has a well-trained sense of what is appropriate; knows the difference between taking a risk and taking a responsible risk; does not fear failure and will go beyond established limits to tackle challenging tasks, even when success is uncertain.
3 **PRACTITIONER:** **Consciously** **Competent**	Draws on past knowledge and thinks flexibly when considering risk factors; educates himself or herself about risks and curbs impulsiveness; accepts setbacks, confusion, and uncertainty as a natural part of a process that leads to a final outcome.
2 **APPRENTICE:** **Consciously** **Incompetent**	Begins to attempt some responsible risks but only if the correct outcome is within easy reach; is trapped by fear and mistrust; is reluctant to accept the challenge of a process in order to find an answer.
1 **NOVICE:** **Unconsciously** **Incompetent**	Will not take risks because the fear of failure is far greater than the desire for venture or adventure; will not play games, attempt new learning, or make new friendships because of a fear of losing, being wrong, or looking stupid.

Name _____ Class _____ Date _____

Rubric for Finding Humor

Rating	Description
4 **EXPERT:** **Unconsciously Competent**	Can see the humorous side of things and create a positive or productive outlook no matter how devastating a situation; is very quick-witted and uses humor to raise the spirits of self and others; is competent at generating funny stories, metaphors, and puns; is quick to laugh at herself or himself and with others.
3 **PRACTITIONER:** **Consciously Competent**	Knows the difference between clowning around and using humor to increase productivity; is able to diffuse situations by adding appropriate humor; tends to use humor; appreciates and understands the humor of others; laughs often at himself or herself and with others; doesn't use humor at inappropriate times.
2 **APPRENTICE:** **Consciously Incompetent**	Is beginning to find humor in some situations; is beginning to move away from offensive humor; is starting to not take himself or herself too seriously; is beginning to appreciate the humor of others without becoming defensive or offended; is learning to distinguish between appropriate and inappropriate humor.
1 **NOVICE:** **Unconsciously Incompetent**	Cannot laugh at self; distorts humor in cases of human differences, ineptitude, injurious behavior, vulgarity, violence, and profanity; uses humor at inappropriate times.

Name _____ Class _____ Date _____

Rubric for Thinking Interdependently

Rating	Description
4 **EXPERT:** **Unconsciously Competent**	Is always empathetic to others in the group; always devotes energy to enhancing group resourcefulness; is always working for the common cause, putting aside independence and ego for the betterment of the group; is all about "we" and "us," not "I" or "me"; is always a team player; focuses on analysis, synthesis, and the evaluation of tasks at hand.
3 **PRACTITIONER:** **Consciously Competent**	Is empathetic to others in the group; is an active participant and works for the common cause of the group; is increasingly more interdependent and sensitive to the needs of others.
2 **APPRENTICE:** **Consciously Incompetent**	Is beginning to contribute to the group; prefers to let others do most of the work; rarely contributes to discussions or participates in active tasks; will opt for working alone if group dynamics become difficult.
1 **NOVICE:** **Unconsciously Incompetent**	Lacks social skills; feels isolated and prefers solitude; says things like "Leave me alone; I'll do it myself," "They don't like me," or "I want to be alone."

Name _____ Class _____ Date _____

Rubric for Learning Continuously

Rating	Description
4 **EXPERT:** **Unconsciously Competent**	Is always open to continuous learning; is always inquisitive about the world and constantly searching for new and better methods and ideas; is always striving for improvement and is prepared to modify and change thinking when new evidence is substantiated; shows humility, commitment, and awe in learning.
3 **PRACTITIONER:** **Consciously Competent**	Is open to continuous learning; has a questioning mind and is eager and inquisitive to learn about the world; strives for improvement and is prepared to modify learning most of the time; is committed; finds opportunities to be amazed; is developing humility in learning.
2 **APPRENTICE:** **Consciously Incompetent**	Is developing an interest in the world; shows some continuous learning in areas of interest but is inclined to give up on expanding ideas if new information isn't readily available.
1 **NOVICE:** **Unconsciously Incompetent**	Does not like learning; shows no interest in independent learning; cannot correctly recall information; lacks questioning, researching, and curiosity skills.

References

Bloom, B. S. (1956). *Taxonomy of educational objectives: The classification of educational goals*. Chicago: Susan Fauer.

Bryan, G. S. (1926). *Edison: The man and his work*. New York: Garden City Publishing.

Budd Rowe, M. (1986). Wait time: Slowing down may be a way of speeding up! *Journal of Teacher Education, 37,* 43–50.

Colman, A. M. (Ed.). (2006). *A dictionary of psychology*. Oxford, UK: Oxford University Press.

Costa, A. (2007). *The school as a home for the mind: Creating mindful curriculum, instruction, and dialogue*. Thousand Oaks, CA: Corwin.

Costa, A., & Kallick, B. (Eds.) (2008). *Learning and leading with habits of mind*. Alexandria, VA: Association for Supervision and Curriculum Development.

de Bono, E. (1999). *Six thinking hats*. Boston: Back Bay Books.

Frangenheim, E. (2005). *Reflections on classroom thinking strategies*. Brisbane, Queensland, Australia: Rodin Educational Consultancy.

Gandhi, M. (1929). *An autobiography or the story of my experiments with truth*. Gujaret, India: Navajivan Trust.

Linton, W. J. (Ed.). (1878). *Poetry of America: Selections from one hundred American poets from 1776 to 1876*. London: George Bell & Sons.

Swartz, R., Costa, A., Beyer, B., Regan, R., & Kallick, B. (2007). *Thinking-based learning: Activating students' potential.* Norwood, MA: Christopher-Gordon.

About the Authors

Karen Boyes is described as Australasia's "Mrs. Education." An expert in effective teaching, learning, and living, she turns research into practical and simple-to-use techniques that create success. She is the founder of Spectrum Education, the New Zealand regional director of the Habits of Mind Institute, and New Zealand's 2001 Business Woman of the Year.

Boyes is the author of *Creating an Effective Learning Environment*, *Study Smart*, *Successful Woman*, and numerous DVDs. Her dynamic presentations provide information that participants can easily integrate. Thousands of teachers have gained renewed energy from her workshops and lectures around the world. In short, she not only educates but also inspires and motivates.

Graham Watts is one of the United Kingdom's leading experts in thinking skills. His knowledge has grown from developing thinking and learning programs in a diverse range of schools around the globe, making his lesson activities tried and tested. His appeal to teachers is his blending of theory with practical ideas that can be used in classrooms.

Watts has published teacher resources in the United Kingdom and the United States and works with teachers around the world in developing skillful thinkers and mindful schools. In addition to speaking at international conferences, he leads professional development days at schools across the United Kingdom and beyond. Recently named a regional director for the Institute for the Habits of Mind, Watts is leading Costa and Kallick's work across many British schools.